RENEWALS 458-4574.
DATE DUE

**WITHDRAWN
UTSA Libraries**

NEW RESEARCH ON LABOR RELATIONS AND THE PERFORMANCE OF UNIVERSITY HR/IR PROGRAMS

ADVANCES IN INDUSTRIAL AND LABOR RELATIONS

Series Editor: David Lewin

Previous Volumes 1–9: Advances in Industrial and Labor Relations

Volume 10: New Research on Labor Relations and the Performance of University HR/IR Programs

ADVANCES IN INDUSTRIAL AND LABOR RELATIONS
VOLUME 10

NEW RESEARCH ON LABOR RELATIONS AND THE PERFORMANCE OF UNIVERSITY HR/IR PROGRAMS

EDITED BY

DAVID LEWIN
*Anderson Graduate School of Management, UCLA,
Los Angeles, USA*

BRUCE E. KAUFMAN
Georgia State University, Atlanta, USA

2001

JAI
An Imprint of Elsevier Science

Amsterdam – London – New York – Oxford – Paris – Shannon – Tokyo

ELSEVIER SCIENCE Inc.
655 Avenue of the Americas
New York, NY 10010, USA

© 2001 Elsevier Science Inc. All rights reserved.

This work is protected under copyright by Elsevier Science, and the following terms and conditions apply to its use:

Photocopying

Single photocopies of single chapters may be made for personal use as allowed by national copyright laws. Permission of the Publisher and payment of a fee is required for all other photocopying, including multiple or systematic copying, copying for advertising or promotional purposes, resale, and all forms of document delivery. Special rates are available for educational institutions that wish to make photocopies for non-profit educational classroom use.

Permissions may be sought directly from Elsevier Science Global Rights Department, PO Box 800, Oxford OX5 1DX, UK; phone: (+44) 1865 843830, fax: (+44) 1865 853333, e-mail: permissions@elsevier.co.uk. You may also contact Global Rights directly through Elsevier's home page (http://www.elsevier.nl), by selecting 'Obtaining Permissions'.

In the USA, users may clear permissions and make payments through the Copyright Clearance Center, Inc., 222 Rosewood Drive, Danvers, MA 01923, USA; phone: (978) 7508400, fax: (978) 7504744, and in the UK through the Copyright Licensing Agency Rapid Clearance Service (CLARCS), 90 Tottenham Court Road, London W1P 0LP, UK; phone: (+44) 207 631 5555; fax: (+44) 207 631 5500. Other countries may have a local reprographic rights agency for payments.

Derivative Works

Tables of contents may be reproduced for internal circulation, but permission of Elsevier Science is required for external resale or distribution of such material.
Permission of the Publisher is required for all other derivative works, including compilations and translations.

Electronic Storage or Usage

Permission of the Publisher is required to store or use electronically any material contained in this work, including any chapter or part of a chapter.

Except as outlined above, no part of this work may be reproduced, stored in a retrieval system or transmitted in any form or by any means, electronic, mechanical, photocopying, recording or otherwise, without prior written permission of the Publisher.
Address permissions requests to: Elsevier Science Global Rights Department, at the mail, fax and e-mail addresses noted above.

Notice

No responsibility is assumed by the Publisher for any injury and/or damage to persons or property as a matter of products liability, negligence or otherwise, or from any use or operation of any methods, products, instructions or ideas contained in the material herein. Because of rapid advances in the medical sciences, in particular, independent verification of diagnoses and drug dosages should be made.

First edition 2001

Library of Congress Cataloging in Publication Data
A catalog record from the Library of Congress has been applied for.

ISBN: 0-7623-0750-1
ISSN: 0742-6186 (Series)

⊗ The paper used in this publication meets the requirements of ANSI/NISO Z39.48-1992 (Permanence of Paper).
Printed in The Netherlands.

CONTENTS

LIST OF CONTRIBUTORS   vii

INTRODUCTION
    David Lewin and Bruce E. Kaufman   ix

CONTINUITY AND CHANGE IN THE STRUCTURE OF
UNION REPRESENTATION IN THE U.S. AIRLINE INDUSTRY,
1969–1999
    David J. Walsh   *1*

LONGITUDINAL STABILITY IN UNION WAGE
DETERMINATION: EVIDENCE FROM THE U.S AUTOMOBILE
ASSEMBLY INDUSTRY, 1970–1999
    Christopher L. Erickson   *31*

EMPLOYEE ACCEPTANCE OF THE CREW CHIEF
PROGRAM IN THE POSTAL SERVICE: AN ANALYSIS
WITH PRE AND POST DATA
    James E. Martin   *51*

THE EVOLUTION OF AN ALTERNATIVE GRIEVANCE
PROCEDURE: THE COLUMBUS TYPOGRAPHICAL UNION
No. 5, 1859–1959
    Howard R. Stanger   *75*

CERTIFICATION OUTCOMES AND RETURNS TO
SHAREHOLDERS IN CANADA
    Felice Martinello, Robert Hanrahan, Joseph Kushner
    and Isidore Masse   *115*

HR/IR PROFESSIONALS' EDUCATIONAL NEEDS AND
MASTER'S PROGRAM CURRICULA
   Philip K. Way   *139*

ARE WE PROPERLY TRAINING FUTURE HR/IR
PRACTITIONERS?: A REVIEW OF THE CURRICULA
   C. Douglas Johnson and James King   *163*

EXECUTIVE INSIGHTS INTO HR PRACTICES AND
EDUCATION
   Cristina M. Giannantonio and Amy E. Hurley   *183*

DEVELOPING NEW PROFICIENCIES FOR HUMAN RESOURCE
AND INDUSTRIAL RELATIONS PROFESSIONALS
   W. Lee Hansen   *209*

LIST OF CONTRIBUTORS

Christopher L. Erickson	Anderson Graduate School of Management University of California at Los Angeles (UCLA)
Cristina M. Giannantonio	Department of Professional Studies Chapman University
Robert Hanrahan	Department of Accounting and Finance Brock University
W. Lee Hansen	Department of Economics and Industrial Relations Research Institute University of Wisconsin
Amy E. Hurley	Department of Professional Studies Chapman University
C. Douglas Johnson	Department of Industrial/Organizational Psychology. University of Georgia
Bruce E. Kaufman	Department of Economics Georgia State University
James E. King	School of Business Samford University
Joseph Kushner	Department of Economics Brock University
David Lewin	Anderson Graduate School of Management University of California at Los Angeles (UCLA)

James E. Martin   School of Business Administration
                           Wayne State University

Felice Martinello   Department of Economics
                           Brock University

Isidore Masse   Department of Economics
                           Brock University

Howard R. Stanger   Business Department
                           State University of New York College at Buffalo

David J. Walsh   Department of Management
                           Miami University

Philip K. Way   University of Cincinnati

INTRODUCTION

David Lewin and Bruce E. Kaufman

The editors are pleased to present the nine chapters that comprise Volume 10 of *Advances in Industrial and Labor Relations* (AILR). Five of these deal with various aspects of union management relations. David J. Walsh examines changes in the structure of union representation in the U.S. airline industry during the last three decades of the 20th century and, over the same period, Christopher L., Erickson analyzes stability in wage determination in the U.S. automobile industry. James E. Martin's study examines factors affecting acceptance of the crew chief program in the U.S. Postal Service, and Howard Stanger's chapter provides a 100-year study of an alternative grievance procedure in a local union. Felice Martinello, Robert Hanrahan, Joseph Kushner and Isidore Masse analyze Canadian union certification outcomes and their effects on shareholder returns. As a set, and apart from their notable individual contributions, these five chapters indicate that research on union-management relations, union representation, financial consequences of unionism, and wage determination, workplace innovation and conflict resolution in unionized enterprises is alive and well.[1]

The next four chapters in this volume deal with the content and pedagogy of human resources (HR) and industrial relations (IR) degree programs in (U.S.) colleges and universities. Initially presented at the 2nd National Conference on Innovative Teaching in HR and IR,[2] these papers, by Philip K. Way, C. Douglas Johnson and James King, Cristina M. Giannantonio and Amy E. Hurley, and W. Lee Hansen, aim to determine whether and to what extent the content of HR/IR degree programs and the competencies of the graduates of those programs match the knowledge and competencies demanded by employers. A close reading of these chapters suggests that knowledge of unionism and competency in union-management relations, contract administration, and the like are decreasingly demanded by employers, and that courses in these and related IR subjects draw fewer and fewer students. By contrast, knowledge of and competency in employee selection, performance management, compensation and reward systems, and other dimensions of HR are increasingly demanded by employers, and courses in these subjects draw more and more students.[3] But the main finding of these chapters is that there remains a significant gap between HR/IR knowledge and competencies demanded by employers and those supplied by degree program curricula. The gap is largest with respect to such behavioral and process competencies as leadership, working in teams, oral and written communication, and integrity/ethics. Therefore, even though they are more HR and less IR-oriented than previously, contemporary HR/IR degree program curricula still tend to emphasize functional specialties and narrow discipline or problem-based bodies of knowledge and competencies.

Taken together, these nine chapters well illustrate what may be termed the 'historic duality' of industrial relations – that is, coverage of all aspects of the employment relationship on the one hand, but a particular emphasis on labor-management relations on the other hand. That this duality is more strongly reflected in HR/IR research than in HR/IR program curricula and teaching, however, is also apparent from the nine chapters included in this volume.

NOTES

1. The chapters by Walsh and Martin are revised versions of papers presented at the Seventh Biennial Bargaining Group Conference, School of Labor and Industrial Relations, Michigan State University, East Lansing, MI, May 12–13, 2000.

2. W.T. Beebe Institute of Personnel and Employment Relations, Georgia State University, Atlanta, GA, June 11–12, 1999.

3. Whether or not knowledge of and competency in workplace dispute resolution has declined as HR/IR degree programs and employers emphasize HR over IR is a matter of some dispute. See David Lewin, IR and HR Perspective on Workplace Conflict: What Can Each Learn from the Other?, *HRM Review*, Vol. 11, 2001, forthcoming.

CONTINUITY AND CHANGE IN THE STRUCTURE OF UNION REPRESENTATION IN THE U.S. AIRLINE INDUSTRY, 1969–1999

David J. Walsh

ABSTRACT

To be effective, unions have to adopt structures that fit the demands of their environments. When key elements of these environments change, there is pressure for union structures to do likewise. Yet, while the U.S. airline industry has seen fundamental changes over the past three decades, the basic contours of union representation, including single-carrier bargaining and craft organization, have remained largely intact. Adjustments to the structure of airline labor have been more subtle and include intensified efforts to organize the unorganized; better coordination among the sub-units of some national unions; and improved cooperation across union and national boundaries.

Airlines are a dramatic example of how established union bargaining power can be undermined by government deregulation . . . Whether the unions have been permanently crippled remains to be seen, and will depend on their future success in organizing the relevant airline workforce, which is rapidly changing, and their willingness to cooperate more closely with one another than in the past (Craypo, 1986, p. 121).

INTRODUCTION

Organization matters. The ability of workers to act concertedly and achieve desired outcomes is heavily influenced by whether they organize, the types of groupings that they form, and the relationships among these organized groups. A representational structure that serves workers well in one environment may be a liability in another, however. The U.S. airline industry has changed substantially over the past three decades. To what extent has the structure of union representation done likewise? Numerous commentators have identified structural change as a necessity if labor is to continue to effectively advance the interests of airline workers (Cappelli, 1987; Wever, 1986; Moody, 1987). Yet, there are also forces that tend to lock existing structures in place and make it difficult for airline labor to act more cohesively.

This chapter considers the nature and sources of union representational structures. It then presents evidence on the structuring, and re-structuring, of airline labor over a three-decade period within which deregulation and many other changes occurred. The ability or inability of unions to re-structure in this important and highly unionized industry may have more general implications for unions attempting to contend with sweeping changes in other industries. There are conspicuous elements of both continuity and change in the structure of airline union representation over this span of time, with the most far-reaching adjustments occurring in response to employment threatening business strategies adopted by carriers.

UNION STRUCTURE

Weber's (1967) seminal work on 'bargaining structure' remains influential. Weber's notion of bargaining structure is appropriately expansive, including informal work groups, election units, negotiation units (i.e., the group of workers included under the same contract), and units of 'direct impact' (i.e., other units whose decisions are directly affected by outcomes of a particular negotiation). Bargaining structure, particularly the negotiation unit, is typically characterized in terms of breadth (range of occupations) and centralization (in relation to corporate structure) (Kochan & Katz, 1988).

Weber's focus is on the scope of individual units rather than on the larger structure resulting from relationships between units. The term 'structure of union representation' is used in this study to make it clear that something broader than 'bargaining structure' is of interest. To be sure, the formal bargaining structure is the starting point for any analysis of union structure in an industry and places constraints on the types of informal structures that are likely to develop.

However, the structure of union representation also includes consideration of patterns of organizing activity, the extent to which union representation is concentrated within a few unions or dispersed across many, the degree of intra-union coordination among the sub-units of international unions, and the presence or absence of a wide variety of inter-union linkages including exchanges of resources, promises of support in strikes, coalitions, federations, and union mergers. It is from this broader perspective that the strengths and weaknesses of a particular union representational structure are best apprehended.

SOURCES OF UNION STRUCTURE

Among the determinants of bargaining structure cited by Weber (1967) are 'market factors', 'representational factors', 'government policies', and 'tactics and power'. Unions have historically aimed to develop bargaining structures that correspond to the markets affecting their members. The strategic objective is to 'take wages out of competition' by ensuring uniformity in labor costs across producers who operate in the same product or labor markets. This allows improvements to be gained for members while minimizing jeopardy to their continued employment. 'Representational factors' pertain to trade-offs between the advantages of larger, more inclusive groupings of workers and the increased heterogeneity of interests and loss of local autonomy that typically accompany consolidation. An obvious example of the influence of government policy on union structure is the National Labor Relations Board's determination of an 'appropriate bargaining unit' for purposes of holding representation elections. The 'election unit', as Weber (1967, p. 14) terms it, is not the last word on bargaining structure as it is often modified by the parties, but it generally defines at least the minimum inclusiveness of negotiation units. Lastly, tactical considerations may lead one or the other party to a bargaining relationship to prefer a particular bargaining structure. One such tactic is 'whipsawing', in which either a union or employer chooses a single, vulnerable target, negotiates favorable terms, and then attempts to extend those terms to a larger set of unions or firms.

Kochan and Katz (1988) elaborate in some useful ways on the determinants proposed by Weber. First, they note that in order 'to achieve a high degree of centralization, unions usually must first organize a large proportion of the product market and then successfully maintain union coverage over time – a tall order' (Kochan & Katz, 1988, p. 124). Second, they observe that centralization in the organizational structure of employers may require a more centralized bargaining structure capable of reaching critical management decision makers. In other words, unions need to be concerned about 'matching up' with the organizational structures of employers, as well as with relevant markets.

This is necessary both to reach the hierarchical level at which corporate decisions are effectively made and also to prevent workers in the various plants or divisions of a large corporation from being played off against one another.

Underlying the notion of 'taking wages out of competition' is the concept of interdependence. The actions and outcomes of one set of parties to a labor-management relationship may have ramifications for other parties (Pennings, 1981). Alternatively, interdependence exists when actors do not control all of the conditions necessary to carry out their actions or to achieve the desired outcomes (Pfeffer & Salancik, 1978). Walsh (1993) has proposed that relations between unions, like other organizations, are fundamentally rooted in their interdependence. This includes the interdependence of bargaining outcomes alluded to above, but also competitive interdependence (e.g., for new members), resource interdependence (e.g., for information, strike support), common problem interdependence (e.g., a threatened plant closing or bankruptcy affecting a number of unions), interdependence through affiliation with the same larger organization (e.g., among affiliates of the same international union), and workflow interdependence (e.g., jurisdictional disputes). There are numerous ways then, in which groups of workers and their unions impinge on, and become relevant to, one another. Environmental changes that affect these interdependencies should affect the ways in which relations between groups of workers and their unions are structured.

Representational structures may come to no longer fit well with the economic environment or corporate structures, yet prove resistant to change. The role of government agencies in establishing units for representational purposes is a basic constraint. Agencies like the NLRB have historically placed a premium on 'stability' in labor relations and resisted re-thinking the types of groupings deemed 'appropriate' (Weber, 1967). The established jurisdictions of unions, particularly where they are linked to a clear craft identity, may render both union leaders and members disinclined to re-think the occupational boundaries of their organizations. Making the structure of union representation more inclusive, regardless of whether that is accomplished by expanding the boundaries of a union or creating linkages across union boundaries, results in a more diverse set of interests to consider and represent. Even when unions are capable of re-structuring themselves, they can expect that employers will most often resist their efforts to wield more power.

UNION REPRESENTATION STRUCTURE IN THE AIRLINE INDUSTRY

Labor relations in the airline industry are governed by the Railway Labor Act. In administering the Act, the National Mediation Board (NMB) establishes the basic contours of union representation through its decisions regarding the occupational and geographic scope of 'crafts and classes'.[1] The NMB has a long-standing policy of only certifying units that are 'system-wide' (i.e., that are co-extensive with the geographic scope of a carrier's route system). Its determinations as to what occupational groupings constitute crafts or classes have varied over the years (Eischen, 1977), but the broad outlines have remained largely unchanged over the span of time with which this study is concerned.[2] Although not legally required by the RLA, bargaining has with few exceptions occurred on a single carrier basis and usually with one craft at a time (Kahn, 1980; Cappelli, 1987). Table 1 shows the formal structure of union representation for the ten largest ('major') carriers (excluding cargo carriers), as of the end of 1999. The essential feature of this matrix is that workers are grouped for representation purposes into units that are both carrier and craft-specific.

The adequacy of union representational structure has been called into question in light of developments since the deregulation of the airline industry. Cappelli's (1985, 1987) analysis of the mis-match between the industry's traditional bargaining structure and the economic realities of the post-deregulation environment has been especially influential. In brief, he argues that single-carrier bargaining aimed at using previously negotiated agreements as the floor for subsequent agreements resulted in relatively generous settlements for airline workers and did not jeopardize their employment because carriers did not compete on the basis of price (fares were set by the Civil Aeronautics Board). With the advent of deregulation, labor costs became a significant factor in determining the competitive positions of carriers (particularly the ability to engage in 'fare wars' with other major carriers) and high cost carriers faced the prospect of employment loss or bankruptcy. Unable to 'take wages out of competition' through multi-carrier bargaining or some other mechanism for ensuring uniformity, airline unions were vulnerable to repeated carrier demands for concessions. While the thrust of his analysis concerns relative labor costs and competitive pressures, Cappelli (1987, 1988) also points to the threats posed by the new business strategies of carriers (e.g., formation of holding companies, mergers, creation of non-union 'alter-ego' carriers).

Cappelli (1985) does not spell out the implications of these changes for union structure in detail, although he points to increased organizing of non-union workers, greater control by international unions over their locals to prevent them from caving in to concession demands, and union coalitions as significant union responses. Craypo (1986) is more specific in prescribing the type of union representational structure that would meet the demands of a changed environment. Necessary changes include organizing the new relevant work force (through jointly planned and executed multi-union campaigns), modifying traditional

Table 1. Union Representation at Major Carriers (excluding cargo carriers), as of September 30, 1999

Carrier	Pilots	Dispatch	F.A's	Mechs	OCFPS	S&S
Alaska	ALPA	TWU	AFA	AMFA	IAM	--
America West	ALPA	TWU	AFA	IBT	TWU	IBT
American	APA	TWU	APFA	TWU	--	TWU
Continental	IACP	TWU	IAM	IBT	--	--
Delta	ALPA	PAFCA	--	--	--	--
Northwest	ALPA	TWU	IBT	AMFA	IAM	IAM
Southwest	SAPA	SAEA	TWU	IBT	IAM/TWU	IBT
TWA	ALPA	TWU	IAM	IAM	IAM	IAM
United	ALPA	IAM	AFA	IAM	IAM	IAM
US Airways	ALPA	TWU	AFA	IAM	IAM/CWA	IAM

Sources: U.S. National Mediation Board. *Fifty-Seventh and Fifty-Eighth Annual Reports* (for the fiscal years ended September 30, 1991 and September 30, 1992). The NMB has since discontinued publishing this information in its annual reports. The 1992 information was updated to 1999 by including subsequent certifications documented in *Determinations of the National Mediation Board* (1993-1999).

The crafts/classifications listed above are pilots, flight dispatchers, flight attendants, mechanics & related, office/clerical, fleet and passenger service, and stock and stores employees. Unions listed as representing the OCFPS groups do not necessarily represent the entirety of those groups and sometimes more than one union represents a segment of this group, as is noted in the table.

- ALPA – Air Line Pilots Association
- APA – Allied Pilots Association
- IACP – Independent Association of Continental Pilots
- SAPA – Southwest Airlines Pilots Association
- TWU – Transport Workers Union
- PAFCA – Professional Airline Flight Control Association
- SAEA – Southwest Airlines Employee Association
- IAM – International Association of Machinists
- AFA – Association of Flight Attendants
- APFA – Association of Professional Flight Attendants
- IBT – International Brotherhood of Teamsters
- AMFA – Aircraft Mechanics Fraternal Association
- CWA – Communications Workers of America

bargaining structures by moving away from pattern-plus negotiations and toward synchronized bargaining, and achieving much greater inter-union cooperation and coordination than in the past. Labeling craft unionism 'an anachronism in a jet-age industry that is going through a drastic restructuring', Moody (1987, p. 9) advocates tactical and structural changes including coordinated bargaining, synchronized contract expiration dates 'throughout the industry', honoring picket lines regardless of legal constraints, aggressive use of secondary boycotts (which are allowed under the RLA), and standardization of wages, benefits, and workrules. Sleigh (1995, p. 222) observes that "[m]ore and more, coalitions and solidaristic actions will have to extend beyond the borders of U.S.-based unions."

These analyses imply that airline unions might attempt to change the formal structure of bargaining, or short of that, adopt less formal mechanisms capable of promoting more uniform terms and conditions of employment across carriers. Informal means of promoting greater uniformity in labor costs across carriers include organizing currently unorganized units; consolidating representation by raiding established units, particularly those held by independent unions; centralizing control over bargaining, so that the sub-units of national unions representing the same crafts at different carriers act more in concert; increasing the exchange of information and support across different unions representing the same craft; and attempting to achieve 'parity' with industry leaders in bargaining. None of these measures 'takes wages out of competition' in the same manner as multi-carrier bargaining, but given the immense obstacles to fundamentally re-shaping the industry bargaining structure, they represent feasible means of accomplishing greater uniformity across carriers.

Since deregulation, it has become much more difficult for airline unions to achieve their ends autonomously and more likely that the actions of one union will have ramifications for others. This increased interdependence goes beyond the intertwining of bargaining outcomes. For example, because carriers now often attempt to operate during strikes (rather than shutting down and collecting MAP subsidies), fostering solidarity across crafts becomes essential, particularly for unions with less bargaining power. Similarly, when all of the unions at a financially distressed carrier are faced with the common problem of potential job loss for their members, the actions of any one union to deal with the problem will affect other unions at the carrier. Mergers or acquisitions create fundamental uncertainty for unions and provide added incentive to organize so that representation rights are less likely to be lost in any corporate combination.

Developments in the 1990s, though less dramatic than the immediate aftermath of deregulation, continue to hold implications for the structure of union representation. On one hand, the solid performance of the industry as a whole in the second half of the decade (see Table 2) diminishes the need for unions to coordinate their activities, insofar as they are not faced with the serious threat of employment loss and bargaining outcomes are less of a zero-sum proposition. Yet, new interdependencies have developed that broaden the universe of relevant other unions. Specifically, carriers have maintained and expanded code-sharing arrangements with regional/commuter lines begun in the 1980s and have formed numerous strategic alliances with foreign carriers. These developments are significant because airline unions must now contend with elaborate networks of carriers,

Table 2. U.S. Airline Industry Statistics, Selected Years 1969–1998.

Year	RPM's* (000,000)	Load** Factor (%)	Net Profit/ Loss ($000)	Employees (FTE)
1969	125,414	50.0	52,752	311,922
1972	152,406	53.0	214,851	301,127
1974	162,919	54.8	321,641	307,318
1977	226,781	61.5	752,536	308,068
1982	259,644	59.0	(915,814)	330,495
1986	366,546	60.3	(234,909)	421,686
1990	457,926	62.4	(3,921,002)	545,809
1994	519,382	66.2	(344,115)	539,759
1997	605,434	70.4	5,169,305	586,509
1998	619,456	70.9	4,893,610	642,499

Sources: Air Transport Association. *The Annual Report of the U.S. Scheduled Airline Industry* (various years)
* Revenue Passenger Miles (RPM's) is a widely used measure of airline industry output.
** Load factor measures the percentage of capacity (Available Seat Miles) utilized by revenue passengers.

potentially capable of shifting routes, services, and equipment – and hence, employment opportunities – amongst themselves.

With code-sharing, flights are listed jointly on computer reservation systems. Major carriers and their regional/commuter partners feed into one another to create 'seamless' air travel. Joint marketing, ticketing, maintenance, and other functions may also be parts of these arrangements. There were some forty-five code-sharing relationships with major carriers in 1993 and these accounted for the lion's share of the traffic flown by regional/commuter carriers (Coleman, 1995). The close integration of major carriers with regional/commuter lines through code-sharing and ownership stakes is increasingly coupled with the acquisition of regional jets capable of displacing wide-bodied jets on routes of up to 1000 miles *(New York Times,* Feb.18, 2000). This means that these smaller carriers, and the unions representing their workers, are now of greater concern to unions at the major carriers. According to ALPA Representation Director Seth Rosen:

> The primary concern regarding this new relationship between the majors and nationals and their affiliated regionals is the allocation of current and future aircraft among the various airlines. Although 19-seat aircraft cannot be considered a threat to 150-seat jets in major markets, the acquisition by regional airlines of larger aircraft increases the potential for problems, including service substitution and alternatives to growth (Rosen, 1988, p. 33).[3]

There is enormous disparity in pay and working conditions between the major and regional/commuter lines. Unions organizing the smaller carriers – and planning to keep those units organized – will have to lessen the disparity, and in the process, reduce the incentive for substitution (*Air Line Pilot*, June 1993; Coleman, 1995; *Air Transport World*, Feb. 1999a). Also, insofar as regional/commuter lines frequently serve as training grounds for the larger carriers, there are obvious advantages if workers moving up to the major carriers are familiar with unions, and preferably, already members of the same union.

The aspect of globalization that has truly taken off in the 1990s is the creation of strategic alliances between U.S. and foreign carriers. In 1998, there were 71 code-sharing relationships in effect between U.S. and foreign carriers, and a much larger number world-wide (Hunnicut, 1998). The prevalence of these arrangements is attributable to such factors as carriers' desire to access new markets relatively cheaply, encouragement by the U.S. government through ready DOT approval and immunity from anti-trust laws, and limitations on foreign ownership of U.S. airlines (making formal mergers impossible) (Hunnicut, 1998; Derchin, 1995). Global carrier alliances threaten labor in much the same way as domestic code-sharing, but on a far larger scale. Former ALPA Intl. President Randy Babbitt declared that "Code-sharing is a wake-up call for pilot groups, who need to recognize the importance of establishing legally enforceable mechanisms that function across national borders" (*Air Line Pilot*, June/July 1997). ALPA is convinced – and is not alone in this belief – that global alliances have resulted in U.S. carriers and their pilots losing a disproportionate share of international flying, particularly on trans-Atlantic routes (*Air Line Pilot*, June/July 1997a; *Air Transport World*, May 1999).

Under these circumstances, increased coordination between airline unions across national boundaries becomes imperative. These alliances pose serious issues for unions (especially, but not exclusively, pilots' unions) regarding the shifting of routes among partner carriers, determining which partner will fly newly-created routes, the potential use of alliance partners to sustain operations during strikes, and consolidation of maintenance facilities, marketing, and ticketing.

CHANGES IN THE STRUCTURE OF UNION REPRESENTATION, 1969–1999

The structural adjustments made by airline labor have been more subtle than any clear departure from the industry's well-established craft tradition and single-carrier bargaining. Instead, changes are to be discerned in the intensity and targets of organizing, the extent to which groups of workers are represented by the same unions and the degree of constraint within those unions (intra-union structuring), and the cohesiveness of relations across the boundaries of unions (inter-union structuring).

ORGANIZING

Relatively little has been written about organizing in the airline industry. Commentators have generally pointed to the high degree of unionization in the industry since the 1940s (Kahn, 1980; Cappelli, 1987) and the high incidence of raiding (Krislov, 1988; Kahn, 1977). In the post-deregulation period, airline unions have had additional motivation to organize. Unorganized units pose a greater threat when the labor costs of carriers have competitive implications. Organizing formerly unorganized units does not by itself 'take wages out of competition', but it at least increases the likelihood that wage rates and other terms and conditions of employment will be relatively equal. The greater probability of a carrier failure or merger in the post-deregulation period also encourages organizing, to lessen reliance on the continued existence of any single carrier and to avoid losing representation rights to another union when units are combined in a merger. While raids on existing units might accomplish some of these purposes, the threat of unorganized, growing carriers can only be met by organizing the previously unorganized. To the extent that regional/commuter carriers have become more consequential, increased organizing of these carriers would also be expected. The most substantial targets, however, for organizing the unorganized, are the large groups of fleet and passenger service and office and clerical workers at the major and national carriers. These groups make up a sizable portion of airline employees and have been relatively impervious to unionization in the past.

Data on union density in the air transport sector (Table 3) suggest that unionization rates have declined somewhat since the early 1970s.[4] However, when

Table 3. Union Density in Air Transportation, Selected Years 1974–1998

Year	Union Members (%)	Covered By Contract (%)
1974*	45.4	N.A.
1977*	47.2	N.A.
1980*	44.8	N.A.
1986	39.7	43.5
1991	37.4	39.4
1996	35.8	38.0
1998	38.2	40.1

Sources: 1974, 1977, and 1980 figures (Kokkelenberg & Sockell, 1985, p. 527); 1986, 1991, and 1996 figures (Hirsch & Macpherson, 1997, pp. 85, 93, 101); 1998 figures (Hirsch & Macpherson, 1999, p. 49).

* These figures are three-year moving averages. Thus, the figure for 1974 combines data for 1973, 1974, and 1975, and so forth.

judged against the backdrop of a near free-fall in private sector union density, airline unions have more than held their ground and the industry remains among the most highly unionized. The figures for 1998 also suggest a possible reversal of the long-term decline.

To what extent does the relative stability of the union presence in the airline industry reflect union organizing activity? Table 4 provides indicators of the extent, targets, and efficacy of airline union organizing over the past three decades. In most of the decade prior to deregulation, the frequency of elections was low. In the years immediately preceding and following deregulation, the number of elections was unusually high. Organizing activity resulting in elections subsided in the late 1980s, but returned to relatively high levels in the late 1990s. Overall, the data suggest that airline unions responded to the numerous incentives to step up their organizing following deregulation, albeit with considerable annual variability.

Table 4. Organizing Activity in the U.S. Airline Industry, Selected Fiscal Years 1970–1999

FY	Elections (n)	Union Win Rate (%)	Net New Members (n)	Raids (%)	Major Carrier (%)	Intl. Carrier (%)
1970	4	50.0	39	25.0	25.0	25.0
1973	10	40.0	0	40.0	20.0	50.0
1977	51	68.6	–241	21.6	13.7	21.6
1980	53	64.2	1761	22.6	5.5	22.6
1983	39	71.8	1054	10.2	5.1	30.8
1986	29	51.7	4933	27.6	17.2	3.4
1989	21	66.7	5068	14.3	14.3	9.5
1992	20	40.0	581	20.0	15.0	5.0
1995	33	57.6	2210	3.0	15.2	0.0
1998	39	61.5	19960	7.7	12.8	0.0
1999	36	75.0	12415	5.6	18.9	2.7

* Figures exclude charters, freight carriers, helicopter services, and airline service companies. Elections resulting in re-runs are counted only in the year in which the results became final. "Raids" are defined here as elections in which an incumbent representative is challenged by another union. Net new members is derived by subtracting from the number of employees in certified units the number of employees gained (or lost) in raids on units with incumbent representatives. Certifications in which units previously enjoyed voluntary recognition by carriers are also discounted. The last two columns capture the percentages of elections involving employees of major carriers and those involving U.S.-based employees of foreign carriers.

Source: U.S. National Mediation Board. *Determinations of the National Mediation Board*, (fiscal years 1969–1997 in print, 1998 and 1999 on-line at www.nmb.gov).

The primary targets for organizing have changed considerably over time. Through the early 1980s, the U.S.-based employees of international carriers were an important focus of organizing. These units tended to be quite small and were composed primarily of passenger service personnel and airline maintenance crews. Since the mid-1980s, the percentage of elections involving employees of the major carriers has remained relatively constant, but the percentage accounted for by employees of foreign carriers has plummeted. This implies that airline union organizing has been increasingly directed toward smaller national and regional/commuter carriers (the omitted groups) since the mid-1980s. This is consistent with the view that these smaller carriers became more relevant following deregulation, because of their potential to increase in size, the possibility that they might threaten employment at the major carriers if allowed to operate in a non-union mode, and the likelihood that they were linked to major carriers through code-sharing arrangements.

Table 4 also points to the prevalence of 'raiding' by airline unions. Until quite recently, raids on incumbent unions made up over a fifth of the elections in a typical year. The recent decline in raiding may be both a cause and consequence of improved relations between airline unions (the re-affiliation of the IBT with the AFL-CIO is no doubt also an important factor). In any event, the prevalence of raiding has historically resulted in meager yields of new members for airline labor. Despite generally impressive union win rates,[5] the propensity to conduct raids on (generally large) units with established representation rather than focus on organizing the unorganized has meant that the number of new members gained each year through organizing has been quite small.[6] The results for 1998 and 1999 represent significant and very hopeful departures from the historical pattern. The outcomes of on-going organizing campaigns at Delta Airlines will have much to do with whether this trend continues (*Daily Labor Report,* Sept. 24, 1999: C-1). In any event, it is clear that while airline unions are organizing the unorganized to a greater extent than in the past, the relative stability of union density in the airline industry derives much more from growth at the already-unionized carriers than from organizing activity.

INTRA-UNION STRUCTURING

While airline workers are represented on a system-wide and craft-specific basis, this leaves open the questions of whether the crafts at a given carrier will be represented by a few or many unions, and whether the same or different unions will represent a craft across carriers.[7] Coordination between crafts or across carriers is enhanced when employee groups are affiliated with the same national unions. Information sharing, common expiration dates and proposals, and picket line support are all more likely under this circumstance. Kahn (1980) observed in the period shortly before deregulation that where a union represented several different crafts at the same carrier, common expiration dates and multi-unit bargaining were typical.

Table 5. Degree of Consolidation in Union Representation at the Major Carriers: 1970, 1979, 1986, and 1999.

	Year			
	1970	1979	1986	1999
Unions Per Carrier (mean)*	3.6	3.6	3.8	3.9
Pilots				
Number of Unions**	2	2	2	4
Dominant Union	ALPA	ALPA	ALPA	ALPA
Proportion***	0.91	0.92	0.90	0.70
Flight Attendants				
Number of Unions	2	7	6	5
Dominant Union	ALPA/ TWU	AFA	AFA	AFA
Proportion	0.50	0.36	0.44	0.44
Mechanics				
Number of Unions	3	3	3	4
Dominant Union	IAM	IAM	IAM	IAM/ IBT
Proportion	0.70	0.73	0.67	0.33
OCFPS				
Number of Unions	5	3	4	3
Dominant Union	IBT/ BRAC	IBT/ BRAC/ ALEA	IBT/ IAM	IAM
Proportion	0.28	0.33	0.33	0.78

Sources: U.S. National Mediation Board. *Annual Report* (fiscal years 1970, 1979, 1986, and 1992). The 1992 information was updated to 1999 with data on subsequent certifications, as documented in *Determinations of the National Mediation Board* (1993-1999).

* This is the average number of different unions representing workers across the six crafts listed in Table 1 (figures for dispatchers and stock & stores employees are not shown here) at each of the major carriers in the specified years. There may have been additional unions representing other, smaller, job groups. The number of major carriers in the industry varied between 10 and 12 over the time between 1970 and 1999.

** This is the number of different unions representing the specified craft or class across all of the major carriers in the specified years.

*** This is the proportion of major carriers at which the 'dominant' union (i.e., the union that represents a craft at the largest number of major carriers) holds representation rights for the specified craft (excluding carriers at which the craft is not represented at all).

Table 5 captures changes in the formal structure of union representation over time, focusing on the extent to which representation is concentrated within a few dominant unions or dispersed among a variety of unions. The average number of different unions representing the primary crafts/classifications at each major carrier remained largely unchanged between 1970 and 1999. TWA is an exception in this regard, as its pilots are represented by ALPA and all of its other unionized employees (including flight attendants), except for dispatchers, are represented by the IAM.

The figures in Table 5 tell different stories depending on the craft being considered. For pilots, ALPA has long been the leading representative. It has engaged in considerable organizing since the early 1980s and now represents pilots at over fifty carriers. Yet, it is worth noting that pilots at three of the major carriers (American, Continental, and Southwest) are represented by independent unions.[8] Independent pilot unions are viable because of the considerable resources and bargaining power that pilots can muster, particularly if the unions restrict their attention to collective bargaining. The independent pilots unions can afford to do so because ALPA maintains such a strong presence defending the interests of pilots in political circles.

In contrast, independent unions of flight attendants emerged in the late 1970s, but had largely disappeared by 1999. Flight attendants were represented by divisions of either ALPA or the TWU prior to the mid-1970's. Flight attendant dissatisfaction with this arrangement grew, resulting in the creation of the AFL-CIO affiliated Association of Flight Attendants and a number of independent flight attendant unions (Nielsen, 1982). These flight attendant unions competed, along with the IBT and TWU, in a flurry of contests in the late 1970s that resulted in highly dispersed representation of flight attendants. By the 1990s, a degree of re-consolidation had occurred, due to carrier mergers (the fate of IUFA at Pan Am), raids by other unions (the IFFA was displaced by the IAM at TWA), and a union merger (the UFA at Continental merged with the IAM). The APFA has remained independent, on the strength of the large number of flight attendants employed at American Airlines (approximately 20,000). The APFA and AFA have discussed merging on a number of occasions and reached an agreement to do so in 1987, only to have it rejected by APFA members (*Daily Labor Report*, Aug. 18, 1987). The AFA represents flight attendants at more carriers (24) than does any other union. At this point, it appears that a flight attendant union either has to be large or has to join with a union that represents other crafts in order to be effective.

Representation of mechanics and related and OCFPS units has gone in opposite directions – perhaps for related reasons. The IAM has seen its role as the chief representative of mechanics and related employees greatly diminished, particularly by challenges from the Aircraft Mechanics Fraternal Association (AMFA). On the other hand, it has emerged in recent years as the primary representative of OCFPS employees. Previously, OCFPS employees were minimally organized and their representation was dispersed across a variety of unions. Consolidation of these groups within the IAM, along with acquisition of representation rights for several flight attendant groups, seemed to point toward a weakening of the strong craft unionism tradition of the airline industry in favor of a quasi-industrial model. However, recent defections, particularly by mechanics, suggest otherwise.

The success of the IAM in consolidating representation across crafts has left them more vulnerable to raids. The Aircraft Mechanics Fraternal Association (AMFA) was formed in the early 1960's. AMFA has argued on several occasions before the NMB – to no avail – that the craft of 'mechanics and related' should be defined more narrowly to include only those mechanics who are licensed and meet other requirements (NMB Case Nos. R-3712, 3713, 3714, decided July 14, 1965). AMFA represented mechanics at a few carriers over the years (e.g., Ozark) and launched unsuccessful raids on IAM mechanics units at United and Northwest (22 NMB 288, Aug. 11, 1995; 19 NMB 94, December 6, 1991). Its fortunes turned in 1990 when it succeeded in displacing the IAM as representative at the Trump Shuttle (17 NMB 196, May 8, 1990). AMFA has enjoyed other victories since, most notably at Alaska (25 NMB 318, April 1, 1998) and Northwest Airlines (26 NMB 269, June 1, 1999). While the source of AMFA's appeal is a matter of debate, it has clearly attempted to differentiate itself as a 'pure' craft union and to convince mechanics that they are better off in their own union where their interests will not be diluted by those of other, more numerous, ground personnel. In one blunt formulation of AMFA's message, National Director O.V. Delle-Femine suggested that support for AMFA stemmed from mechanics feeling that ''ramp service workers are on their backs'' (*Daily Labor Report*, March 9, 1990, p. A-6). More recently, Delle-Femine has stated:

> At both airlines [American and United], I think mechanics want to see the industrial mentality thrown out ... The mechanics want to have their own union where they are the majority and they run their own affairs (*Daily Labor Report,* July 12, 1999, p. A-9).

According to Delle-Femine, the IAM's successful 1998 organizing campaign in which it gained representation rights for 18,000 passenger service employees 'really perturbed the mechanics ... Man did that help this drive. Now they are a firm minority' (*Daily Labor Report*, July 12, 1999, p. A-9).

AMFA's recent successes – and its on-going efforts at other carriers including United and Delta – have captured the attention of the IAM and TWU. The IAM responded by creating two new District Lodges for mechanics and related employees only (IAM FaxLink, April 23, 1999). The TWU has initiated a similar 'self-determination' initiative whose purpose is 'to provide the Mechanic & Related membership with additional options by establishing sister locals where they would be the majority representative' (TWU, n.d.). These recent developments clearly evidence the difficulty of creating more inclusive structures when important sub-groups feel that this compromises their autonomy and power.

Even when workers at different carriers are represented by sub-units of the same international unions, coordination and cooperation do not automatically follow. In the airline industry, formal representation rights are generally held by the international unions, but sub-units of the international unions generally have the primary responsibility for bargaining and representing the workers at given carriers. These sub-units include ALPA and AFA Master Executive Councils (MEC's), IAM District Lodges, and TWU and IBT locals. The extent to which these sub-units operate autonomously or within tight constraints imposed from above has direct bearing on whether the representation of airline workers is as fragmented as it first appears. Given the heightened interdependence of airline unions and their need in the post-deregulation era to negotiate more uniform contract provisions (or at least to not adopt concessionary terms that would then be thrust upon other employee groups), one avenue for increasing coordination is to centralize decision-making within international unions. This would reduce the discretion of units representing employees at particular carriers to make decisions adversely affecting other groups. The clearest indication of a move in this direction is found in the internal dynamics of ALPA.

Following its fairly tepid response to deregulation legislation and several rounds of concession bargaining, the ALPA International began to assert greater control in the mid-1980s (Walsh, 1994). Its actions have included creating guidelines for concessionary and crisis bargaining, increased training of negotiators, vesting greater policy making authority in the Executive Board, creating a major contingency fund to be allocated only at the initiation of the ALPA International President or Executive Council, cracking down on excess expenditures by MEC's, initiating a 'Shared Vision Program' intended to highlight pilots' common identity as ALPA members, investigating the possibilities of 'coordinated bargaining' across carriers, establishing a 'No B-scale Committee' with the aim of eliminating two-tier wage structures at all ALPA carriers, formulating a 'global pilot strategy' to deal proactively with the effects of industry globalization (*Air Line Pilot*, Dec. 1992), and creating a National Scope Clause Review Committee (to deal with the conflict between the job security concerns of pilots at major carriers and the desire of regional carrier pilots to see their carriers grow (*Air Line Pilot*, June/July 1997b).

To be sure, all of this has left ALPA more coordinated and less like the loose confederation that it was prior to deregulation. Still, coordination in bargaining across carriers remains informal and highly variable. There are formidable obstacles to increased international union control within ALPA. One of these is the widely varying financial circumstances of ALPA carriers. The strong allegiance of pilots to their own carriers is another fundamental constraint. This tendency is reinforced by the importance of carrier-specific seniority in determining central aspects of a pilot's work life such as pay, equipment flown, and scheduling (Cappelli, 1985). The fact that MEC's, the major sub-units of ALPA responsible for representing pilots, do not mix pilots from more than one carrier, further encourages pilots' preoccupation with the affairs of their own carriers. Lastly, the continued viability and popularity of independent pilot unions carries the implicit threat that MEC's could break away from the International and form their own independent pilots unions (as occurred at American Airlines in the 1960's and more recently at Continental).

Aligning the interests of pilots at major and commuter carriers is a difficult, but not intractable, problem. A creative attempt to negotiate terms favorable to both groups is language in the Northwest pilot's agreement linking the number of regional jets at Northwest code-sharing partners to the number of wide-body jets maintained by Northwest (Daily Labor Report, Sept.15, 1998). Pilots at Northwest Airlines main commuter code-sharing partner, Mesaba Express, pledged to not do any struck work during the Northwest Airlines pilots' strike in March 1998 (Interview, William Zoller, ALPA NWA MEC Chair, July 1, 1999). Both Northwest and Mesaba shut down rather than attempt to operate during the strike. In January 1999, the ALPA pilots at Delta met with representatives from each of the carrier's regional/commuter code-sharing partners (Atlantic Southeast, Business Express, Comair, Skywest, and Trans States). ALPA Delta MEC Chairman Capt. Charles S. Giambusso explained that '[b]ecause our respective airlines have such close ties, we believe it's beneficial for the pilot groups to maintain close contact and work together whenever possible' (ALPA News Release, January 13, 1999). The group is aiming toward a written 'protocol agreement' affirming support for mutual goals, patterned after the types of agreements the union has reached with pilot groups at international code-sharing partners. One dividend accruing from this contact is that the ALPA group at Delta has found it easier to keep track of the number of regional jets being used by Delta code-sharing carriers due to simply being able to ask the involved unions, rather than having to wrest the information away from the carriers (Interview with Charles S. Giambusso, Delta ALPA MEC Chair, August 18, 1999).

Other, more far-reaching, forms of solidarity may be beyond the capability of ALPA to orchestrate. For example, ALPA was confronted with several major strikes during the 1980s (at Continental, United, and Eastern). In each case the striking pilots requested a nation-wide 'suspension of service', but none was forthcoming (*Air Line Pilot*, Sept. 1989). The largely strike-free 1990s have not tested the limits of strike support within ALPA. Despite occasional discussion of such solidaristic bargaining goals as a single, nation-wide seniority list for pilots and 'flow-through' agreements to ensure the hiring of commuter pilots when positions open up at major carriers, the first issue remains a non-starter and the latter has seen relatively little implementation.

INTER-UNION STRUCTURING

While inclusion within the same organizations may be the surest means of facilitating cooperation and coordination between groups of workers across crafts or carriers, it is still quite possible for cooperative relations to be maintained across union boundaries. To the extent that this potential is realized, the flexibility of union structure is maximized. Despite an apparently 'fragmented' structure of representation, solid cross-union ties allow the individual unions to cooperate on matters of joint concern, while still enjoying the advantages of autonomy and a relatively homogenous set of interests to represent.

Systematic evidence on the quantity and quality of relations among airline unions in the period prior to deregulation is lacking, but it appears that the reputation of airline unions for insularity was warranted (Walsh, 1994; Craypo, 1986). In the tumultuous decade following deregulation the frequency and intensity of interactions across the boundaries of airline unions increased. Coalitions were formed at a number of carriers, including Pan Am, Eastern, Frontier, Republic, Ozark, U.S. Air, and TWA (*Flightlog*, Summer 1984). Presented with serious threat to the continued employment of all of their members and pressed for concessions, these unions worked together closely (albeit with considerable friction), sometimes engaged in joint bargaining with the carriers, and attempted to influence acquisitions. Along craft lines, the Coalition of Flight Attendant Unions was formed in 1984, bringing together the AFA and numerous other unions representing flight attendants (*Flightlog*, July 1989). The coalition focused on political issues, particularly flight attendant duty time legislation. A large-scale mobilization of airline labor took place in 1989 in response to the threat posed by Frank Lorenzo and his attempt to break the Machinists union. While not producing the hoped for outcome, the mobilization around the Eastern Airlines strike included inter-union transfers of funds, picket line support, sympathy strikes by the ALPA Eastern MEC and TWU Local 553, and a high level of AFL-CIO involvement. A systematic study of relations among airline unions found considerable inter-union activity in the latter 1980s, including various forms of communication and information sharing, and joint action to achieve common goals (Walsh, 1994).

Were the findings from the late 1980s an aberration influenced by the extraordinary event of the Eastern Airlines strike, or has the level of inter-union contact been maintained or expanded since then? A follow-up study was conducted in 1999.[9] To the extent that the results are comparable, they suggest that airline unions continue to have contact with about the same number of other unions representing workers at major carriers, that coalition formation and other joint activity may have subsided among this group of unions, and that union officers now view inter-union relations as being more important to their own union's effectiveness. Thus, while respondents in 1989 reported direct communication or contact with an average of 11.7 other unions also representing workers at a major carrier during the previous two years, respondents in 1999 reported an average of 11.5 unions with which they had direct communication or contact.[10] In terms of joint action, respondents in 1989 reported having engaged in joint action with an average of 3.7 other unions, compared to an average of 2.9 reported by respondents in 1999.[11] Respondents in 1999 seemed to be more convinced of the importance of relations with other airline unions. On a four point scale ranging from 'not important at all' to 'very important', 1999 respondents rated the importance of ties with other airline unions more highly (a mean of 3.24) than had 1989 respondents (a mean of 2.48).[12]

Much of the coalition activity reported by study respondents came out of the Coalition of Flight Attendant Unions. Despite the demise of a number of independent flight attendant unions since the 1980s and continuing competition among unions representing flight attendants, this coalition has sustained itself and remains active on political and regulatory issues. In a new development, the Coalition of Airline Pilot Associations (CAPA) was formed in 1997 (*Daily Labor Report*, Dec. 18, 1997).[13] Thus far, CAPA has pressed the FAA to issue pilot flight, duty, and rest time regulations and has obtained agreements from member unions not to perform struck work (*Daily Labor Report*, Oct. 14, 1997; *Daily Labor Report*, Dec. 18, 1997). While any joining together of pilots' unions is a potentially significant development, the absence of ALPA from the coalition is noteworthy.

It is the growth of cross-national alliances between airline unions, corresponding to the creation of global carrier alliances, that is the most significant departure from not only the pre-deregulation period, but also from the 1980s. Prior to the 1990s, contacts between airline unions and their international counterparts were quite limited, occurring primarily through international federations such as the International Transport Workers' Federation (ITF) and the International

Federation of Airline Pilots Associations (IFALPA). IFALPA dealt almost exclusively with air safety issues.

In October 1992, ALPA issued its 'Global Pilot Strategy' intended to deal proactively with the challenges posed by globalization (*Air Line Pilot*, January 1993). The strategy emphasizes the importance of alliances with pilot unions outside of the U.S. and of equalizing basic terms of employment:

> When global alliances are struck, we must ensure a harmonization of work rules and pay scales of corporately allied pilot groups so that we maintain the 'level of the playing field' to prevent one pilot group from being played off against another (*Air Line Pilot*, December 1992: 17).

ALPA's focus on globalization has taken two other interesting turns. First, in 1997, ALPA's Board of Directors authorized the creation of an independent 'International Pilot Services Corporation'. The purpose of this entity is to share ALPA's expertise on a range of issues – for a price – with pilots' unions throughout the world (*Air Line Pilot*, June/July 1997b). ALPA's expertise is frequently sought by other unions (*Air Line Pilot*, January 1997). ALPA's international negotiating seminars have trained more than 150 pilot negotiators from numerous countries (*Air Line Pilot*, June/July 1997c). Whether this means that there is a substantial market to purchase these services[14] and what this novel business arrangement would do to traditional notions of labor solidarity remain interesting questions. The second development is a merger in 1997 between ALPA and the Canadian Air Line Pilot's Association (*Air Line Pilot*, February 1997). The two unions had entered into a 'Joint Services Agreement' in 1995. The formal merger process was no doubt accelerated by financial problems that emanated from the departure of Air Canada pilots from CALPA in 1995.

ALPA pilots at Northwest have been pioneers in cross-border airline labor alliances. KLM and Northwest entered into a comprehensive alliance in 1992, including not only code-sharing but a substantial KLM equity stake (later reduced) in Northwest (*New York Times*, July 31, 1997). This expanded with the additions of Alitalia and Continental into the 'Wings Alliance'. The Northwest ALPA MEC has worked especially closely with the Dutch pilots union (VNV). The groups meet on a regular basis and have signed several 'protocols', agreeing to a fair distribution of flying opportunities on Atlantic routes and pledging to present their respective carriers with common demands on a number of issues (*Air Line Pilot*, March/April 1993). In 1993, KLM pilots obtained an agreement with their carrier to hire 40 furloughed Northwest pilots, to be employed until positions re-opened at Northwest (*Air Line Pilot*, January 1993). During KLM negotiations in 1995, the Northwest pilots passed resolutions offering funds and pledging to not perform any struck work (Interview, Steve Zoller, ALPA Northwest MEC Chair, July 1, 1999). During

KLM negotiations in 1997, the Northwest pilots stepped up their support, threatening to suspend all Atlantic flights if KLM went ahead with an outsourcing proposal. The ALPA International Executive Board backed up this threat by authorizing the disbursement of up to $200,000 to pay for legal expenses that the Northwest MEC might incur due to a sympathy strike on behalf of KLM pilots (*Air Line Pilot*, June/July 1997b). In ALPA's 1998 strike against Northwest, the KLM pilots were enjoined by a Dutch court from engaging in a sympathy strike, but they provided funds and promised not to perform any struck work. This labor alliance has been extended to include the IACP (Continental) and ANPAC (Alitalia) (*ALPA News Release*, April 19, 1999).

International airline labor alliances have formed around all of the largest global carrier alliances. The 'Oneworld Cockpit Crew Coalition' claims to be the largest coalition of alliance partner pilots and includes the ten unions that represent pilots at the alliance's carriers. (*Daily Labor Report*, Mar. 26, 1999).[15] Pilot unions associated with the carriers that have created the 'Atlantic Excellence Alliance' (Delta, Austrian Airlines, Finnair, Sabena, and Swissair) have formed the Global Pilot Alliance (and subsequently added the pilot's union from TAP Air Portugal). This alliance has agreed to meet at least three times a year, to support each group's bargaining goals aimed at reducing disparities in compensation packages, to work toward harmonization of safety rules across nations, to negotiate language prohibiting the performance of struck work, and to support the Portuguese pilots in their efforts to obtain flight time/duty time provisions consistent with those of the other member unions (Delta ALPA MEC, December 5, 1997; December 3, 1998). The 'Star Alliance' (United Airlines, Lufthansa, SAS, Air Canada, Thai, Varig, Air New Zealand, and Ansett) has also spawned a labor alliance.

Pilot unions have been at the forefront of global airline labor alliances, but other crafts have also been involved. The ITF has taken a strong interest in the globalization of the airline industry and it has organized numerous meetings for pilot, flight attendant, and ground crew unions. An ITF-sponsored meeting in 1994 focused on flight/duty time limits for flight attendants and resulted in the signing of a mutual support agreement between AFA, the British Airways flight attendants (BASSA), and Qantas flight attendants (FAAA) (*Flightlog*, 1994). Flight attendant unions have had to confront the issue of globalization in a more immediate way than other groups because several carriers with extensive international operations (e.g., United, American) use 'foreign nationals' based in other countries as flight attendants. Interestingly, and by voluntary agreement between the AFA and United, flight attendants based in other countries are covered under their labor agreement. AFA has agreements with flight attendant unions in Germany (Lufthansa) and France (Air France) that provide for a form of joint representation of these workers. If disputes arise under the contract, then AFA will deal with them. Matters relating to legal rights are dealt with by the other unions (Interview with Patricia Friend, AFA Intl. Pres., August 12, 1999).

CONCLUSION

In the face of turmoil and change, airline labor has taken significant steps toward re-structuring itself. Previously non-union groups have been organized; representation of some crafts is more consolidated than previously; strike support is more likely; some international unions, particularly ALPA, have made major strides in reigning in their sub-units; a number of coalitions have been formed and some have withstood the test of time; and inter-union ties now reach broadly across national boundaries. Yet, the industry's bargaining structure remains unchanged; airline unions have scarcely taken wages out of competition; the representation of some crafts, particularly mechanics, has become more dispersed; independent unions retain a significant presence, particularly among pilot groups and through the resurgence of AMFA; some coalitions have lapsed or suffered from serious disputes among their members; and most global alliances among airline unions are very new and untested. In light of the apparent need, why hasn't there been more change in the structure of union representation?

One answer is that the problem of taking wages out of competition has, at least partially, been taken care of by others. Carriers also have an interest in limiting the effects of competition. They have become quite proficient at locking up regions of the country with mega-hubs and code-sharing alliances and in avoiding all-out fare wars. To the extent that carriers remain successful in circumscribing competition, the possibility of employment losses being generated by labor cost disparities becomes more remote. In the immediate aftermath of deregulation, carriers faced with severe financial problems argued for the uniqueness of their circumstances and attempted to ratchet down concessions agreed to at other carriers. In the more munificent environment of recent years, carriers have sought to limit increases by arguing that a fair outcome is parity with other carriers.[16] The chances of producing outcomes that roughly approximate parity across carriers are enhanced by the substantial control that NMB mediators exert over the bargaining process. The popularity of 'interest-based bargaining' may also lend itself to greater uniformity insofar as a more analytical, information-based approach to bargaining is utilized.[17] Should the financial situation of the industry turn drastically for the worse or non-union new entrants buck the odds and establish themselves, then we might see unions attempt to go further to equalize labor costs across carriers. Of course, under those circumstances carriers may be decidedly less interested in maintaining parity.

While competitive pressures emanating from differential labor costs may currently be too remote to have a decisive influence on union structure, carrier business strategies, particularly organization into holding companies, bankruptcy filings, mergers and acquisitions, code-sharing relationships with regional/commuter carriers, and entry into global carrier alliances, have had a major impact on union structure. Unions have seen the necessity of matching the new structures being created by carriers. The threats to employment, continued representation, and bargaining leverage posed by these arrangements are large and immediate. One problem that this poses is that it puts airline unions in the position of continually reacting to carrier business strategies. In a very real sense, union organization is always a derivative of prior organization by employers, but the fluidity of some of these arrangements, particularly global carrier alliances[18] makes them an unstable basis for inter-union relationships as well.

Lastly, numerous obstacles stand in the way of any further re-structuring of airline labor. The NMB's definitions of acceptable crafts or classes are unlikely to change and will thus continue to provide the template upon which union representational structure is based. The strong craft orientations of many airline unions limit the prospects for consolidation in representation. The grouping of workers into sub-units (e.g., ALPA and AFA MEC's) that include only workers from a single carrier also tends to reinforce preoccupation with the affairs of those individual carriers at the expense of a broader outlook. Raiding among airline unions has declined, but not disappeared in recent years. Competition over members both interferes with cooperative relations and also feeds the desire to negotiate contract terms superior to those negotiated by a union's rivals. Ultimately, given the obstacles to change and the sacrifice of autonomy that is typically involved, more fundamental re-structuring will have to await clearer indications that the current representational structure does not permit unions to successfully advance the interests of airline workers.

NOTES

1. The NMB affects the structure of representation in other ways. For example, it decides when and if carriers have merged and constitute single carriers for representation purposes (see 14 NMB 388, July 31, 1987 for a statement of current procedures).

2. Significant change did occur in the NMB's treatment of office and clerical, fleet and passenger service workers. Its 1980 decision in *Japan Air Lines* (7 NMB 217) firmly

established that, contrary to earlier policy, each of the three groupings constitutes a craft or class for representation purposes.

3. A recent lawsuit by ALPA against Delta Airlines for substituting regional jets flown by Comair on some Delta Shuttle routes is one indication that the pilots' worries are far from academic (*Daily Labor Report*, April 29, 1999).

4. Although the figures are all based on data from the CPS, differences in the methods used may affect their comparability. In light of the general view that the airline industry is heavily unionized, one might wonder why the density figures are not even higher. No doubt, union density is greater among the major carriers than for the industry as a whole. However, since the smaller carriers also employ many fewer people than do the majors, lower unionization rates at the smaller carriers can only be part of the story. More important are the limited extent of unionization at one of the largest carriers, Delta, and the fact that the single largest craft or class – office/clerical, fleet and passenger service employees – is less fully organized than other groups, even at the major carriers. The exact size of the OCFPS group is difficult to estimate, but Air Transport Association figures for employment by craft show that 'service personnel' (not including mechanics) and 'office employees' comprised 52.5% of total industry employment in 1997 (*ATA Annual Report*, 1998).

5. The mean annual union win rate in representation elections over the thirty year period was a healthy 67.4%.

6. Over the thirty year period, the mean annual number of employees involved in representation elections was 12,261 and the mean annual number of new members was 2810, a yield of about 23%.

7. The degree of cohesiveness within bargaining units is also relevant here, but is difficult to track in any systematic way over time. It has been suggested that a recent spate of contract rejections (e.g., flight attendants at Northwest and American Airlines) stems not only from the heightened expectations of union members during relatively prosperous times, but also from the presence of factions within unions using the internet to rally opposition to the union leaderships and the tentative agreements (*Daily Labor Report* , March 20, 2000; *Air Transport World*, May 2000). According to the Airline Industrial Relations Conference, one-third of the 108 tentative agreements reached with airline unions during 1996–1999 were rejected by their members (*Air Transport World*, May 2000). Sick-out's, refusal of overtime assignments, and other actions that have led carriers to pursue legal remedies against airline unions (e.g., against the APA at American Airlines, the IBT at Northwest Airlines, ALPA at Comair) may also signal increasing difficulty in reigning in the actions of individuals and groups (*Air Transport World*, March 2000).

8. Independent union is not a precise term. In this study, I use it to refer to unions that are not AFL-CIO affiliates and that represent employees at no more than a couple of carriers.

9. The same methodology was used in both the 1989 and 1999 studies (see Walsh, 1994 for details), but there were fewer respondents and questions regarding inter-union relations in the 1999 study. The survey was conducted using phone interviews. Respondents were the top officers (or their designees) of unions representing workers at the major carriers. Eighteen (out of 38 – response rate of 47%) respondents were interviewed. Each was sent a written copy of the questions beforehand, which also included a listing of other unions in the industry to which the respondent could refer during the interview. The relatively low response rate was disappointing and appears to have resulted in large part from the high level of bargaining activity going on in 1999, including a number of rejections of tentative agreements.

10. The same wording was used in both surveys and is as follows: "With which of the unions listed has [name of respondent's union] had any *direct communication or contact* (e.g., letters, telephone calls, meetings, etc.) during the past two years?"

11. The wording of the item in both surveys was "With which of the unions listed has [name of respondent's union] carried out some form of *joint action* (worked together to achieve a common goal, such as in joint lobbying, joint legal action, forming a coalition, etc.) during the past two years?"

12. The wording of the item was "Overall, *how important* are the ties that [name of respondent's union] has with other union's representing airline workers in terms of [name of respondent's union]'s ability to get its job done? (1) not important at all (2) somewhat important (3) quite important (4) very important" This endorsement of the importance of relations with other unions is in line with the findings of a recent study sponsored by the International Transport Workers Federation (ITF) in which personnel from 56 unions representing workers at 36 airlines around the world were surveyed. The researchers found relatively high levels of support (between 70 and 75% of respondents) for the effectiveness of several forms of inter-union cooperation (cross-border union cooperation, union cooperation across alliance partners, and inter-union cooperation at the national level) as trade union strategies (ITF, 1998).

13. Coalition member unions include the Allied Pilots Association (American), the Independent Association of Continental Pilots, the Air Canada Pilots Association, the Independent Pilots Association (UPS), the FedEx Pilots Association, the Southwest Airlines Pilots Association, and the Teamsters.

14. Among the early customers were pilot groups at Aer Lingus, Aero Litoral, Air France, KLM, and TAP (for help with analysis of airline financial and business plans), Aer Lingus (bargaining strategies), and Cathay Pacific (scheduling analysis) (ALPA, January 2000).

15. The carriers and unions are American Airlines (Allied Pilots Association), British Airways (British Airline Pilots Association), Cathay Pacific (Hong Kong Aircrew Officers Association), Qantas (Australian and International Pilots Association), Japan Airlines (Japan Airlines Flight Crew Union), Finnair (Finnish Air Line Pilots Association), Iberia (Sindicate Espanol de Pilotos de Lineas Aereas), Lan Chile (Lan Chile Pilots Union), Argentina Airlines (Association de Pilotos de Lineas Aereas) and Lot Polish Airline (Polish Airline Pilots Association).

16. Recent negotiations between US Airways and the AFA highlighted the carrier's attempts (resisted by the AFA on the grounds that it would result in concessions) to advance a formula of "parity plus one percent" (*Daily Labor Report*, May 2, 2000). Parity was at issue in a double-sense; parity with other flight attendant groups and also acceptance of the same approach by all of the union's at U.S. Airways. Parity issues also loomed large in the 1997 agreement between United and the AFA. The lengthy (10 year) contract includes a wage arbitration provision that can be invoked in 2001 to ensure that United's rates maintain a specified relationship to other flight attendant groups. Additionally, flight attendants won parity with pilots in the hotel accommodations provided during lay-overs (Interview with Kevin Lum, former United AFA MEC Chair, July 20, 1999).

17. The NMB has been a vigorous proponent of interest-based bargaining (*Daily Labor Report*, May 5, 1998). Eleven of the eighteen union officers interviewed for this study (61%) reported having tried IBB and most indicated a willingness to do it again. Interestingly, several respondents acknowledged that while using IBB had been a positive

experience for the negotiators, members' discomfort with the process may have been a factor in low support for tentative agreements.

18. Global carrier alliances have been very fluid (Oster and Strong, 1998). A Goldman Sachs report indicated that out of 121 new alliances formed in 1997, 102 were dissolved within two years (*Air Transport World,* April 1999). There is a wide-spread belief that the alliance phenomenon may be short-lived, giving way to either formal mergers (if ownership limitations are eliminated) or more permissive bi-lateral agreements between nations (*Air Transport World,* February 1999; April 1999).

ACKNOWLEDGMENTS

An earlier version of this chapter was presented at the 7th Biennial Bargaining Group Conference, School of Labor and Industrial Relations, Michigan State University, May 12–13, 2000. Thanks to conference participants for their helpful comments.

REFERENCES

Air Line Pilots Association

Dolan, D. (2000). Challenge 2 – ALPA Must Effectively Deal with Industry Globalization. <http://www.alpa.org/internet/prescorner/hup_1-2000/challenge_2htm>.

Air Line Pilot

Duffy, H. A. (1989, September). President's Forum. *Air Line Pilot, 58,* 2.
Martinez, E., Jr. (1992, December). ALPA In Evolution. *Air Line Pilot, 61,* 12–17, 53.
Martinez, E., Jr. (1993, January). Global Pilot Strategy: Positioning for Progress. *Air Line Pilot, 62,* 12–15.
DiNunno, G. (1993, March/April). Global Alliances Begin. *Air Line Pilot, 62,* 25–26.
Mark, R.. (1993, June). Regional Pilots: Lifestyles of the Not So Rich and Famous. *Air Line Pilot, 62,* 12–15.
(no author) (1997, January).. ALPA Discusses ESOP's With British ALPA Pilots. *Air Line Pilot, 66,* 51.
Roberts, B. (1997, February). A Historic Union. *Air Line Pilot, 66,* 10–13.
Blattner, L. (1997a, June/July). Code-Sharing: Realities of a Global Pilot Strategy – Part II. *Air Line Pilot, 66,* 17–19.
DiNunno, G. (1997b, June/July). ALPA Leaders Set New Goals. *Air Line Pilot, 66,* 20–23.
Woerth, D. (1997c, June/July). Gathering on the Nile. *Air Line Pilot, 66,* 36–7.

ALPA News Releases

(Nov. 17, 1998). One World Alliance Pilots Meet, Set Uniform Safety Standards As Goal, Release No. 98.86. <http://www.alpa.org/internet/news/>,
(Jan. 13, 1999). Delta Pilots Meet with Domestic Code-share Carrier Pilots, Release No. 99.05. <http://www.alpa.org/internet/news/>.
(April 19, 1999). Wings Alliance Pilots Sign Protocol Pledging Mutual Support, Release No. 99.23. <http://www.alpa.org/internet/news/>.

ALPA Delta MEC News Releases
(Dec. 5, 1997). International Coalition of Pilots Meets in Washington, Plans Activities.
    <http://www.dalpa.com/public/releases/971205.htm >.
(Dec. 3, 1998). Global Pilot Alliance Strengthens Pact Provisions.
    <http://www.dalpa.com/public/releases/981203.htm >.

Air Transport Association
(no author). (March 4, 2000). Chapter 10. The Future of Aviation, *Airline Handbook*.
    <http://www.air-transport.org/public/Handbook/CH10.htm>
(numerous years). *Annual Report of the U.S. Scheduled Airline Industry*.
    <http://www.air-transport.org/public/industry/>

Air Transport World
Moorman, R. W. (1999a, February). A Fair Shake. *Air Transport World, 36*, 33–36.
Feldman, J. M. (1999b, February). Disappearing Act. *Air Transport World, 36*, 25–30.
Flint, P. (1999, April). Alliance paradox. *Air Transport World, 36*, 33–34, 36.
Flint, P. (1999, May). Trafficking in myths. *Air Transport World, 36*, 52.
Moorman, R. W. (2000, March). Throwing down the gauntlet. *Air Transport World, 37*, 49–51.
Feldman, J. M. (2000, May). Rejection dejection. *Air Transport World, 37*, 81–83.

Association of Flight Attendants
Flightlog
Puchala, L. (1984, Summer). Coalitions – Airline Unions Are Working Together. *Flightlog, 22*, 4.
(no author). (1989, July). FAA Promises to Investigate Flight Attendant Fatigue. *Flightlog, 27*, 11.
(no author). (1994, Spring). International Update: International Solidarity, Certification and Duty Time Top ITF Agenda. *Flightlog, 32*, 7–8.

Cappelli, P. (1985). Competitive Pressures and Labor Relations in the Airline Industry. *Industrial Relations 24*, 316–38.
Cappelli, P. (1987). Airlines. In: D. B. Lipsky & C. B. Donn (Eds.),. *Collective Bargaining in American Industry* (pp. 135–86). Lexington, MA: Lexington Books.
Coleman, W. S. (1995). Airline Globalization and Regional Airlines. In: P. Cappelli (Ed.). *Airline Labor Relations in the Global Era* (pp. 74–78). Ithaca, NY: ILR Press.
Craypo, C. (1986). *The Economics of Collective Bargaining*. Washington, DC: Bureau of National Affairs.

Daily Labor Report
Flight Attendants at American Airlines To Merge With AFL-CIO Affiliated Union. (1987, August 18). *Daily Labor Report*, pp. A11–12.
Mediation Board Mails Ballots To Mechanics On Trump Shuttle. (1990, March 9). *Daily Labor Report*, p. A-5.
Coalition of Unionized Pilots Targets Safety Improvements As Top Priority. (1997, October 14). *Daily Labor Report*, p. D-11.
Unionized Pilots Pledge Solidarity In Event Of Pilot Strike Or Lockout. (1997, Dec. 18) *Daily Labor Report*, p. D-12
Prah, P. M. (1998, May 1). Pilots' Unions At 15 Airlines Worldwide Consider Responses To Carrier Alliances. *Daily Labor Report*, p. D-18.
Prah, P. M. (1998, May 5). NMB: Dubester Says Focus on Preventive Mediation Is Showing Results In Rail, Airline Bargaining. *Daily Labor Report*, p. D-25.

Wolski, M. (1998, September 15). Northwest Pilots Ratify Contract; End 15-Day Strike Against Carrier. *Daily Labor Report*, A-9.
Pilot Unions Form Coalition To Explore New Ways To Address Global Concerns. (1999, March 26). *Daily Labor Report*, p. A-13.
Tumey, B. (1999, April 29). Pilots' Union Sues Delta Over Using Regional Airline For Shuttle Flights. *Daily Labor Report*, p. A-5.
Wolski, M. (1999, May 11). Alitalia To Join Northwest, KLM Partnership; Unions Sign Protocol Fostering Cooperation. *Daily Labor Report*, p. A-10.
Bologna, M. (1999, July 12). Independent Union Seeks To Represent Aircraft Mechanics At United, American. *Daily Labor Report*, p. A-9.
Tumey, B., & Ginsbach, P. (1999, September 24). Unions Courting 55,000 Delta Employees In Drives To Become First Bargaining Agents. *Daily Labor Report*, p. C-1.
Ginsbach, P. (2000, March 20). NMB: Chairman Hopeful On US Airways Dispute; Agency Sees Expansion In ADR Requests. *Daily Labor Report*, p. B-1.
Ginsbach, P. (2000, May 2). AFA Members Ratify US Airways Pact By 78 Percent; Raises Total 11 Percent. *Daily Labor Report*, p. A-11.

Derchin, M. (1995). What Went Wrong?. In: P. Cappelli (Ed.), *Airline Labor Relations in the Global Era* (pp. 13–17). Ithaca, NY: ILR Press.
Eischen, D. E. (1977). Representation Disputes and Their Resolution in the Railroad and Airline Industries. In: C. E. Rehmus (Ed.), *The Railway Labor Act at Fifty* (pp. 23–70). Washington, DC: National Medication Board.
Hirsch, B. T., & Macpherson, D. A. (1997, 1999 editions). *Union Membership and Earnings Data Book*. Washington, DC: Bureau of National Affairs.
The Impact of Recent Alliances, International Agreements, DOT Actions, and Pending Legislation on Air Fares, Air Service, and Competition in the Airline Industry: Hearings before the Subcommittee on Aviation of the House Committee on Transportation and Infrastructure, 105th Cong., 2nd Sess. (April 30, 1998), pp. 476–92 (prepared statement of Charles A. Hunnicutt).

International Association of Machinists
New Mechanic and Related District Lodge. FaxLink (April 23, 1999) http://www.iamaw.org/departments/communications/.

International Transport Workers' Federation
Blyton, P., Lucio, M., McGurk, J., & Turnbull, P. (1998). *Contesting Globalisation: Airline Restructuring, Labour Flexibility, and Trade Union Strategies*. (Report prepared in cooperation with the International Transport Workers' Federation) <http://www.itf.org.uk/PRESS/conglob.html>.

Kahn, M. L. (1977). Labor-Management Relations in the Airline Industry. In: C. E. Rehmus (Ed.), *The Railway Labor Act at Fifty* (pp. 97–128). Washington, DC: National Mediation Board..
Kahn, M. L. (1980). Airlines. In: G. C. Somers (Ed.), *Collective Bargaining: Contemporary American Experience* (pp. 315–72). Madison, WI: Industrial Relations Research Association.
Kochan, T. A., & Katz, H. C. (1988). *Collective Bargaining and Industrial Relations*. Homewood, IL: Irwin.
Kokkelenberg, E. C., & Sockell, D. R. (1985). Union Membership In The United States, 1973–1981. *Industrial and Labor Relations Review, 38*, 497–528.

Krislov, J. (1988). Representation Elections in the Railroad and Airline Industries, 1955–1984. *Labor Law Journal, 39*, 242–46.

Moody, K. (1987, June). Go-It-Alone Mentality Hurts Airline Unions In Era Of Deregulation. *Labor Notes*, pp. 8-9.

National Mediation Board

National Mediation Board. (various years). *Annual Report.*

National Mediation Board. (various years). *Determinations of the National Mediation Board.* (fiscal years 1969–1997 in print; 1998 and 1999 on-line <http://www.nmb.gov/.>).

New York Times

Northwest Air to Buy Back 19% Stake Held by KLM. (1997, July 31). *New York Times*, p.: C-2.

Morrow, D. J. Twilight of Turboprops? (2000, February 18). New York Times, pp. C-1, 6.

Nielsen, G. P. (1982). *From Sky Girl To Flight Attendant.* Ithaca, NY: ILR Press.

The Impact of Recent Alliances, International Agreements, DOT Actions, and Pending Legislation on Air Fares, Air Service, and Competition in the Airline Industry: Hearings before the Subcommittee on Aviation of the House Committee on Transportation and Infrastructure, 105th Cong., 2nd Sess. (April 30, 1998), pp. 526–43. (Prepared statement of Clinton V. Oster, Jr. and John S. Strong).

Pennings, J. M. (1981). Strategically Interdependent Organizations. In: P. C. Nystrom & W. H. Starbuck (Eds.), *Handbook of Organizational Design, 1*, 433–55. New York: Oxford University Press.

Pfeffer, J., & Salancik, G.R. (1978). *The External Control of Organizations.* New York: Harper & Row.

Rosen, S. D. (1988). A Union Perspective. In: J. T. McKelvey (Ed.), *Cleared For Takeoff* (pp. 11–35). Ithaca, NY: ILR Press.

Sleigh, S. R. (1995). The Difficulty of Sticking Together in Tough Times. In: P. Cappelli (Ed.), *Airline Labor Relations in the Global Era* (pp. 212-22). Ithaca, NY: ILR Press.

Transport Workers Union

(no date). Self-Determination – Questions and Answers. Viewed June 4, 1999 <http://www.Twu513.org/resturcture/QandA.htm>.

Walsh, D. J. (1993). The Labor Movement as an Interorganizational Network. In: S. B. Bacharach, R. L. Seeber & D. J. Walsh (Vol. Eds.),. Research in the *Sociology of Organizations*: Vol. 12, Special Issue on Labor Relations and Unions (pp. 245–78). Greenwich, CT: JAI Press.

Walsh, D. J. (1994). *On Different Planes.* Ithaca, NY: ILR Press.

Weber, A. R. (1967). Stability and Change in the Structure of Collective Bargaining. In: L. Ulman (Ed.), *Challenges to Collective Bargaining* (pp. 13-36). Englewood Cliffs, NJ: Prentice-Hall.

Wever, K. R. (1986). Changing Union Structure and the Changing Structure of Unionization in the Post-Deregulation Airline Industry. *Proceedings of the Thirty-Ninth Annual Meeting, December 28–30.* Madison, WI: Industrial Relations Research Association.

LONGITUDINAL STABILITY IN UNION WAGE DETERMINATION: EVIDENCE FROM THE U.S. AUTOMOBILE ASSEMBLY INDUSTRY, 1970–1999

Christopher L. Erickson

ABSTRACT

This chapter focuses on the following conceptualization of union wage determination: that wage provisions in union contracts manifest significant longitudinal stability, or 'wage rules' that hold across bargaining rounds despite differences in industry and company profits and prospects. The contracts between the major U.S. automobile assemblers and the UAW union over the period 1970–1999 are examined and found to provide support for this hypothesis. Particularly notable is the apparent return to a variant of the previous wage rules in the 'post-concession' era since the mid-1980s. Possible explanations for the emergence and persistence of such rules and implications for union wage determination, the overall wage structure, and the analysis of other economic aspects of human behavior are also discussed.

INTRODUCTION

This study examines the proposition that patterns of institutionalized wage rules may prevail in collective bargaining relationships over long periods of time. In other words, the possibility that there may not only exist pattern bargaining, or cross-sectional stability, but as well longitudinal stability, or a set of wage rules, norms, or protocols that hold across bargaining rounds and are violated only in times of extreme crisis. In essence, this proposition posits that wages are generally one of the many factors held constant in the constraints of complex labor negotiations; that incremental changes come over other (non-wage) aspects of the compensation package, if it all; to put it starkly, that union wages are usually not determined by labor and product market conditions in a given negotiation.

I will attempt to establish the existence of a '3% plus COLA' wage rule among the largest company-union pairs in the U.S. automobile assembly industry, a rule violated during the 'concession bargaining' period of the early 1980s, but apparently returned to in a somewhat different form in the 1990s. While longitudinal stability in the post-war era has been examined before (e.g. Katz (1985), Piore and Sabel (1984)), this study documents its re-appearance in the bargaining rounds of the mid-1980s through late-1990s. I will also address some of the possible explanations for the emergence and persistence of the '3% plus COLA' wage rule and implications for union wage determination, the overall wage structure, and the analysis of other economic aspects of human behavior.

UNION WAGE OUTCOMES AS BASED ON WAGE NORMS OR RULES (LONGITUDINAL STABILITY)

The strand of theory on union wage determination emphasized here posits that there is longitudinal stability of wage determination across time periods, independent of short-term economic conditions. Variants of this approach have been articulated in Katz (1985), Piore and Sabel (1984), and Reder and Neumann (1980).

First, it is useful to briefly describe the different wage clauses of a typical union contract. Union contract wage clauses in the United States in the post-World War II era typically contain at least two main conceptually separate components: the Annual Improvement Factor (AIF), or base wage increase, and the Cost-of-Living Adjustment (COLA), which indexes wages to changes in some cost-of-living index (usually the CPI), with payments coming at specified dates over the life of the contract.

Katz (1985) provides an analysis of wage rules as one aspect of the collective bargaining system in the automobile industry. He argues that "formula-like mechanisms have been used to set wages in collective bargaining agreements in the auto industry since the GM-UAW agreement in 1948. The formula wage-setting mechanisms regularly included in the national contracts are an annual improvement factor (AIF) and COLA. The AIF increased wages at 2 to 3% per year, while the COLA automatically raised hourly wages in accordance with increases in the nationwide consumer price index" (p. 14). He also notes the various amendments to wage rules, including periodic revisions, diversions to pay for fringe benefits, COLA caps, and skilled trades adjustments. Yet, he concludes that "all of these cases modified either the COLA or AIF but did not alter the structure or central importance of the wage formulas. On the whole the important fact was how rigidly the wage rules were applied." Finally, he points out the functions served by wage rules: orderly adjustment of wages during multiyear agreements, reduction of the potential scope of disagreement over compensation, provision of structure for negotiations, provision of political stability for labor and management leaders, and reduction of the likelihood that overt conflict might break out in the face of a negotiations impasse.

Piore and Sabel (1984) posit long-term stability of wage rules over the post-war period, based on the wage-setting formula negotiated between General Motors and the UAW in 1948:

> The formula established as the standard for wage setting the long-run, economywide increase in labor productivity [3% at the time] plus the change in the consumer price index; wages, it was agreed, should rise by this amount every year. Given that labor productivity adjusted for price changes is a measure of productive capacity, consistent and uniform application of the formula to all wages and salaries would ensure that private-consumer purchasing power would expand at the same rate as national productive capacity. The complex of labor-relations and wage-setting institutions generalized the formula in precisely this way.
>
> Within the mass-production industries, the automobile settlement was spread through the institutional links between the major national unions. Each of these industries – and within them, most companies – conducted separate negotiations; but the negotiations were tied together in 'orbits of coercive comparison', which forced all unions to follow similar patterns. Because the industries were large and important in the national economy – and strikes, therefore, of great consequence – the negotiations received wide press coverage and the settlements were highly visible. Rank-and-file union members used these highly publicized settlements as a measure to judge their union leaders: settlements in one industry became a standard that other union leaders had to meet in order to prove their prowess at the bargaining table (p. 80).

Thus, their argument goes, the wage rule of '3% AIF plus COLA', based on the average growth rate of labor productivity, was institutionalized and spread through pattern bargaining, providing the standard against which settlements were judged in the post-war period and serving as a regulatory mechanism for the macro-economy.

Reder and Neumann(1980) conceptualize collective bargaining as "a series of bargains in which the bargainers learn about one another's behavior patterns during the bargaining process and develop conventions (protocols) to guide subsequent bargaining activity" (p. 868). They further characterize repeated collective bargaining encounters involving the division of an uncertain joint product: "we assume that the division process consists of establishing a set of rules or a formula governing division of an imperfectly predictable joint product during a specified time period. These rules or formulae are expressed in a collective-bargaining agreement or contract" (p. 870). "Finally, and most important, a protocol relates the wage rates, fringes, etc., that are to be paid to those set in certain other collective-bargaining agreements and to movements in the cost of living" (p. 871).

Thus, we might say that 'what employers and unions do' is to take actions so as to attempt to reduce uncertainty and address contingencies; given that complete contracts are impossible, the parties attempt to reduce the number and scope of issues to be contended. It seems a reasonable extension of Reder and Neumann's work to postulate that protocols might tie wages to past agreements or to some historically developed rule such as '3% plus COLA', effectively rendering wages as one of the factors held constant in the constraints of a complex labor negotiation.

These viewpoints suggest a 'path dependence' in union wage determination (David (1985)), with the wage determination system in the post-war decades being heavily dependent on choices made in the immediate post-war years. Thus, it is worth examining the sources of support for the watershed 1948 GM-UAW settlement. Katz (1985) found that the idea for AIF (initially 3 cents rather than 3%) plus COLA was thought up by General Motors President Charles Wilson during a hospital stay. While we may never know his precise motivation, or whether he (or anyone else) could have anticipated the long-term congruence of the 3% wage rule with the average growth rate of labor productivity in the economy, it was certainly true that the '3% plus COLA' wage rule resonated with the Keynesian ideology of the UAW in the Walter Reuther era, increasing the chances of its acceptance by both sides.

This Keynesian inclination is evident in one of the union's initial statements on the 1948 settlement: they described the novel AIF portion of that agreement as "a gesture toward keeping the workers' purchasing power abreast of the increased output resulting from technological advance in the national economy" (as quoted in Ross (1949), p. 5). An even more explicitly Keynesian sentiment was put forth in an economic brief by Reuther filed with the War Labor Board in 1945: "Increased production must be supported by increased consumption, and increased consumption will be possible only through increased wages" (as quoted in Lichtenstein (1995), p. 222). Another economic brief presented by the UAW to GM in 1945 argues that "Manufacturers of automobiles and other durable goods have a major responsibility in building purchasing power for the products of the entire economy ... unless these industries begin now to lead the way toward a far larger spending power in the hands of the people than we have ever known, their brief boom will collapse and they will carry themselves and the nation back to a depression with nineteen million unemployed" (UAW (1945: 53)).[1] The '3% AIF plus COLA' wage rule was thus consistent with the UAW's stated aspiration to keep wages (and purchasing power) growing at the same rate as productivity, an aspiration that was likely influenced in large measure by the depression and the Reuther/CIO ideology of corporatism and was clearly consistent with Keynesian economics.

We can therefore conceptualize the 'bargain' between labor and capital primarily in terms of the predictability and stability it provided for both sides. General Motors got labor peace, while the UAW was guaranteed a steady and predictable growth in wages. Under Keynesian assumptions, the steady increase in wages, and the associated growth in overall purchasing power through the links to other sectors and workers, should have provided additional predictability for General Motors in terms of demand for its products, as well as obvious benefits for the economy as a whole. Thus, in the immediate post-war era, the '3% plus COLA' wage rule seemingly made sense for both parties.

Whatever the initial impetus for the emergence of the '3% plus COLA' wage rule, additional possible explanations for the *persistence* of wage rules relate to the individual psychology involved in the formation of bargaining 'focal points' and anchoring points more generally, as well as customary behavior (see, for example, Schelling (1960) and Tversky and Kahneman (1974) for discussions of anchoring in negotiations and in the formation of probability estimates, and Piore (1972) for a discussion of customary behavior in unionized wage setting). The basic notion is that once '3% plus COLA' was the settlement term for a few settlements, custom set that as the standard that formed the starting (or focal) point for future negotiations and against which future settlements were judged. How could the parties and, perhaps more important, their constituents, decide where to set their initial demands and evaluate whether a settlement was favorable or not in a world of seemingly ample rents, particularly when the parties had essentially decided to keep the companies' books closed during the negotiations?

At the very least, once '3% plus COLA' had been established as the customary settlement, it probably formed an 'anchoring point', the assumed 'normal' level at the start of the next round of negotiations. And, being the customary settlement, deviating from it would have likely antagonized the workers who had grown accustomed to it. Thus, it is possible that the costs of violating rank and file norms of longitudinal fairness outweighed the benefits of determining wages more rationally (in terms of achieving a bargaining equilibrium) rather than just increasing real wages according to a simple, repetitive rule.[2]

The rationale for longitudinal wage stability in the above-cited works varies from the provision of structure to negotiations, to the provision of labor peace, to the existence of psychological anchors, to functionally forming the basis for macroeconomic stabilization. The common element of this approach is the hypothesized existence of rules, norms, or protocols providing longitudinal stability in union wage determination: i.e. similarity of contract terms across bargaining rounds through the adherence to simple rules such as '3% plus COLA'.

While this proposition involving longitudinal stability was always controversial, even many of those who accepted that it existed for most of the post-war era argued that it had fundamentally broken down during the 'concession bargaining' era of the early 1980s (see, for example, the debates among Dunlop (1982), Freedman (1982), Freeman (1986), Mitchell (1985), and Vroman and Abowd (1988)). The basic empirical questions, then, are whether there is evidence of the existence of '3% plus COLA' in the union contracts before the 1980s, whether it broke down during the 'concession bargaining' era of the 1980s, and whether it has returned after that crisis. Thus, I now turn to the evidence for the existence of the '3% plus COLA' wage rule in the contracts negotiated between the UAW and the 'Big 3' automakers between 1970 and 1999.

THE PORTIONS OF CONTRACTED WAGE INCREASES AND OTHER ISSUES IN THE REPORTING OF CONTRACT CLAUSES

I propose a particular method for investigating the nature of union wage determination: a qualitative analysis of the collectively bargained contract clauses, as opposed to statistical analysis of summary measures of ex-ante predicted or ex-post realized wage outcomes.[3] Recall from above that union contract wage clauses in the United States in the post-World War II era typically contain at least two main conceptually separate components: the Annual Improvement Factor (AIF), or base wage increase, and the Cost-of-Living Adjustment (COLA), which indexes wages to changes in some cost-of-living index (usually the CPI).[4] The contention here is that meaningful information for evaluating the nature of union wage determination can be obtained by separately analyzing the different parts of the contract clauses, rather than compounding them into one number, thereby confounding the effects of the AIF and the COLA.

When one looks at the actual contracts, one fact becomes apparent: the terms in which the wage outcomes are reported vary widely across the contracts. Some specify wage increases in terms of percentage increases, others specify the increases in terms of cents-per-hour increases by wage levels or labor grades, and still others just present wage tables with new wage levels that will take effect at given dates over the life of the contract. In general, each bargaining unit's contract follows the same basic terminology as the previous contract for that bargaining unit. When one looks at the variety of contracts negotiated in a given round, at first glance it seems as though they have little to do with each other at all in terms of the wage clauses.

But, an important clue lies in the reports of these contract terms in the BLS publication *Current Wage Developments* (now *Compensation and Working Conditions*) and the BNA publication *The Daily Labor Report*. These reports, based on information from the negotiators and newspaper accounts of the settlements, tend to report the settlements in a common form, such as "3% plus 20 cents first year increase, 3% second and third year increases ..." When these reports are checked against the actual form in which the increases are recorded in the contract, which vary widely across the different union-company pairs as noted above, they do, indeed, match up. Thus, it is important to note that what I mean by contract terms under this approach are, in fact, a translation of the contract terms into a similar form, generally as reported in *Current Wage Developments*. Thus, *Current Wage Developments* is more than just an alternative source of contract wage settlement information; it is also important as a source of TRANSLATION of those terms into a common language, presumably the language of the negotiators that was widely known at the time of the negotiation and was shared with the negotiators' constituents.

RESULTS AND INTERPRETATION

The sample chosen here is the 'Big 3' automakers, General Motors, Ford, and Chrysler, all represented by the UAW. This industry was often argued by those in the 'pattern bargaining school' to form the core of one of the main 'orbits of coercive comparison' of the union wage settlement system during the heyday of the 'New Deal Industrial Relations System', with agricultural implements and aerospace contracts generally closely following the key auto settlement in a given bargaining round, and contracts in other industries either following the terms of this pattern to a lesser extent or following their own orbits of coercive comparison. This has clearly been one of the prominent industries for union wage determination (and U.S. industrial history more generally). This was also the industry analyzed earlier by Levinson (1960) and Katz (1985).

The period chosen is the set of contract rounds between 1970 and 1999. Industrial relations researchers tend to argue that the 1970s represented the tail-end of the 'New Deal System', when industrial relations practices maintained their stability and continuity with the past while the economic conditions enabling these practices deteriorated and radically changed all around them (Kochan, Katz and McKersie (1986)). The 1980s represented the break-up of this system, with 'concession bargaining' and other crises of the early 1980s, followed by the last few years, which are still very much open to interpretation. Thus, I argue that this choice of the automobile assembly industry in the 1970s, 1980s, and 1990s is most sensible in that it allows for the interpretation of both the previous system as well as the developments of the last two decades within a well-defined core industry, yet remains tractable.

Table 1 presents the wage settlements in the automobile assembly industry from the 1970–71 bargaining round through the 1999 bargaining round. The first, second and third year increases presented are general wage increases (or AIF), except when designated as 'ls', for 'lump sum' payment.[5] The COLA formulas indicate the increase for a given change in a Consumer Price Index (CPI). Thus, '1 ¢ / 0.3 (1967)' means 'one cent increase for each 0.3-point rise in the 1967 CPI'. The table also presents the approximate number of workers covered by each contract, as reported by the BLS, the BNA, and newspaper reports. Together, the contract terms and employment numbers can give us a sense of the extent of increase in the 'wage bill' (or total wage cost to the company) from contract to contract.

There are many interesting clues here regarding the extent of pattern bargaining, and previous studies of wage determination in this industry have examined the extent of cross-sectional stability (see, for example, Levinson (1960), Katz (1985), Budd (1992, 1997), and Erickson (1996)). Yet, I posit that simple visual inspection suggests another insight: that, not only have the contracts among the three major assemblers tended to resemble each other (manifesting cross-sectional, within-bargaining round stability, or pattern bargaining), but, except for a few rounds in the early 1980s, they also manifest significant longitudinal, or cross-bargaining round stability in the form of a '3% plus COLA' wage rule.

When one looks at the settlements of the 1970s, *every* contract at all three companies provided 3% AIF in the second and third years, with somewhat more variance in the first – suggesting that '3% AIF plus COLA' was a wage norm or rule during that period. The frequent variation from 3% in the first year is a complicated issue, often involving 'COLA travel', or the money not paid under the COLA system over the final quarter of the previous contract.[6] In addition, the first year increase was sometimes specified in terms of cents per hour rather than (or in addition to) percentage terms.

The contracts of the early-1980s, a time of crisis by most standards, do not suggest anything even remotely resembling '3% plus COLA'. However, Katz

Table 1. Automobile Industry Contract Wage Terms

Bargaining Round	General Motors UAW	Ford UAW	Chrysler UAW
1970–71:			
Settlement Date	11/12/70	12/7/70	1/19/71
1st Year Increase	49 ¢ – 61 ¢	49 ¢ – 61 ¢	49 ¢ – 61 ¢
2nd Year Increase	3 %	3 %	3 %
3rd Year Increase	3 %	3 %	3 %
COLA	1 ¢ / 0.4 (1957–59)	1 ¢ / 0.4 (1957–59)	1 ¢ / 0.4 (1957–59)
Workers Covered	400,000	161,000	110,000
1973:			
Settlement Date	11/19/73	10/26/73	9/17/73
1st Year Increase	3 % + 12 ¢	3 % + 12 ¢	3 % + 12 ¢
2nd Year Increase	3 %	3 %	3 %
3rd Year Increase	3 %	3 %	3 %
COLA	1 ¢ / 0.3 (1967)	1 ¢ / 0.3 (1967)	1 ¢ / 0.3 (1967)
Workers Covered	415,000	185,000	115,000
1976:			
Settlement Date	11/19/76	10/5/76	11/5/76
1st Year Increase	3 % + 20 ¢	3 % + 20 ¢	3 % + 20 ¢
2nd Year Increase	3 %	3 %	3 %
3rd Year Increase	3 %	3 %	3 %
COLA	1 ¢ / 0.3 (1967)	1 ¢ / 0.3 (1967)	1 ¢ / 0.3 (1967)
Workers Covered	390,000	170,000	115,000
1979:			
Settlement Date	9/14/79	10/4/79	10/25/79
1st Year Increase	3 % + 24 ¢	3 % + 24 ¢	3 % + 24 ¢
2nd Year Increase	3 %	3 %	3 %
3rd Year Increase	3 %	3 %	3 %
COLA	1 ¢ / 0.26 (1967)	1 ¢ / 0.26 (1967)	1 ¢ / 0.26 (1967)
Workers Covered	462,000	190,000	123,000

Table 1. (Continued)

Bargaining Round	General Motors UAW	Ford UAW	Chrysler UAW
1982–83:			
Settlement Date	3/22/82	2/11/82	12/9/82, 9/5/83
1st Year Increase			3%
2nd Year Increase			
3rd Year Increase			
COLA	1 ¢ / 0.26 (1967)	1 ¢ / 0.26 (1967)	1 ¢ / 0.26 (1967)
Profit Sharing	yes: 0% – 10% (of profits)	yes: 0% – 15% (of profits)	
Workers Covered	320,000	105,000	47,000
1984–85:			
Settlement Date	9/27/84	10/14/84	10/23/85
1st Year Increase	9 ¢ – 50 ¢	8 ¢ – 47 ¢	9 ¢ – 50 ¢
2nd Year Increase	2.25% ls	2.25% ls	2.25% ls
3rd Year Increase	2.25% ls	2.25% ls	3%
COLA	1 ¢ / 0.26 (1967)	1 ¢ / 0.26 (1967)	1 ¢ / 0.26 (1967)
Profit Sharing	yes: 0% - 10% (of profits)	yes: 0% - 15% (of profits)	
Workers Covered	350,000	115,000	70,000
1987–88:			
Settlement Date	10/8/87	9/17/87	5/4/88
1st Year Increase	3 %	3 %	3% ls
2nd Year Increase	3% ls	3% ls	3% ls
3rd Year Increase	3% ls	3% ls	
COLA	1 ¢ / 0.26 (1967)	1 ¢ / 0.26 (1967)	1 ¢ / 0.26 (1967)
Profit Sharing	yes: 0% – 16% (of profits)	yes: 0% – 16% (of profits)	yes: 0% – 16% (of profits)
Workers Covered	335,000	104,000	64,000

Table 1. (Continued)

Bargaining Round	General Motors UAW	Ford UAW	Chrysler UAW
1990:			
Settlement Date	9/17/90	10/7/90	10/30/90
1st Year Increase	3 %	3%	3%
2nd Year Increase	3% ls	3% ls	3% ls
3rd Year Increase	3% ls	3% ls	3% ls
COLA	1 ¢ / 0.26 (1967)	1 ¢ / 0.26 (1967)	1 ¢ / 0.26 (1967)
Profit Sharing	yes: 6% - 17% (of profits)	yes: 6% – 17% (of profits)	yes: 6% – 17% (of profits)
Workers Covered	227,000	100,000	60,000
1993:			
Settlement Date	10/24/93	9/16/93	10/4/93
1st Year Increase	3 %	3%	3%
2nd Year Increase	3% ls	3% ls	3% ls
3rd Year Increase	3% ls	3% ls	3% ls
COLA	1 ¢ / 0.26 (1967)	1 ¢ / 0.26 (1967)	1 ¢ / 0.26 (1967)
Profit Sharing	yes: 6% – 17% (of profits)	yes: 6% – 17% (of profits)	yes: 6% – 17% (of profits)
Workers Covered	260,000	96,000	60,000
1996:			
Settlement Date	11/2/96	9/14/96	10/3/96
1st Year Increase	$2,000 ls	$2,000 ls	$2,000 ls
2nd Year Increase	3%	3%	3%
3rd Year Increase	3%	3%	3%
COLA	1 ¢ / 0.26 (1967)	1 ¢ / 0.26 (1967)	1 ¢ / 0.26 (1967)
Profit Sharing	yes: 6% – 17% (of profits)	yes: 6% – 17% (of profits)	yes: 6% – 17% (of profits)
Workers Covered	215,000	105,000	72,000

Table 1. (Continued)

Bargaining Round	General Motors UAW	Ford UAW	(Daimler) Chrysler UAW
1999:			
Settlement Date	10/13/99	10/24/99	9/27/99
1st Year Increase	3% + $1,350 ls	3% + $1,350 ls	3% + $1,350 ls
2nd Year Increase	3%	3%	3%
3rd Year Increase	3%	3%	3%
4th Year Increase	3%	3%	3%
COLA	1 ¢ / 0.25 (1967)	1 ¢ / 0.25 (1967)	1 ¢ / 0.25 (1967)
Profit Sharing	yes: 6% – 17% (of profits)	yes: 6% – 17% (of profits)	yes: 6% – 17% (of profits)
Workers Covered	185,000	100,000	75,000

Wage increase numbers are AIF base wage increases, except those designated 'ls' for 'lump sum' payment. COLA formulas listed are cents-per-CPI point; the year listed in the COLA rows is the base year of the relevant CPI index. Ranges in the profit sharing row denote the percentage of profits to be paid out, contingent on the level of profits.

(1985), for example, argues that such seemingly unnecessary practices as the inclusion of a COLA clause in the one-year contract negotiated at Chrysler in 1982 suggests that the structure of the traditional wage rule was consciously maintained.

Then, in the late 1980s and early 1990s, something like the '3% plus COLA' rule seemed to return, but with the contracts generally providing a first year wage increase of 3% and second and third year lump sum payments of 3%. In 1996, the contracts called for second- and third-year wage increases of 3% (as in the contracts of the 1970s), with a first-year lump sum payment. In 1999, the 4-year contracts provided for 3% wage increases every year, and an additional bonus of $1,350 in the first year.

These findings suggest the following interpretations. '3% AIF plus COLA' held as a wage rule or norm through the 1970s, particularly in the second and third years of the contracts. This interpretation is modified by the fact that the first year increase in addition to the 3% showed some variation across the bargaining rounds, as discussed above. The 'concession' contracts of the early 1980s represented a break from this previous system, with the contracts generally specifying no wage increases and adopting profit sharing clauses. But, after the crises of the early 1980s, the automobile assembly industry seems to have returned to something like '3% plus COLA', albeit with profit sharing in place and the 3% provided by lump sum payments rather than wage increases in the second and third years of the contracts in the 1987, 1990, and 1993 rounds, a return to 3% second and third year AIF wage increases in the 1996 round, and 3% AIF wage increases in every year of the 4-year 1999 contracts. At the very least, this table suggests that some significance has been attached to '3%' as the typical yearly wage increase in addition to the COLA, both before the 'concession bargaining' era of the early 1980s and again in recent rounds.

Additional insights can be gained by examining the distribution of AIF increases in Budd's(1992) data, presented in Fig. 1. These are contracted AIF percentage wage increases (though sometimes inferred in percentage terms from average hourly earnings in the industry) for the UAW contracts negotiated across a variety of industries over the periods 1955–79 and 1987–90. The mean of this distribution of yearly percentage AIF increases is 3.04%, the standard deviation is 1.52%, and the median is 2.79%. The Budd data thus indicates a tendency to 3% as the mean of the distribution of AIF increases over the last few decades in UAW contracts more generally.[7]

In sum, '3% plus COLA' appears to have constituted an important regularity in union wage determination among the major company-union pairs in this

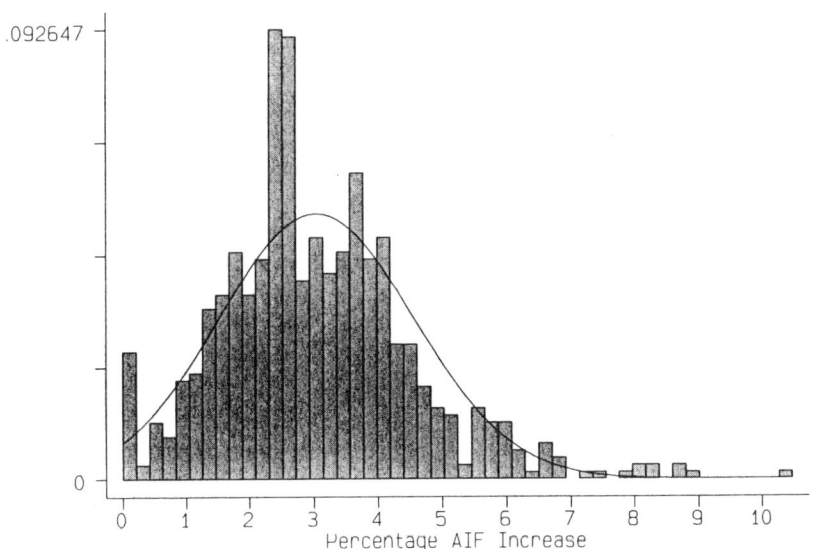

Fig. 1. Distribution of AIF Increases, Negotiated UAW Wages, 1955–79 & 1987–90
Source: Data from Budd (1992)

industry, seemingly forming a 'focal point' for subsequent negotiations. These findings thus suggest that wage determination is not a function of short-term labor market, firm, or industry conditions during non-crisis periods when the rules are actively in place; rather, wage increases seem to have been based to a large extent on past practice. Despite the fact that both company and industry profits, as well as such factors as worker productivity and union strength, varied from contract round to contract round and company to company up until 1980, the contracted growth rate of wages was essentially stable among these companies. But, this did not hold in a time of crisis such as the early 1980s when there were apparently not enough rents available to meet the customary settlement.[8] This brings us back to regulation theory: the idea that once the customary settlement had been established, it persisted as long as it was consistent with the macroeconomic and individual companies' competitive environments.[9]

The return to something resembling '3% plus COLA' in the 1990s seems a testament to the staying power of such customary rules. And, along with the contract terms evidence presented in Table 1, there is also some additional qualitative evidence for a return to the previously longitudinally stable wage rule in the 1990s: The UAW, in reporting its 1996 contract with Ford, said that: "'We're back to two AIFs for the first time since 1979', [UAW President] Yokich told the Ford Council. He was referring to the 3% Annual Improvement Factor raises that the union had traditionally won from the Big Three before the auto industry fell into hard times in the 1980s" (UAW(1996)).

The return to something resembling the earlier wage rule is even more notable given that the contracts in the 1990s maintained the profit sharing formulas adopted during the crisis period of the early 1980s. Apparently, at this point, the companies were willing to return to a modified version of the previous rule *in addition to* profit sharing. Obviously, the existence of profit sharing provides the companies with flexibility in compensation determination above and beyond the wage rules: in 1998, for example, the average profit sharing payout at Chrysler was $7,400, but only $200 at GM (Katz and Darbishire (2000), p. 36). Note as well in Table 1 the drop in the number of workers covered by the contracts by approximately half at all three companies from the peak in 1979 to 1990. Perhaps this drop in employment was one of the factors that made the return to something resembling the historic '3% plus COLA' formula more palatable to the companies, given that it represented a much smaller increase in the overall wage bill (as, of course, did the substitution of 3% lump sum payments for 3% AIF increases, over the longer term).[10] Note as well that productivity advances and capital stock increases in automobile manufacturing may have reduced unit labor costs during the 1980s, and that the successes at the NUMMI and Saturn experimental plants may have provided coercive comparisons contributing to the return to a modified version of the previous wage rule.[11]

Additional coercive comparisons may have come from the growing non-union portion of the automobile industry. Figure 2 presents real average hourly earnings (at 1982–84 prices) for production workers in both automobiles and all durable goods manufacturing over the period 1970–96. While this data does not allow us to separately analyze union and non-union earnings,[12] it does indicate that automobile industry earnings remained well above earnings for other production workers in the economy during this period, even with the concessions at the unionized companies.

CONCLUSIONS AND LARGER CONSEQUENCES

First and foremost, consideration of the existence of wage rules suggests that we might want to re-think the extent to which union wages have been determined on the basis of short-term product and labor market conditions. Many studies of union compensation concentrate on wages alone, and those based on

Fig. 2. Real Average Hourly Earnings for Production Workers in Automobiles and Durable Goods, 1970–96. *Source: U.S.B.L.S.*

the U.S. often use the same source of data as was used here to construct the contract data in Table 1, *Current Wage Developments* – now *Compensation and Working Conditions* (e.g. Budd (1992, 1997), Currie and McConnell (1992), Vroman and Abowd (1988)). At the very least, perhaps more emphasis should be put on other aspects of the compensation package: perhaps marginal compensation determination takes place more among benefits or even work rules than over wages.[13]

Second, these findings are consistent with the view that we should consider post-war U.S. union wage determination in the context of the 'New Deal Industrial Relations System' in which many aspects of the unionized employment relationship were based on rigid and longitudinally stable rules. This system acted to limit contingencies, increase predictability, and lower uncertainty, ambiguity, and conflict. It had very little flexibility, and the pay part of it was no exception. In essence, the postwar bargain as regards compensation can be conceptualized as, in exchange for labor peace and the agreement that unions would NOT ever demand a look at the financial books, employers gave unions a stable 3% + COLA yearly wage increase: 'You (the workers) have no say over the strategic direction of the firm, we (the employers) guarantee you a stable rule regarding the increase of real wages, and we take the residual'. The gains to the parties came primarily in the form of stability and predictability. And, whatever led to the emergence of the rules in the late 1940s, other factors such as customary behavior and psychological anchoring could well have contributed to their long-term persistence, even after (and if) the initial impetuses for the wage rules became obsolete.

In sum, these findings suggest that we should take seriously the notion that union wage determination has been based on simple, repetitive rules, as were many other aspects of U.S. industrial relations in the post-war period.[14] It is intriguing, however, that in the 1990s, when many argue that the old system is dead or dying, there seems to have been a return to something resembling the previous wage rule.

But, absent a complete return to the old rule, an important question raised by all of this is: What determines which of the 'constraints' on flexible wage determination are released in a time of crisis such as the early 1980s? And, even more: What is the nature and extent of the type of 'crisis' that leads to the release of these constraints? Is it driven by the company's actual ability to pay? Perhaps by possibility of layoff or other severe economic hardship for the 'median voter' in the union local? Or, by the various other factors that lead to an increase in management's bargaining power, such as the political climate of the early 1980s as evidenced by the PATCO air traffic controllers' strike and subsequent employee dismissals? These are important questions for future research.

Third, these findings clearly have macroeconomic consequences, suggesting a possible source of wage rigidity (as discussed in Piore and Sabel (1984)). A contract with a COLA clause and an AIF determined by past practice suggests wages that are responsive to inflation but little else, such as differences in firm or economy-wide performance. The experience of the early 1980s perhaps suggests more responsiveness in times of crisis, but the experience of the 1990s documented here suggests a return to rigidity, albeit with some amount of profit sharing now in place. The existence of rigid wage rules also constitutes a possible partial explanation for the PERSISTENCE of inter-industry wage differentials (which is an enduring puzzle in the wage determination literature). The question of where initial differences in wages across industries come from remains unanswered, but the existence of wage rules does give a partial explanation for how they could persist, particularly if '3% plus COLA' has been followed in contracts negotiated in other industries (as asserted by Piore and Sabel (1984)), and to the extent that non-union wages are pegged to the union sector in given industries (through, for example, specialized wage surveys or union threat effects).

Finally, this interpretation of union wage determination might give us reason for pause about the applicability of marginal decision making theory to other aspects of human behavior. Some recent findings suggest that, even in the non-union sector, 'non-competitive' issues such as fairness are most important in determining wages (see, for example, Bewley and Brainard (1993)). If we would expect anything to be determined on the basis of market conditions, wages (even in the union sector) would probably be high on most of our lists. This analysis suggests the possibility that the adoption of simple rules results in a wide range of issues being 'locked up' in the constraints facing decision makers such as union and management negotiators, as argued by Reder and Neumann (1980). In any case, another important question for future research is the extent to which such simple longitudinal rules exist in other realms of repetitive negotiation.

NOTES

1. Note, however, that Reuther remained unhappy about General Motors' unwillingness to link its pricing policies to wage increases. The nature of the essential 'bargain' struck between the union and the companies in the post war era will be discussed below. See Lichtenstein (1995) for a detailed explanation of the nature of the UAW ideology as regards wages in the Reuther era.

2. Consider the following quotes taken from the film *Final Offer*, the documentary account of the negotiations between General Motors and the UAW in Canada in 1984, the round when Candian automobile contracts first broke from '3% plus COLA'. During

the ratification meeting with the UAW negotiating committee, one local union leader states "You want to tell the membership that they can't get what they had for thirty years ... they can't get 3% with the money that this corporation's making?" Another member of the committee says that "I'll likely be with those pensioners another year from now and I'm giving my gut feeling. I don't like to give up that 3% ... I've seen it for years and years and years and I don't want my kid or my son-in-law or the other guys having to give it up" (National Film Board of Canada (1985)).

3. See Erickson (1996) for a more detailed discussion of this approach.

4. See Katz (1985) for further explication of these two components. The wage clauses can also contain other portions, such as profit sharing clauses, incentive systems, lump sum payments, etc. Note that I am not including benefits here, nor even less tangible and comparable items such as work rules.

5. See Bell and Neumark (1992), Erickson and Ichino (1994), and Erickson (1992) for discussions of lump sum payments.

6. Thus, the cents-per-hour paid in addition to the 3% in the first year of these contracts might well be properly placed in the same category as the COLA (from the previous contract!) rather than the AIF.

7. The discrepancies from exactly 3% in the Budd data could represent genuine deviations from the wage rule due to such factors as crisis bargaining, contracts without COLA clauses, or other deviations in bargained outcomes; alternatively, the discrepancies could represent coding issues, such as the difficulty in treating such things as 'COLA travel', which often goes into the first year AIF of the new contract rather than the third year COLA of the previous contract (as discussed above); the treatment of timing of payments and contract settlements, especially where retroactivity is common when strikes occur; or the inference of percentage wage increases from average cents-per-hour wage increases and industry average hourly earnings.

8. Or, alternatively, when the companies saw the benefits of breaking from the historical wage rule as outweighing the costs; see the discussion below.

9. Levinson (1960), in his study of pattern bargaining in this industry in the early post-war era, argued that bargaining pairs follow the industry pattern except in times of crisis, when attempting to meet the pattern is likely to drive the firm out of business. The argument here is that not only patterns, but also longitudinally stable wage rules hold as long as they are economically (and perhaps politically) viable.

10. See Erickson and Ichino (1994) for a discussion of the long-term advantages of AIF wage increases relative to lump sum payments for workers, given compounding and 'permanence' issues.

11. Saturn workers, for example, generally receive higher profit sharing payouts compared to workers at other General Motors plants because Saturn's profit sharing formula factors in standards such as product quality, while the formula at traditional GM plants relies exclusively on profits (Evenoff (1999)). One possibility is that matching Saturn's profit sharing system might not be feasible or advisable at other GM plants, but that consideration of the overall compensation at the Saturn plant could lead to demands for higher wages and lump sum payments at the traditional plants.

12. For the entire durable goods sector, Neumark and Wachter (1995) found that the union/non-union wage differential decreased by 4% from 1973 to 1989. Katz and Darbishire (2000) report that in 1994 the hourly wage for assemblers in Nissan transplants was about $3.00 less than for assemblers at General Motors, and that in 1996 the

hourly wage for assemblers at a BMW transplant was $1.74 less than for assemblers at General Motors (p. 32).

13. Just to give one example, in the 1996 round the pattern-setting Ford-UAW agreement, in addition to the wage provisions, provided for increases in monthly pension benefits, sickness and accident benefits, life insurance benefits, and tuition assistance benefits. It also provided guarantees of overall employment levels at the company for the first time. Mitchell (1980) and Erickson (1996) discuss the role of fringe benefits in deviations from wage patterns. An important question for future research involves the extent to which benefits are in fact determined on the basis of patterns and/or longitudinally stable rules.

14. Note that this conceptualization of the 'post-war bargain' may well be consistent with a 'strategic HR management' perspective, insofar as the company 'strategy' in the post-war era was to maintain control over production, predictability of costs, and the overall strategic direction in terms of product design, marketing, number of units produced, etc. In a sense, one might think of 'strategic HR management' in this instance as the company opting for predictability and stable rules on the labor side in exchange for total strategic control over all other aspects of the enterprise.

ACKNOWLEDGMENTS

I thank Sanford Jacoby, Harry Katz, Daniel J.B. Mitchell, and Michael Piore for their comments on earlier drafts, as well as seminar participants at the U.C.L.A. Department of Economics and the New York State School of Industrial and Labor Relations at Cornell University. I also thank John Budd for the use of his data on UAW wage outcomes.

REFERENCES

Bell, L., & Neumark, D. (1992). Lump-Sum Payments and Profit Sharing Plans in the Union Sector of the United States Economy. *The Economic Journal, 103*, 602–619.

Bewley, T., & Brainard, W. (1993). A Depressed Labor Market, As Explained by Participants. Working paper, Yale University.

Budd, J. W. (1992). The Determinants and Extent of UAW Pattern Bargaining. *Industrial and Labor Relations Review, 45*, 523–539.

Budd, J. W. (1997). Institutional and Market Determinants of Wage Spillovers: Evidence from UAW Pattern Bargaining. *Industrial Relations, 36*, 97–116.

Bureau of National Affairs. *Collective Bargaining Bulletin.* Various Issues.

Bureau of National Affairs. *The Daily Labor Report.* Various Issues.

Bureau of National Affairs (1998). Wage Patterns in Automobiles. In *Collective Bargaining Negotiations and Contracts* (pp. 18:401–18:431). Washington: BNA.

Currie, J., & McConnell, S. (1992). Firm-Specific Determinants of the Real Wage. *Review of Economics and Statistics, 74*, 297–304.

David, P. A. (1985). Clio and the Economics of QWERTY. *American Economic Review, 75*, 332–37.

Dunlop, J. (1982). Working Toward a Consensus. *Challenge, 25*, 26–34.

Erickson, C. L. (1992). Wage Rule Formation in the Aerospace Industry. *Industrial and Labor Relations Review, 45*, 507–522.

Erickson, C. L. (1996). A Re-Interpretation of Pattern Bargaining. *Industrial and Labor Relations Review, 49*, 615–634.

Erickson, C. L., & Ichino, A. C. (1994). Lump Sum Bonuses in Union Contracts. *Advances in Industrial and Labor Relations, 6*, 183–218.

Evanoff, T. (1999). Strikes Shrink GM Profit Sharing. *Detroit Free Press*, January 21, p. 1C.

Freedman, A. (1982). A Fundamental Change in Wage Bargaining. *Challenge, 25*, 14–17.

Freeman, R. (1986). In Search of Union Wage Concessions in Standard Data Sets. *Industrial Relations, 25*, 131–145.

Katz, H. C. (1985) *Shifting Gears*. Cambridge: MIT Press.

Katz, H. C., & Darbishire, O. (2000). *Converging Divergences: Worldwide Changes in Employment Systems*. Ithaca: Cornell University Press.

Kochan, T., Katz, H., & McKersie, R. (1986). *The Transformation of American Industrial Relations*. New York: Basic Books.

Levinson, H. M. (1960). Pattern Bargaining: A Case Study of the Automobile Workers. *Quarterly Journal of Economics, 74*, 296–317.

Lichtenstein, N. (1995). *The Most Dangerous Man in Detroit: Walter Reuther and the Fate of American Labor*. New York: Basic Books.

Mitchell, D. J. B. (1980). *Union, Wages, and Inflation*. Washington: Brookings Institution.

Mitchell, D. J. B. (1985). Shifting Norms in Wage Determination. *Brookings Papers on Economic Activity, 2*, 575–608.

National Film Board of Canada (1985). *Final Offer*. San Francisco: California Newsreel for the National Film Board of Canada.

Neumark, D., & Wachter, M. L. (1995). Union Effects on Non-union Wages: Evidence from Panel Data on Industries and Cities. *Industrial and Labor Relations Review, 49*, 20–38.

Piore, M. J. (1972). Fragments of a 'Sociological' Theory of Wages. Industrial Relations Research Association *Proceedings of the 25th Annual Meeting*, 286–295.

Piore, M. J., & Sabel, C. F. (1984). *The Second Industrial Divide*. New York: Basic Books.

Reder, M. W., & Neumann, G. R. (1980). Conflict and Contract: The Case of Strikes. *Journal of Political Economy, 88*, 867–886.

Ross, A. M. (1949). The General Motors Wage Agreement of 1948. *The Review of Economics and Statistics, 31*, 1–7.

Schelling, T. C. (1960). *The Strategy of Conflict*. Cambridge: Harvard University Press.

Tversky, A., & Kahneman, D. (1974). Judgment Under Uncertainty: Heuristics and Biases. *Science 185*, 1124–1131.

United Automobile Workers (1945). Purchasing Power for Prosperity. Econonomic Brief presented to the General Motors Corporation.

United Automobile Workers (1996). UAW-Ford Workers Lead the Way for '96: UAW Wins Breakthroughs in Job Security, Pensions, Education. Electronic Press Release.

U.S. Department of Labor. *Current Wage Developments*. Various Issues.

Vroman, W., & Abowd, J. (1988). Disaggregated Wage Developments. *Brookings Papers on Economic Activit,y 1*, 313–346.

EMPLOYEE ACCEPTANCE OF THE CREW CHIEF PROGRAM IN THE POSTAL SERVICE: AN ANALYSIS WITH PRE AND POST DATA

JAMES E. MARTIN

ABSTRACT

This study evaluates the implementation of a crew chief program. Data from surveys administered both before and after trials in six cities were analyzed. Using an exchange theory model and qualitative literature on workplace teams, hypotheses were generated concerning the pre-existing workplace climate, crew chief role and relations, and differences between those who became crew chiefs and regular mail processors. Greater acceptance was predicted by stronger management support of the program, crew chiefs not behaving as junior supervisors, and viewing the position as desirable and as a promotion. However, the hypothesis relating the pre-existing climate to program acceptance was not supported.

INTRODUCTION

Our nation's industries have been faced with increased competitive pressures, both domestic and international. These pressures, as the corporate restructuring in the automobile industry and elsewhere indicate, are not unique to any one company (cf. Hitt et al., 1998; Holley & Jennings, 1997; Klein & Sorra, 1996; Kochan et al., 1986; Zahra, 1998). One outcome of these pressures in recent years is that many organizations have embarked on major design and work innovations incorporating changes in technology (Batt & Applebaum, 1995; Hunter & Lafkas, 1998; Macy & Izumi, 1993; Osterman, 1994, 2000). The introduction of new technologies within organizations frequently is accompanied by innovations to the employment structure and human resource practices (Osterman, 1994, 2000). Only recently, however, has research begun to examine how these innovations are related to various criteria of effectiveness or how they might potentially influence employee attitudes (Campion et al., 1996; Macy & Izumi, 1993).

In the past, the influence of technological innovations on employees has often been overlooked. For example, in the Postal Service, the new technologies associated with increasing automation and the resulting workplace changes have embittered employees (Goodin, 1992b). As Blackler and Brown noted (1985: 213), "there is an important need to seek to influence opinion and practice to ensure that the technologies are used to increase peoples' opportunities for self-determination at work rather than simply to seek ways in which the new technologies can smoothly be introduced." Therefore, it is useful to conduct research examining how the introduction of new technologies and the accompanying changes in employment structure affect employees.

One innovation resulting from or accompanying the introduction of technological change is the institution of the 'crew chief' position in unionized workplaces (Luby, 1995). Luby has defined the position as a lead position in the bargaining unit, with enhanced authority and responsibilities, which has replaced supervisors and their duties. In many ways, the crew chief position is similar to a team leader position as found in bargaining units in the automobile industry (Babson, 1993; MacDuffie, 1995; Rinehart et al., 1995), but is not attached to a fixed team. Although the use of crew chiefs is not currently widespread, their introduction at American Airlines, and the resulting transformation in the nature of supervision, positively affected the work environment and satisfaction of the average employee (Luby, 1995). Thus, greater understanding of the crew chief position and its introduction into the workplace is warranted, as other organizations, such as the Postal Service, where technological innovation has greatly changed mail processing, are considering implementing this workplace innovation (General Accounting Office, 1994).

Given the apparent dearth of quantitative research examining the acceptance of the crew chief (or team leader) position in a unionized setting, the purpose of the present investigation is to examine the factors associated with acceptance of a crew chief program in such a setting. This endeavor should serve to increase understanding of the position and facilitate the development of recommendations to increase the acceptance of crew chiefs by bargaining unit employees. In turn, the increased acceptance of crew chiefs (and team leaders) by employees should result in their increased usage. Therefore, this study is designed to be an evaluation of a set of crew chief trials. This study reports the results of an exploratory study using data from employees who became crew chiefs, and from those regular employees who did not. Survey data was collected both before and after a crew chief program was implemented in six cities. It uses a model of the relevant predictors of overall crew chief program acceptance to develop and test hypotheses.

THE MODEL

Previous research has used several different theoretical perspectives to study workplace innovations. The model used here incorporates exchange theory (e.g., Blau, 1964), which suggests that interpersonal relationships involve reciprocal exchanges of rights and responsibilities. Reciprocity norms govern these relationships (Gouldner, 1960), with employees generally believing that they should help those who have helped them in the past or whom they expect to help them in the future. Organizational psychologists (e.g., Levinson, 1965) have extended the exchange concept to person-organization relationships, suggesting that organizational reciprocity motives strongly influence behavior. Thus, it is believed social exchange processes direct person-organization relationships (Eisenberger et al., 1986), including those between the union and its members (Shore et al., 1994; Sinclair & Tetrick, 1995).

Contemporary exchange models often characterize person-organization relations as psychological contracts in which employees develop assumptions about their obligations to their employer and their employer's obligations to them (Rousseau, 1995). Graham (1991) suggests that these contracts vary from strong to weak relational ties. Employees with strong relational ties identify with the employer, share the collective values of the employer, and feel strongly obliged to stay with their employer and to work beyond their formal job requirements. In contrast, those with weak relational ties exchange involvement only for very exactly defined short-term benefits. Thus, social exchange models suggest that employees' perceptions of the nature of their relationship with their employer influence their conduct. In addition to using social exchange theory as the broad framework in which to examine the introduction of workplace innovations, the model developed in this investigation draws on the case study and descriptive literature on teams, team leaders, and crew chiefs to develop some specific predictions. Therefore, taken together, this model can be used to make predictions regarding the acceptance of a crew chief program.

Workplace Climate

There is some agreement that workplace or organizational climate can be conceptualized as employee perceptions concerning salient characteristics of the work context (Schneider, 1990). Several authors have argued that the initial workplace climate is an important consideration in the successful implementation of change. Cooke (1990) discusses at length the climate-related variables of trust and commitment in a study of labor-management cooperation. He operationalized trust in the context of a union-management relationship in several ways, including sharing information, consulting, following through on promises, and living up to one's roles and responsibilities. Cooke defined commitment as meaning "to obligate or bind to some course of action." (p. 125). He concluded that without trust or commitment, a joint labor-management cooperative innovation was unlikely to succeed in the long run. Klein and Sorra (1996) included "climate for implementation" in their integrative model of the determinants of the effectiveness of organizational implementation. While their climate concept was related to the actual innovation implementation, they argued that it is the climate that determines whether the innovation is successfully implemented. A third relevant approach to climate and innovation comes from the work of Tracey et al. (1995), who related the pre-existing climate and organizational culture to the acquisition of behaviors from training. Studies have found that a more positive climate is associated with more effective workplace innovations (e.g., Cooke, 1990; Macy et al., 1989; Tracey et al., 1995).

Broad climate indicators in the union-management innovation literature include commitment to the employer and union (Batt & Applebaum, 1995; Macy & Izumi, 1993), workgroup climate or commitment (Applebaum & Batt, 1994; Macy & Izumi, 1993), and the assessment of supervisory behaviors or climate (Batt & Applebaum, 1995; Macy & Izumi, 1993). Other studies of workplace innovation have noted that an important narrow climate indicator was satisfaction with advancement opportunities (Ondrack & Evans, 1986). Advancement opportunities are an important issue with such innovations, as there may be an effect of the innovation on the career line and number of available positions in the workplace (Ondrack & Evans, 1986; Osterman, 1994, 2000).

As set forth in this study, workplace climate thus concerns the pre-existing perceived psychological climate within which the crew chief program was introduced. This factor comprises the perceptual variables of workgroup climate, supervisory climate, and general work climate. The concepts included in this facet of the model have been extensively studied in relation to workplace innovations (Applebaum & Batt, 1994; Macy et al., 1989; Spreitzer et al., 1999). Consistent with exchange theory and the notion of psychological contracts (Rousseau, 1995), these studies have found that more effective forms of participation and employee empowerment are associated with more positive workplace climates as assessed by employee attitudes and perceptions.[1]

Hypothesis 1. The more positive the workplace climate prior to initiating the crew chief program, the greater will be the acceptance of the program by the crew chiefs and the regular employees.

Crew Chief Relations

The second factor in the model is the relations the crew chief has with the supervisors and management, and builds on the team leader and crew chief literature. The existing findings in that literature are consistent with exchange theory, and suggest that a more positive climate of supervision and management is related to more effective crew chiefs and team leaders (Luby, 1995; Robertson et al., 1993; Shaiken, 1995). Support by supervisors and managers appears related to the acceptance/effectiveness of the crew chief role (Babson, 1995; Luby, 1995; MacDuffie, 1995; Robertson et al., 1993), since without such support, it is harder to carry out the relevant role duties. The general literature on workplace innovation and program implementation notes that it is important that management support the innovation if it is to have a good chance of being successful (e.g., Batt & Applebaum, 1995; Macy & Izumi, 1993; Rodgers et al., 1993). Babson (1995) and Robertson et al. (1993) also discuss the importance of a specific form of support; having adequate numbers of employees in the workplace to insure the acceptance of the team leader concept. Without adequate staffing, the team leader is responsible for filling in for the missing employees, and thus is not functioning as a team leader. Overall, consistent with exchange theory, management support of the crew chief program represents a positive psychological contract with the employees that should increase the acceptance of the program.

Hypothesis 2. The more positive relations and support that the supervisors and management are perceived to have with the crew chiefs and crew chief program, the greater will be the acceptance of the crew chief program.

Crew Chief Role

The third factor in the model is the role of the crew chief and the crew chief program. There is also much discussion in the literature of the relevant role of the position incumbent and the quality of the relationship between the position incumbent and other employees (Babson, 1995; Luby, 1995; MacDuffie, 1995; Rinehart et al., 1995). The CAMI (CAMI is a joint venture of GM and Suzuki in Ontario) report (Robertson et al., 1993) discussed the ambiguity surrounding the role of the team leader in terms of whether he/she was supposed to be concerned with production or concerned with people. The union members wanted the bargaining unit position to be concerned with the people, and not with trying to get members to work harder. Babson (1993) found that if the team leader acts as a junior supervisor, he/she will likely not be accepted by the rank and file and may even be voted out of the position. Rinehart, Huxley and Robertson's (1995) research at the CAMI plant, which described the team concept as not having met the company's expectations for success, found that few employees aspired to be a team leader. In contrast, Luby (1995) reported that at American Airlines, where crew chiefs had positively affected the workplace, employees actively sought the crew chief position. Overall, these findings suggest that, in exchange theory terminology, crew chief emphasis on the relational component of work, rather than on the structural supervisory component, should be associated with a positive psychological climate, and would result in greater acceptance of the crew chief program.

Hypothesis 3. The more positive the view of the role and position of the crew chief, the greater will be the acceptance of the crew chief program.

Differences between Crew Chiefs and Regular Mail Processors

There is also literature that suggests there should be differences in attitudes and motivations between the regular employees and those holding the position of crew chief, with those promoted to the position having generally more positive attitudes. Lieberman's (1956) classic longitudinal study found that employees who moved into leader roles, either in the union or in management, shifted their former attitudes to identify with their new position. Qualitative research also reports differences in the attitudes of team leaders and team members concerning the overall program, its relations with management, and its role (Rinehart et al., 1995; Robertson et al., 1993). Exchange theory also suggests that attitude differences should exist between mail processors and those who were promoted to crew chief. More specifically, since crew chiefs ultimately receive more direct benefits from the crew chief program than regular employees do, they would likely feel more positive about the position.

Hypothesis 4. The attitudes toward the crew chief program, its relations with supervisors and management, and its role will be more positive for the crew chiefs than for the regular employees.

METHOD

Setting and Surveying

Study background. The work innovation studied in this paper resulted from the 1990–1991 contract negotiations and interest arbitration between the American Postal Workers Union (APWU) and the United States Postal Service (USPS). At that time, the parties established a memorandum of understanding concerning establishing a trial program for 'crew chiefs' in automated mail processing. The parties agreed in their 1991 memorandum of understanding to establish a national level APWU-USPS task force to explore the crew chief concept and to help evaluate the trial program. Crew chiefs were to be a bargaining unit position patterned after crew chiefs or team leader positions existing in some successful private sector organizations, such as American Airlines and Auto Alliance (Mazda) (Babson, 1993, 1995; Luby, 1995). Employees in crew chief positions were assigned the primary responsibility for the oversight of other bargaining unit employees in the highly automated mail processor positions, including the direction of employees in the work unit, work assignments, administrative support and scheduling of overtime. One-year crew chief trials were established in six automated mail Processing and Distribution Centers in different parts of the country. The memorandum of understanding stated that "At the conclusion of these trial programs and tests, the parties will meet to decide whether the program should be expanded, remain at the status quo, or be terminated due to lack of success in relation to the parties' goals of greater opportunity for craft employees and improved efficiency for the USPS." (Collective Bargaining Agreement Between APWU, AFL-CIO and USPS, 1991: 138–139). The APWU contracted with the author to help evaluate the crew chief trials in automated mail processing.

The national task force selected the sites where trials were to take place and developed the job descriptions and training for the crew chiefs. Several criteria were used to select the sites. First, they were to be spread geographically around the country. Second, the local APWU affiliates had to express an interest in participating in the trials. Third, management members of the national task force had to have confidence that the local management would actually implement the crew chief concept, and allow crew chiefs to fulfill their duties as described in the memorandum of understanding. Crew chiefs began functioning at the first site in July 1992. Before the trials could begin at the next site, a new Postmaster General, who had recently taken office, announced a major reorganization of the USPS. While the details of that reorganization, which separated the mail processing functions from the customer service functions, were being formulated and taking effect, the introduction of further trials was suspended. However, the Time-1 surveying had already been completed in three cities. In early November 1992, the work on the project began again, and the Time-1 surveying was completed. Crew chiefs began functioning in the five remaining cities beginning January 1993.

A meta-analysis by Macy and Izumi (1993) of 131 North American field studies of such workplace transformations found that only 9% fully involved a union. Thus, the situation studied here differs from other workplace transformations because not only was the union, the APWU, involved as a full partner, but also because the union was the initiating party. As a result of the surveying and other assessments, the union concluded that the crew chief program was a success, in that the union members wanted it continued. However, the program was suspended due to disputes during the 1994 bargaining.

The jobs. Mail processors work on machines using technological advances that have completely replaced the older letter-sorting machines (LSMs). The LSMs used 17 employees to sort up to 43,200 letters hourly (Halliday, 1992). Today, all mail processors work on optical character reader (OCR), bar code sorter (BCS) and delivery bar code sorter (DBCS) machines. These machines are highly automated and can process up to 30,000 pieces of mail an hour and have replaced the much less automated LSMs (Goodin, 1992b). The actual mail processor work tasks are rigidly defined, as at NUMMI, a joint General Motors-Toyota venture, whose employees are represented by the UAW (Adler, 1995; Brown et al., 1991). The mail processors feed the mail to the machine and clear out the sorted mail. These technological changes have not been well accepted by the postal employees due to the perception that jobs were being lost (Goodin, 1992b). It was predicted there would be a doubling of employees in mail processor positions by 1998 (APWU, 1992), which would partially replace some of the LSM positions lost. If the parties accepted crew chiefs on a permanent basis, the number of mail processors would increase by an additional 10–15% beyond that doubling. The union was interested in crew chiefs because it had noticed that the ratio of supervisors to clerks had been increasing. Thus, by creating the new position, that ratio would decrease. The APWU also believed that the organization of Postal Service work created an "unnecessarily adversarial and bureaucratic workplace environment" (Arbitration Proceedings: USPS and National Association of Letter Carriers and APWU, Opinion and Award, 1991: 15). Thus, it thought that crew chiefs would improve the work climate, similar to what had occurred at American Airlines.

The addition of the crew chief between the employees and supervisors and the reduction in the number of supervisors on the workplace floor changed the organizational hierarchy for the mail processors. Using the terminology of Macy and Izumi (1993), the 'action-lever' of this field experiment represented a structural design change in the operation and control of the six Processing and Distribution Centers. In Osterman's (1994) terms, the establishment of the crew chief position represented a change in the internal labor market within the USPS, because mail processors could now move up to a higher level position still inside the bargaining unit. While the reorganized mail processor work shared some similarities with self-directed work teams, it did not meet the accepted definition of such (see Osterman, 1994) for several reasons. First, the crew members did not supervise their own work or make their own decisions about its pace and flow. Further, the crew was not an intact team, as the crew members usually rotated and often did not have the same crew chief from day-to-day. The qualitative evaluation of crew chiefs by the General Accounting Office (GAO, 1994) concluded with a recommendation that the crew chief program be expanded as one approach to implementing self-managed work units. While the supervisors were not eliminated, they were removed from the mail processing operation. In the Postal Service, supervisors are unionized. Thus, many opposed the crew chief program because, if made permanent, fewer supervisors would be needed (GAO, 1994). Indeed, the National Association of Postal Supervisors opposed the crew chief initiative (Goodin, 1992a).

Survey questions. The research team developed a survey instrument that was both relevant to employees holding mail processor positions and psychometrically sound. Wherever possible, standard scales or items and scales adapted from previously published work were used. The resulting Time-1 survey variables used here consisted primarily of various facets of commitment, attitudes toward supervision, and perceptions of workgroup relations. In addition, there was a page of demographic items and some descriptive items about the workplace. After lengthy discussions with members of the national task force and our participation in several site visits, several sets of items relating to the crew chiefs were added to the 1993 Time-2 survey. As part of the crew chief evaluation, different surveys were given to crew chiefs and to regular mail processors who were not crew chiefs. While there were many common items on both surveys, the crew chief survey had items describing their role behaviors that the mail processors would not be aware of. Similarly, the mail processor survey had items describing the way the crew chiefs were perceived.

Two questions, selected by the union to summarize the member attitudes concerning crew chiefs and the crew chief program, assessed the dependent variable. The first question was: "Overall, how do you feel about the crew chiefs as they function in your Postal Installation now?", with five response choices, ranging from "Very Satisfied" to "Very Dissatisfied". The second question was: "My overall opinion of the crew chief program is that it should:," with the following five response choices; "Remain as is," "Be changed only slightly," "Be changed only moderately," "Be changed greatly," or "Be discontinued." These two questions were combined into a single scale called Crew Chief Program Acceptance (total sample alpha = 0.86, inter-item correlation = 0.70).[2]

Procedures. With the cooperation of the USPS, all employees holding the mail processor position and/or crew chief position were surveyed during their working hours in the six cities in both 1992 and 1993. Because the Time-1 surveys were administered before the crew chief trials had been established, all employees, all of whom were then in the mail processor position, received the identical survey with no mention of the term 'crew chief'. A total of 477 were surveyed. The Time-2 surveys were administered in 1993 after the crew chiefs had been in place for almost a year, except for the first site, where the time lag was longer; 538 mail processors and 74 crew chiefs filled out surveys. Using standard matching techniques, 167 mail processor and 41 crew chief surveys were matched from Time-1 to Time-2. The remainder were not employed at both times. Some of the multivariate sample sizes were slightly smaller due to missing data.

ANALYSES

To guard against potential misinterpretation of the results due to pre-existing differences, both by city and by employee, the hypothesis testing controlled for these differences. Macy et al. (1989) argued that employee demographic differences are important primarily to the extent that they affect initial attitudes, and thus should be controlled for. Further, a major Postal reorganization took place while the Time-1 surveying was in progress. Thus, the analyses controlled for this through a dummy variable dichotomizing the six cities into a variable representing the first three sites surveyed (before reorganization) and the second three sites surveyed (after reorganization) of sites surveyed (*City, survey wave*). The latter variable and selected employee demographics were entered as controls on step 1 in the regression equations.

Then, on the second step, six perceptual climate variables as measured at Time-1 were entered. These included two three-item scales adapted from Martin and Peterson (1987), loyalty to the local APWU union and loyalty to the USPS (both facets of commitment), which have been widely used in studies of union member commitment (cf. Magenau & Martin, 1999). Two scales related to supervisory behavior, a three-item *Supervisory Climate* scale adapted from Smith (1976), and a three-item *Supervisor Production Orientation* scale adopted from Cammann et al. (1983). The former assesses the perceived relationship between supervision and work performance, while the latter assess how much the supervisor is concerned with production, and is similar conceptually to the concept of 'initiating structure' from Fleishman and Harris (1962). A five-item *Workgroup Climate* scale was developed for this study from the items of Berthiaume and Martin (1991) (two items assessing loyalty to one's workgroup), and items from Koys and DeCotiis (1991) and Litwin and Stringer (1968) (items assessing warmth and cohesion within the immediate workgroup). There was also a one-item scale assessing *Satisfaction with Advancement Opportunities* developed for this study. On the third step, variables developed especially for this study assessing the crew chief relational concepts (*Supervisor Works Well With and Supports Crew Chief, Supervisor Does Not Undercut Crew Chief, Management Supports Crew Chief Program, and Adequate Staffing*) and the crew chief role concepts (*Crew Chief Position is a Promotion, I Know Crew Chief Role, Crew Chief is Part of Management, and Would Like to be (continue as) Crew Chief*) were entered. The scale reliabilities for both the mail processor and crew chief groups are shown in Appendix A.

The first three hypotheses were tested through a three-step hierarchical regression with the variables assessed at Time-1 entered on the first two steps as described above. This enabled them to serve as control variables prior to entering the third step, Time-2 variables assessing the relations of the crew chief and the crew chief program with supervision and management, and the crew chief's role, into the regression analysis. Hypothesis four was tested by running a one-way multivariate analysis of variance (MANOVA) on the variables, both the independent predictors and the dependent variable, between the regular mail processors and those holding the position of crew chief. This was followed by univariate t- tests. Because of the small sample size for the crew chiefs and the resultant lack of power, regression results significant at the 0.10 level will be reported for analyses involving crew chief data beyond the more traditional level of 0.05. In addition, the correlation results were examined.

RESULTS

Table 1 shows the correlations among all the variables examined in the study for both the regular mail processors and the crew chiefs, and shows which variables are associated with Crew Chief Program Acceptance at the zero-order level. Looking at the crew chief results first, there is little support for Hypothesis 1, that a positive workplace climate prior to initiating crew chiefs is positively related to acceptance of the crew chief program. Only one of the six variables was as predicted, with one opposite to the predictions. Hypothesis 2, that positive relations and supervisor and management support for the crew chief program are positively related to acceptance was supported. As Table 1 indicates, three of the four relational variables were significant in the predicted direction. Hypothesis 3, that a more positive view of the role and position of the crew chief is positively related to acceptance, was supported by two of the four role-related variables. The results in Table 1 indicate a similar pattern of support for the first three hypotheses for the mail processors as for the crew chiefs. As the pattern of correlations suggest, there was little support for Hypothesis 1, moderately high support for Hypothesis 2, and stronger support for Hypothesis 3.

Hypothesis 4 stated that the attitudes toward the crew chief program, its relations with supervisors and management, and its role will be more positive for the crew chiefs than for the regular employees. The MANOVA results indicate significant differences between the mail processors and the crew chiefs (multivariate F (20, 177) = 7.70, $p < 0.001$) in support of Hypothesis 4.[3] Table 2 presents the means, standard deviations and the results of the follow-up univariate t-tests on the variables used in testing that hypothesis. Further, because this study had exploratory elements, the same is presented for the other variables examined in the study, plus *Satisfaction with Advancement Opportunities* as assessed at Time 2. The means indicate that, as hypothesized, the crew chiefs are significantly ($p < 0.01$) more favorable to the crew chief program than the mail processors. Overall, the crew chiefs have slightly favorable attitudes toward the program while the mail processors have slightly negative attitudes. Significant differences occurred for more than half the predictor variables, with generally more positive attitudes among the crew chiefs. As predicted by Hypothesis 4, where differences were found in the relational and role-related variables, the crew chiefs were uniformly more positive.

The other variables also showed some differences. As mail processor seniority was used in the selection criteria for crew chiefs, it is not surprising that seniority was higher for crew chiefs. The climate variables show some important

Table 1. Correlation of Variables: Mail Processors Above Diagonal, Crew Chiefs Below Diagonal[a]

	1	2	3	4	5	6	7	8	9	10	11	12	13	14	15	16	17	18	19	20
1	**1.00**	0.16	0.00	0.09	0.09	−0.22	0.04	0.07	0.23	−0.01	0.14	−0.04	0.19	0.07	0.23	0.13	0.44	0.25	−0.24	0.29
2	0.01	**1.00**	0.04	0.03	0.01	−0.06	0.00	0.00	0.03	0.03	0.11	0.03	−0.12	0.07	−0.02	0.08	0.19	0.02	0.04	0.03
3	0.01	−0.22	**1.00**	−0.05	0.24	−0.04	−0.03	−0.05	0.09	0.03	−0.06	−0.03	0.02	0.00	0.12	−0.08	−0.17	0.02	−0.04	0.05
4	−0.23	0.20	0.01	**1.00**	−0.23	−0.16	−0.13	−0.06	−0.02	−0.06	−0.06	−0.11	0.10	0.04	0.07	0.03	0.06	0.23	−0.08	−0.16
5	0.14	−0.22	0.44	−0.06	**1.00**	−0.03	0.13	0.22	0.07	0.20	0.07	0.09	0.04	−0.00	0.11	0.00	0.10	−0.01	0.08	0.07
6	−0.11	−0.21	0.10	−0.30	0.02	**1.00**	0.07	0.02	−0.30	−0.12	−0.16	0.14	−0.18	0.03	−0.19	−0.35	−0.10	−0.08	0.01	−0.04
7	0.22	0.08	0.06	−0.37	0.14	0.08	**1.00**	0.22	0.09	0.21	0.07	0.27	0.02	0.14	0.17	0.12	0.10	−0.06	−0.00	0.10
8	−0.29	−0.06	0.17	−0.16	0.09	0.11	0.37	**1.00**	0.16	0.53	0.06	0.21	0.07	0.18	0.16	0.05	0.10	−0.02	−0.18	0.08
9	0.17	−0.02	−0.19	0.12	−0.32	0.01	0.11	−0.10	**1.00**	0.42	0.16	0.08	0.13	−0.02	0.09	0.09	0.05	0.18	0.01	0.09
10	0.14	−0.08	−0.21	−0.17	−0.11	−0.06	0.21	0.11	0.30	**1.00**	0.10	0.40	0.04	0.16	0.14	0.03	0.16	−0.05	−0.02	0.05
11	0.12	−0.05	−0.03	−0.26	0.02	−0.01	0.40	0.44	0.07	0.22	**1.00**	0.18	0.17	0.05	0.25	0.14	0.05	0.13	0.13	0.07
12	−0.16	0.19	−0.32	−0.20	−0.06	−0.02	0.34	0.01	0.04	0.47	0.14	**1.00**	0.08	0.14	0.11	−0.04	0.11	0.05	0.12	−0.08
13	0.27	0.13	−0.09	−0.32	0.10	0.00	0.16	−0.02	0.09	0.19	0.15	0.32	**1.00**	0.28	0.26	0.09	0.13	0.21	0.07	0.13
14	0.31	0.22	0.00	−0.16	0.22	−0.06	0.17	−0.22	0.03	−0.09	−0.06	0.13	0.60	**1.00**	0.26	0.13	0.11	0.08	0.08	−0.03
15	0.40	0.08	−0.15	−0.13	0.00	−0.16	0.02	−0.30	0.15	0.25	0.02	0.37	0.41	0.57	**1.00**	0.10	0.05	0.25	0.10	0.17
16	0.00	0.27	−0.12	−0.07	0.03	−0.31	0.16	0.14	−0.27	0.04	0.12	0.01	−0.28	−0.21	−0.13	**1.00**	0.09	0.09	0.07	0.02
17	0.25	0.12	−0.18	−0.18	−0.06	−0.34	0.27	−0.09	0.18	0.53	0.09	0.35	0.34	0.44	0.40	−0.06	**1.00**	0.06	−0.04	0.36
18	0.27	0.01	0.17	0.18	0.14	−0.07	0.12	−0.10	−0.10	−0.03	0.08	−0.13	0.04	0.10	0.15	−0.10	0.09	**1.00**	−0.09	0.14
19	0.09	0.03	−0.01	−0.11	−0.21	0.02	−0.02	0.07	0.24	0.34	−0.06	−0.04	−0.12	−0.18	0.14	−0.13	0.07	0.19	**1.00**	0.00
20	−0.12	−0.01	−0.17	−0.24	−0.19	0.03	0.23	0.09	0.11	0.06	0.21	−0.13	0.22	0.23	0.17	−0.11	0.24	0.34	0.16	**1.00**

VARIABLES:

1. Crew Chief Program Acceptance
2. Race (white = 1, nonwhite = 2)
3. Tenure as Mail Processor
4. Gender (male = 1, female = 2)
5. Age
6. City, Survey Wave
7. Work Group Climate
8. Supervisory Climate
9. Union Loyalty
10. Postal Service Loyalty
11. Supervisor Production Orientation
12. Satisfaction with Advancement Opportunities
13. Supervisor Works Well With and Supports CC
14. Supervisor Does Not Undercut CC
15. Management Supports CC Program
16. Adequate Staffing
17. CC Position is a Promotion
18. I Know CC Role
19. CC is Part of Management
20. Would Like to be (continue as) CC

[a] $n = 159$ for mail processors, rs > .11, $p < 0.05$, one-tailed tests. $n = 39$ for crew chiefs, rs > 0.21, $p < 0.05$, one-tailed tests.

Table 2. T-tests of Differences Between Mail Processors and Crew Chiefs

Variable	Mail Processors Means n=167	Crew Chiefs Means n=41	t-ratio
Demographic and City			
Race, percent nonwhite	37	30	0.87
Tenure as Mail Processor, years	4.34	5.23	2.21*
	(2.25)	(2.53)	
Gender, percent female	43	37	0.76
Age	39.86	40.27	0.27
	(8.62)	(8.22)	
City, percent first wave	49	51	0.24
Workplace Climate			
Workgroup Climate[a]	2.86	2.73	0.82
	(0.89)	(0.99)	
Supervisory Climate[a]	2.51	2.14	2.28*
	(0.97)	(0.70)	
Union Loyalty[b]	3.40	3.33	0.26
	(1.76)	(1.74)	
Postal Service Loyalty[b]	4.05	3.42	2.19*
	(1.67)	(1.60)	
Supervisor Production Orientation[b]	4.19	4.23	0.13
	(1.79)	(1.36)	
Satisfaction with Advancement Opportunities (Time 1)[a]	2.15	2.02	0.56
	(1.28)	(1.33)	
Satisfaction with Advancement Opportunities (Time 2)[a]	2.58	2.61	0.10
	(1.43)	(1.34)	
Crew Chief Relations			
Supervisor Works Well With and Supports CC [a]	3.90	4.68	2.70**
	(1.66)	(1.64)	
Supervisor Does Not Undercut CC [b]	3.40	4.46	3.50**
	(1.71)	(1.87)	
Management Supports CC Program [b]	2.73	3.29	2.61**
	(1.22)	(1.27)	
Adequate Staffing [b]	2.74	3.56	2.46*
	(2.07)	(1.03)	
Crew Chief Role			
CC Position is a Promotion [a]	2.48	3.37	3.86**
	(1.32)	(1.28)	
I Know CC Role [a]	3.65	4.24	2.72**
	(1.28)	(1.09)	
CC is Part of Management [a]	3.46	2.90	2.88**
	(1.11)	(1.15)	
Would Like to be (continue as) CC [a]	2.01	4.22	11.04**
	(1.19)	(.94)	
Crew Chief Program Acceptance [a]	2.48	3.51	4.76**
	(1.28)	(1.08)	

* $p < 0.05$, ** $p < 0.01$

[a] 5-point scale, higher values more positive, [b] 7-point scale, higher values more positive. Standard deviations are in parentheses.

differences. *Supervisory Climate and Postal Service Loyalty* were more positive for the mail processors. An examination of the two sets of means for *Satisfaction with Advancement Opportunities* indicated no difference at either time. At Time-1, there was slight dissatisfaction with advancement opportunities. However, an analysis with *t*-tests for paired samples found that *Satisfaction with Advancement Opportunities* significantly increased for both mail processors and for crew chiefs *(p < 0.01)*, to become neutral to positive.

The small sample sizes in relation to the number of predictors incorporated in this study raises concerns with the issue of multicollinearity. To address these concerns, the potential of multicollinearity was assessed by regressing each predictor on the remaining predictors. For two of these regressions for the crew chiefs, the multiple R exceeded 0.80, the point identified by Kim and Kohurt (1975) where multicollinearity becomes a problem. Thus, the regression analyses were re-run omitting variables which had not been significant predictors. The results in terms of the significant variables, beta weights and variance explained were almost identical. Thus, multicollinearity was deemed not to be a problem, as it did not affect the results.

Table 3 shows the results of the two three-step regression analyses, one for mail processors, and the other for crew chiefs. Out of a total of nine significant predictors at the third step, only one was the same in both regressions. For both groups, greater management support of the crew chief program predicted more positive overall crew chief program acceptance. Differences between the crew chief and mail processor regressions can also be seen in the changes in R^2 at step 2 and step 3. The R^2 change from the addition of the Time-1 climate variables to the regressions was much larger for the crew chiefs (0.38, $p < 0.05$) than for the mail processors (0.07, < 0.10). In contrast, the R^2 change from the addition of the role and relationship variables to the regressions was much larger for the mail processors (0.28, $p < 0.001$) than for the crew chiefs (0.18, *ns*).

While the two regressions indicate that the pre-existing climate is important, there is only mixed support for Hypothesis 1. Three of the six climate predictors were significant for the crew chiefs. However, two of them had negative signs, suggesting that for crew chiefs at least, a poorer *Supervisory Climate* at Time-1, and less *Satisfaction with Advancement Opportunities* at Time-1, were associated with greater Time-2 acceptance of the crew chief program. On the other hand, a more positive view of the *Workgroup Climate* at Time-1 was associated with greater Time-2 acceptance of the crew chief program. For the mail processors, a more positive *Union Loyalty* and more negative *Postal Service Loyalty* at Time-1 were associated with greater Time-2 acceptance of the crew chief program.

Table 3. Regression of Crew Chief Program Acceptance on Demographic, Climate, and Crew Chief Variables.[a]

Variable	Mail Processors ($N = 159$)			Crew Chiefs ($N = 39$)		
	Step 1 beta	Step 2 beta	Step 3 beta	Step 1 Beta	Step 2 beta	Step 3 Beta
Race	0.14+	0.14+	0.10	0.06	0.15	0.21
Tenure as Mail Processor	−0.03	−0.03	−0.01	−0.02	−0.04	−0.01
Gender	0.08	0.10	0.03	−0.29	−0.27	−0.32
Age	0.11	0.10	0.08	0.15	0.21	0.08
City, Survey Wave	−0.19*	−0.14	−0.05	−0.19	−0.13	−0.11
R^2 at step 1	0.08			0.11		
Workgroup Climate		0.04	−0.02		0.32+	0.45*
Supervisory Climate		0.12	0.01		−0.53**	−0.38*
Union Loyalty		0.24**	0.24**		0.11	0.06
Postal Service Loyalty		−0.22*	−0.23*		0.28	0.29
Supervisor Production Orientation		0.07	0.05		0.15	0.07
Satisfaction with Advancement Opportunities		−0.01	0.00		−0.51**	−0.78**
R^2 Change at step 2		0.07+			0.38*	
Supervisor Works Well With and Supports CC			0.05			0.16
Supervisor Does Not Undercut CC			0.02			−0.20
Management Supports CC Program			0.17*			0.49*
Adequate Staffing			0.04			−0.09
CC Position is a Promotion			0.35**			−0.03
I Know CC Role			0.06			0.18
CC is Part of Management			−0.27**			−0.12
Would Like to be (continue as) CC			0.10			−0.27
R^2 Change at step 3			0.28**			0.18
Total R^2 (Adjusted R^2)	0.08(.05)	0.15(0.08)	0.42(0.34)	0.11(−0.03)	0.49(.28)	0.67(0.33)
Overall F	2.69*	2.30*	5.35**	0.79	2.37*	2.00+

[a] Variables entered in steps 1 and step 2 were collected at Time-1. Variables entered in step 3 were collected at Time-2.
+ $p < 0.10$, * $p < 0.05$, ** $p < 0.01$.

Hypothesis 2 stated that the relations the supervisors and management have with the crew chiefs and crew chief program will be positively related to acceptance of the crew chief program. There is some support for this hypothesis. In each regression, greater management support of the crew chief program was related to more crew chief program acceptance. There was also support for Hypothesis 3 among the mail processors but not among the crew chiefs. Two of the four role-related variables were significant predictors for the mail processors, while none were predictors for the crew chiefs.

DISCUSSION

The present study generally supported the hypothesized model based on exchange theory for both crew chiefs and mail processors, with the general exception of the climate variables. While the pre-existing climate was more important for crew chiefs than mail processors in explaining variance in the dependent variable, the differences in climate found between the two groups is consistent with exchange theory. For crew chiefs, greater acceptance of the crew chief program was predicted by a perception of a more favorable workgroup climate, less favorable supervisory climate, and lower satisfaction with their advancement opportunities. Further, crew chiefs had less positive attitudes than the mail processors about the supervisory climate. These results are consistent with the view that crew chiefs more accepting of the crew chief program were motivated to become crew chiefs to improve their situation, i.e., their advancement opportunities and the supervisory climate. Indeed, satisfaction with advancement opportunities increased for both groups over time. This finding gives a strong indication of success of one union goal, greater advancement opportunity for employees, at least at the perceptual level.

The structure of the pre-existing climate predictors for mail processors can be explained by the fact that the crew chief program was a union-sponsored innovation, which was opposed by many first-line supervisors (Goodin, 1992a). Thus, those mail processors with higher *Union Loyalty* and lower *Postal Service Loyalty* were more accepting of the crew chief program, possibly seeing it as an exchange that would benefit the union and make it easier to confront their employer. These results are consistent with the view that the crew chief program was seen more as a union than an employer program.

There was support for Hypothesis 2 concerning the relational variables. The only common predictor for both groups was that management supports the crew chief program. The need of management to support workplace innovations in order for them to be successful follows themes in the existing team leader and program implementation literature (Batt & Applebaum, 1995; Macy & Izumi,

1993; Rodgers et al., 1993). At the zero-order level, mail processors who viewed the supervisors as working well with and supporting the crew chief were more supportive of the crew chief program. The same relationship held for the crew chiefs, but not being undercut by the supervisor was also important for the latter. Adequate staffing did not appear to be an issue for the crew chief respondents, but was for mail processors.

Relatively strong support was found for Hypothesis 3, as all four role-related variables were related to greater crew chief acceptance for the mail processors at the zero-order level, as were two of the four for the crew chiefs. This is consistent with the prior literature and exchange theory. In the regressions, *Crew Chief is Part of Management* was a significant negative predictor for the mail processors. This is supportive of the team leader literature that says that persons in such positions should not function as a junior supervisor or an arm of management (Babson, 1993; Robertson et al., 1993). Where crew chiefs are seen as part of management, that violated the psychological contract that crew chiefs are bargaining unit employees, and not part of management. At the zero-order level for crew chiefs, those more accepting of the crew chief program were more likely to think becoming a crew chief is a promotion and to understand the role. There was no relationship for the other two role-related variables.

As predicted by Hypothesis 4, the views of the crew chief program were more positive for the crew chiefs than for the mail processors. There was a significantly greater acceptance of the program among the crew chiefs and almost all of the relational and role-related variables were more positive among the crew chiefs. The application of exchange theory suggests that the very fact that crew chiefs have been promoted to crew chief would lead them to have more favorable attitudes about the position and the crew chief program. There also was a different structure of predictors between the two groups, with only one common predictor in the regressions. The only other common relationships of relational and role-related variables were found at the zero-order level.

CONCLUSIONS

The differences in means found between the crew chiefs and mail processors are not unexpected. Both these differences and the differences in the regression results can be explained by exchange theory, with those individuals assuming the crew chief positions having more positive attitudes toward and a different structure of attitudes concerning the position. This study is also one of the few studies of a workplace innovation where the union was the primary mover (Macy & Izumi, 1993). That may explain the relationships of the two climate variables for the mail processors, positive for *Union Loyalty* and negative for *Postal Service*

Loyalty. It is also important to note that most of the conclusions from the descriptive team leader and crew chief literature were supported, at least at the zero-order level, and none were contradicted (Babson, 1995; Luby, 1995; MacDuffie, 1995; Rinehart et al., 1995; Robertson et al., 1993).

This study has several limitations. The small sample size (particularly for the crew chiefs) suggests some caution in interpreting the regression results. A concern with comparing the two regressions is that the variables may not have homogeneous variances across the two groups. Lack of homogeneity could point to range restrictions and thus affect certain relations among the variables. The results of the Bartlett-Box F test for homogeneity of variance revealed the two groups only differed on three variables, the two Time–1 supervisory variables, and *Adequate Staffing*. Thus, while it is possible that differences in the predictors across the two regressions were attributable to differences in the variances, it is unlikely for two reasons. First, very few variables had heterogeneous variances, and second, the variances for the dependent variable passed the test for homogeneity (Bartlett-Box $F(1,35591) = 2.10$, ns).

Another limitation is that it is not known how the loyalty measures would predict in an environment where the overall labor-management climate was less adversarial (GAO, 1994). Further, the post-trial data were collected while the crew chief trials were relatively new. It is not known whether the results would remain similar over a longer period of time. However, the results appear robust enough to offer the first quantitative support for many of the conclusions from the descriptive team leader and crew chief literature (Babson, 1995; Luby, 1995; MacDuffie, 1995; Rinehart et al., 1995; Robertson et al., 1993). Using that literature, and the results from the mail processors, confidence is increased in any recommendations concerning crew chiefs and crew chief programs. The only common predictor of crew chief program acceptance by both mail processors and crew chiefs was that management is perceived to support the program. This conclusion is repeated in most of the innovation literature (e.g., Greenwood & Hinings, 1996; Klein & Sorra, 1996; Rodgers et al., 1993). Thus, management support is critical to the acceptance of such a program. Further conclusions can be drawn from the mail processor results. To be accepted by regular employees, crew chiefs should not be seen as junior supervisors or an arm of management. The position should also appear desirable to hold, as mail processors more interested in becoming a crew chief were more supportive of the program. By making the position part of a career ladder, the crew chief position also becomes attractive.

It is hoped that this study will offer some guidance to others who want to study the role of team leaders or crew chiefs in work organizations, and show how such programs may operate to have increased acceptance by employees. The model based on exchange theory should be helpful in guiding such research.

If the results of this study replicate, data from surveys of team leaders or crew chiefs themselves will not likely tell us much about how to increase acceptance of such an innovation by the regular rank-and-file employees. Data from the regular employees themselves are necessary to achieve this end. This research gives ideas on how crew chiefs can make the use of increased technology more acceptable to the workforce. Since unions and employers are likely to continue changing the employment structures as they implement technological innovations, the results from this study provide useful information for avoiding pitfalls.

NOTES

1. Studies are most commonly concerned with changes in the variables assessing these concepts (e.g., Macy & Izumi, 1993) to determine if an innovation was successful. Existing research is not generally concerned with what the climate was before the innovation was instituted. The reason for this appears to be that most studies of workplace innovations do not examine the identical innovation at multiple sites across different shifts.
2. The reliability shown in Table 2 is slightly lower for the mail processors, and substantially lower for the crew chiefs. The latter is likely a function of the small sample size.
3. A multivariate analysis of covariance (MANCOVA) covarying the demographic variables and city, survey wave, (multivariate $F(15, 177) = 12.16$, $p < 0.001$), followed by univariate F-tests, found essentially the same differences in the attitudinal variables between the two groups.

ACKNOWLEDGMENTS

A version of this chapter was presented at the Seventh Biennial Bargaining Group Conference, May 13, 2000, at Michigan State University, East Lansing, Michigan. This article was supported by a Wayne State University School of Business Administration Spring/Summer 1999 Faculty Development Grant. The author would like to thank Dawn Palace, Richard Peterson, Robert Sinclair, and Michael Sherman for their helpful comments on earlier versions of this chapter.

REFERENCES

Adler, P. (1995). Democratic Taylorism: The Toyota production system at NUMMI. In: S. Babson (Ed.), *Lean Work: Empowerment and Exploitation in the Global Auto Industry* (pp. 207–219). Detroit, MI: Wayne State University.

Applebaum, E., & Batt, R. (1994). *The new american workplace: Transforming work systems in the United States.* Ithaca, NY: ILR Press.

Tracking changes in the postal workforce. (1992, March). *The American Postal Worker*, p. A10.

Arbitration Proceedings: USPS and National Association of Letter Carriers and APWU, Opinion and Award (1991).

Babson, S. (1993). Lean or mean: The MIT model and lean production at Mazda. *Labor Studies Journal, 18*(2) Summer, 3–24.

Babson, S. (1995). Lean production and labor: Empowerment and exploitation. In: S. Babson (Ed.), *Lean work: Empowerment and exploitation in the global auto industry* (pp. 1–40). Detroit, MI: Wayne State University.

Batt, R., & Applebaum, E. (1995). Worker participation in diverse settings: Does the form affect the outcome, and, if so, who benefits? *British Journal of Industrial Relations, 33*, 353–378.

Berthiaume, R. A., & Martin, J. E. (1991). Organizational commitment: The effect of workgroup commitment on turnover. Paper presented at the 99th Annual Convention of the American Psychological Association, San Francisco, CA.

Blackler, F., & Brown, C. (1985). Evaluation and the impact of information technologies on people in organizations. *Human Relations 38*, 213–231.

Blau, P. (1964). *Exchange and power in social life.* New York: Wiley.

Brown, C., Reich, M., & Stern, D. (1991). Skills and security in evolving employment systems: Observations from case studies. Mimeo, Institute of Industrial Relations, University of California-Berkeley.

Campion, M. A., Papper, E. M., & Medsker, G. J. (1996). Relations between work team characteristics and effectiveness: A replication and extension. *Personnel Psychology, 49,* 429–452.

Cooke, W. N. (1990). *Labor-management cooperation: New partnerships or going in circles.* Kalamazoo, MI: Upjohn.

Cammann, C., Fichman, M., Jenkins, Jr., G. D., & Klesh, J. R. (1983). Assessing the attitudes and perceptions of organizational members. In: S. E. Seashore, E. E. Lawler III, P. H. Mirvis and C. Cammann (Eds.), *Assessing organizational change: A guide to methods, measures, and practices* (pp. 71–138). New York, NY: John Wiley & Sons.

Collective Bargaining Agreement Between APWU, AFL-CIO and USPS, November 21, 1990–November 20, 1994 (1991).

Eisenberger, R., Huntington, R., Hutchison, S., & Sowa, D. (1986). Perceived organizational support. *Journal of Applied Psychology, 75,* 51–59.

Fleishman, E. A., & Harris, E. F. (1962). Patterns of leadership behavior related to employee grievances and turnover. *Personnel Psychology, 15,* 43–56.

General Accounting Office, U.S. (1994). U.S. Postal Service: Labor-management problems persist on the workroom floor, Volumes I & II, Washington, DC: Superintendent of Documents.

Gouldner, A. W. (1960). The norm of reciprocity. *American Sociological Review, 25,* 165–167.

Greenwood, R., & Hinings, C. R. (1996). Understanding radical organizational change: Bringing together the old and new institutionalism. *Academy of Management Review, 21,* 1022–1054.

Goodin, M. (1992a). Postal work force is in transition. *Crain's Detroit Business*, February 24, 14.

Goodin, M. (1992b). Workplace changes embitter workers. *Crain's Detroit Business*, February 24, 14.

Graham, J. W. (1991). An essay on organizational citizenship behavior. *Employee Responsibilities and Rights Journal, 4,* 249–270.

Halliday, J. (1992). Postal Service goal: Total automation. *Crain's Detroit Business*, February 24, 1992, 16.

Hitt, M. A., Keats, B. W. & DeMarie, S. M. (1998). Navigating in the new competitive landscape: Building strategic flexibility and competitive advantage in the 21st century. *Academy of Management Executive, 12,* 22–42.

Holley, W. H., & Jennings, K. M. (1997). *The labor relations process* (6th ed.). Hinsdale, IL: Dryden Press.

Hunter, L. W., & Lafkas, J. J. (1998). Information technology, work practices and wages. In: *Proceedings of the Fiftieth Annual Meeting*, Industrial Relations Research Association. Madison, WI: IRRA, 110–117.

Kim, J., & Kohurt, F. J. (1975). Multiple regression analysis: Subprogram regression. In: N. H. Nie, C. H. Hull, J. G. Jenkins, K. Steinbrenner, & D. H. Brent (Eds.), *Statistical package for the social sciences* (2nd. ed.). New York: McGraw-Hill.

Klein, K. J., & Sorra, J. S. (1996). The challenge of innovation implementation. *Academy of Management Review, 21*, 1055–1080.

Kochan, T. A., Katz, H. C., & McKersie, R. B. (1986). *The transformation of American industrial relations*. Basic Books: New York.

Koys, D. J., & DeCotiis, T. A. (1991). Inductive measures of psychological climate. *Human Relations, 44*, 265–285.

Levinson, H. (1965). Reciprocation: The relationship between man and organization. *Administrative Science Quarterly, 9*, 370–390.

Lieberman, S. (1956). The effects of changes in roles on the attitudes of role occupants. *Human Relations, 9*, 385–402.

Litwin, G. H., & Stringer, R. A. (1968). *Motivation and organizational climate*. Boston, MA: Harvard University: Division of Research, Graduate School of Business Administration.

Luby, A. M. (1995). The decline of control management in aircraft maintenance. In: P. Cappelli (Ed.), *The new frontier: Airline labor relations in the global era* (pp. 201–211). Ithaca, NY: ILR Press, Cornell University.

MacDuffie, J. P. (1995). Workers' roles in lean production: The implications for worker representation. In: S. Babson (Ed.), *Lean work: Empowerment and exploitation in the global auto industry* (pp. 54–69). Detroit, MI: Wayne State University.

Macy, B. A., & Izumi, H. (1993). Organizational change, design, and work innovation: A meta-analysis of 131 North American Field Studies – 1961–1991. *Research in Organizational Change and Development, 7*, 235–313.

Macy, B. A., Peterson, M. F., & Norton, L. W. (1989). A test of participation theory in a work re-design field setting: Degree of participation and comparison site contrasts. *Human Relations, 42*, 1095–1165.

Magenau, J. M., & Martin, J. M. (1999). Dual and unilateral loyalty: Methodological, conceptual and practical issues. *Advances in Industrial and Labor Relations, 9*, 183–210.

Martin, J. E., & Peterson, M. M. (1987). Two-tier wage structures: Implications for equity theory. *Academy of Management Journal, 30*, 297–315.

Ondrack, D. A., & Evans, M. G. (1986). Job enrichment and job satisfaction in quality of working life and nonquality of working life sites. *Human Relations, 39*, 871–899.

Osterman, P. (1994). How common is workplace transformation and who adopts it? *Industrial and Labor Relations Review, 47*, 173–188.

Osterman, P. (2000). Work re-organization in an era of restructuring: Trends in diffusion and effects on employee welfare. *Industrial and Labor Relations Review, 53*, 179–196.

Rinehart, J., Huxley, C., & Robertson, D. (1995). Team concept at CAMI. In: S. Babson (Ed.), *Lean work: Empowerment and exploitation in the global auto industry* (pp. 220–234). Detroit, MI: Wayne State University.

Robertson, D., Rinehart, J., & Huxley, C. (1993). *Japanese production management in a unionized auto plant*. CAW-Canada Research Department, Willowdale, Ontario.

Rodgers, R., Hunter, J. E., & Rogers, D. L. (1993). Influence of top management on management program success. *Journal of Applied Psychology, 78,* 151–155.
Rousseau, D. M. (1995). *Psychological contracts in organizations: Understanding written and unwritten agreements.* Thousand Oaks, CA: Sage.
Schneider, B. (1990). *Organizational climate and culture.* San Francisco, CA: Jossey-Bass.
Shaiken, H. (1995). Experienced workers and high-performance work organization: A case study of two automobile assembly plants. In: *Proceedings of the Forty-Seventh Annual Meeting* (pp. 257–266). Industrial Relations Research Association, Madison, WI: IRRA.
Shore, L., Tetrick, L. E., Sinclair, R. R., & Newton, L. (1994). Validation of a measure of perceived union support. *Journal of Applied Psychology, 79,* 971–979.
Sinclair, R. R., & Tetrick, L. E. (1995). Social exchange and union commitment: A comparison of union instrumentality and union support perceptions. *Journal of Organizational Behavior, 16,* 669–680.
Smith, F. J. (1976). Index of organizational reactions (IOR). *JSAS Catalog of Selected Documents in Psychology 6,* 54, No. 1265.
Spreitzer, G. M., Noble, D. S., Mishra, A. K., & Cooke, W. N. (1999). Predicting process improvement in an automotive firm: Explicating the roles of trust and empowerment. *Research on Managing Groups and Teams, 2,* 71–92.
Tracey, J. B., Tannenbaum, S. I., & Kavanagh, M. J. (1995). Applying trained skills on the job: The importance of the work environment. *Journal of Applied Psychology, 80,* 239–252.
Zahra, S. A. (1998). Competitiveness and global leadership in the 21st century. *Academy of Management Executive, 12,* 10–13.

APPENDIX A

Scale Reliabilities for Mail Processors and Crew Chiefs

Variable	Mail Processors α	Crew Chiefs α
Workgroup Climate	0.81	0.87
Supervisory Climate	0.85	0.63
Union Loyalty	0.93	0.91
Postal Service Loyalty	0.87	0.88
Supervisor Production Orientation	0.90	0.76
Supervisor Works Well With and Supports CC	0.72	0.70
CC is Part of Management	0.60	0.89
Crew Chief Program Acceptance	0.78	0.55

THE EVOLUTION OF AN ALTERNATIVE GRIEVANCE PROCEDURE: THE COLUMBUS TYPOGRAPHICAL UNION NO. 5, 1859–1959

Howard R. Stanger

INTRODUCTION

The grievance arbitration procedure is of paramount importance to union members and management alike.[1] It affords workers a degree of workplace participation and industrial democracy while simultaneously stabilizes labor-management relationships by resolving workplace disputes in an orderly manner, without interrupting production.[2] Lewin and Peterson (1988) note the many functions served by grievance arbitration procedures. First, they ensure compliance with the collective bargaining agreement. Second, they are adjudicative in that they resolve outstanding complaints.[3] The third function is administrative, in that grievance representatives resolve grievances and set precedents for future ones. The importance of shop-floor relations, the site of most grievance activity, is noted by historian David Brody (1993: 177), who argues that

> what happens on the shop floor is not a secondary affair in the lives of working people. On the contrary, it engages their innermost sense of self-worth and honor.

Currently, grievance arbitration procedures are a ubiquitous feature of collective bargaining agreements in the United States. For example, in a recent survey, the Bureau of National Affairs found them to exist in all of the 400 contracts sampled (BNA, 1992). But this was not always so. In the early 1930s, it is estimated that fewer than 8 to 10% of all agreements provided for grievance arbitration. By the outset of World War Two, this number increased to 62%, and continued to rise throughout and after the war. For example, the percentage rose to 73% in 1944, 89% by 1952, and between 90 to 95% by 1960 (Brody, 1993, Nolan & Abrams, 1983b, 876; Slichter et al., 1960). The widespread incorporation of grievance procedures came in the wake of a concentrated burst of union growth and stabilization between the late 1930s and 1960. During this time, a system of 'workplace contractualism' emerged to govern shop-floor relations between industrial unions and their employers (Brody, 1993).[4]

Research on grievance procedures has been ongoing since World War Two, but has become more widespread and sophisticated since the early 1980s. This increase in scholarship has come in response to the paucity and major weaknesses of earlier studies, i.e., among other things, research designs and the lack of theoretical grounding. The most sophisticated of these examinations was conducted by Lewin and Peterson (1988). Combining surveys, interviews and archival records for three years, they tested their Systems Model of grievance procedures in four industries and sectors, using six measures of grievance procedure effectiveness.[5] Their study, and those undertaken by others since, has greatly increased our understanding of contemporary grievance arbitration procedures.[6] Nevertheless, we still know very little about how these procedures evolved and operated over long periods of time. This is an omission noted in Peterson's (1992) literature review in which he encourages researchers to identify

> the environmental and internal forces over the period studied that may have influenced the operation of the union grievance process in firm(s) studied. The grievance process fits into a broad framework of workplace relations at a given point in the history of a given society (155).

This study attempts to fill in some of the void by tracing the evolution of a grievance procedure in the Columbus Typographical Union No. 5, from its rebirth in 1859 to 1959, when it celebrated its centennial anniversary. This period was one of industry and union growth and stability. After 1960, the printing and publishing industry underwent a dramatic technological revolution that changed labor-management relations and, to some extent, the manner in which grievances were handled.[7] The union's rich records permit an examination of the factors that shaped and impacted the workings of the grievance procedure.

Examination of a craft union's grievance procedure provides an alternative to the more extensively studied industrial union grievance procedure that became pervasive by the end of World War Two. A few notable differences emerge from this study. First, the incorporation of formal dispute resolution procedures came about voluntarily and internal to the industry, unlike in other notable and pioneering industries. Second, the Columbus union maintained a high degree control over the grievance procedure. For example, for many decades, the rules required that a discharged printer remain on the job until a higher appeals body upheld the discharge. In most workplaces, including other unionized composing rooms, the reverse held. Third, over the one hundred-year period under study a viable system of peer review of grievances operated with the blessing of all concerned parties. Peer review complemented the high degree of informality, conciliation and cooperation between labor and management that characterized the Columbus experience. These latter features – peer review, informality, conciliation, and cooperation – have become desired objectives in many unionized environments today. Moreover, this study demonstrates that peaceful labor relations can exist in highly competitive industries, and shows that adversarialism is neither inevitable in labor-management relations nor the grievance procedure.

Another implication of this study is that it will also shed new light on the historiography of grievance arbitration procedures and, perhaps, provoke some discussion about reclaiming a viable, competing grievance arbitration model.

To situate better the experience of the Columbus Typographical Union, it is first necessary to review the literature on the historical development of grievance arbitration in the United States.

GRIEVANCE ARBITRATION IN HISTORICAL PERSPECTIVE

Review of Historical Surveys

No definitive history has yet been written on the history of labor arbitration in the United States. Edwin Witte (1952) wrote the first major survey on the subject, a highly descriptive account. This became the standard treatment of arbitration until Robin Fleming's (1965) short descriptive overview. He divides the American experience with arbitration into three distinct periods. The first covers the period from 1865, when Pittsburgh's iron puddlers arbitrated wages in the first recorded arbitration case, to the onset of World War Two in 1941. The second period runs from 1941 to the *Lincoln Mills* case in 1957.[8] It was this period that witnessed the widespread incorporation of grievance arbitration clauses in labor contracts. The last period, after 1957, was marked by the legalization of arbitration, which embedded arbitration firmly in industrial relations practices. Over the years, outsiders were instrumental in resolving 'emergency' situations, while private parties established mechanisms to handle day-to-day affairs.

The most comprehensive survey of labor arbitration was written by Nolan and Abrams (1983a & b), who provide a different organizing framework. In their first paper, covering the years between 1865 and 1941, they investigate to what degree was labor arbitration created and operated outside the realm of state-sanctioned law, and to what degree was labor arbitration mature and accepted before World War Two. Their papers incorporate works by Witte (1952) and Fleming (1965).

They reach a few key conclusions about the pre-1941 period. First, the onset of strikes or labor unrest in general led either the government or important public figures to intervene and establish arbitration procedures. This was the case in the 'pioneering' industries such as railroads, anthracite coal mining, and the needle trades (clothing, millinery and hosiery). Thus, they refute a common misperception of the exaggerated autonomy of labor arbitration.[9] The only exception was in newspapers, where the threat of technological displacement led the typographical union and newspaper publishers to establish arbitration procedures voluntarily.

Second, labor boards created during World War One exposed the parties to dispute resolution by outside parties, even though many boards resolved only interest disputes and preferred mediation to arbitration. This experience led to the emergence of labor arbitration almost in its modern form between the wars. 'By the 1930s', Nolan and Abrams (1983a, 412) write,

> arbitration was understood in its modern sense as involving grievance cases. The development of the (labor) agreement not only made the distinction between interest and grievance arbitration meaningful, but also made grievance arbitration almost a necessity.[10]

But it was the Federal government's encouragement of arbitration during World War II, combined with the negotiation of grievance arbitration clauses by the new industrial unions and major manufacturers that solidified grievance arbitration in American industrial relations. In short, they contend,

> well before the start of World War II labor and management were largely convinced that grievance arbitration could be mutually advantageous ... American labor arbitration had come of age by 1941 (421).[11]

In the sequel, Nolan and Abrams (1983b) focus on the 'Maturing Years' of arbitration, 1941 through the early 1980s. In its mature form, labor arbitration became more structured and focused on contractual grievances, while the role of the arbitrator was limited by the terms of the contract.

> In place of a freewheeling expert, the modern arbitrator sits almost as a judge, trying to determine the intentions of the parties from the document they signed and the ways they have conducted themselves under that agreement (p. 629). By 1983, arbitration was fully mature.[12]

While the precise date of the birth of modern grievance arbitration may be debated – the late 1930s versus during World War Two – scholars agree that arbitration practices in the needle trades (clothing and hosiery) and automobiles have shaped contemporary practices. There are no studies available indicating what happened to dispute resolution procedures in some of the other pioneering industries such as railroads, coal mining and printing. However, while these industries probably continued their earlier practices of dispute resolution, the sudden upsurge in industrial unionism redirected the attention of scholars, policymakers and labor professionals away from the pioneering industries and toward the emergent Congress of Industrial Organizations (CIO).

Robert Zieger documents the dramatic growth in industrial unionism beginning with the successful unionizing drives in automobiles and steel during the late 1930s. For example, the UAW increased its membership from about 165,000 in 1939 to over one million by 1944. The Steel Workers Organizing Committee grew to include over 700,000 members. The CIO's electrical and shipbuilding unions drew in 432,000 and 209,000 members, respectively. By 1939, Zieger notes the CIO represented 3.5 million members; during the Second World War, labor's ranks, including the American Federation of Labor, swelled by five million (Zieger, 1994, 60, 84). As the CIO captured the attention of the nation, coal mining, railroads and the needle trades were in slow decline in the postwar years (Lichtenstein, 1993). The printing industries, always small, were dwarfed by heavy industry. The ITU reached its peak in membership in 1959 with slightly more than 100,000 members.

Moreover, in the industrial core of American industry dispute resolution procedures also removed conflict from the shop floor and transferred it to quiet offices where higher level union and company representatives attempted to negotiate settlements. The centralization of dispute resolution matched that of the parties' own centralized administrative structures (Atleson, 1998). In contrast, the printing industries were highly decentralized and the parties preferred to resolve conflicts locally. This system did not fit the industrial relations model being solidified in heavy industry surrounding the World War Two period.

Given this dramatic episode in American labor history, it is no wonder that interest in the seemingly anachronistic workings of craft unionism waned. In the era of industrial unionism, the automobile industry held center stage. Still, as Nolan and Abrams (1983a) argue, "(t)he coal, newspaper and clothing industries were also important in shaping American labor arbitration" (382).

The next section illustrates how the industrial union model of arbitration, typified by the experience of the automobile industry, came to be. Following this, we will document the experience of the printing industries (newspaper and commercial printing) and then detail the experience of the Columbus Typographical

Union's grievance procedure to reveal an alternative model of dispute resolution rooted in craft unionism and heretofore overlooked by scholars.

Clothing, Hosiery and Automobiles

The origins of modern day grievance arbitration can be traced back to the experiences of the clothing industry during the 1910s, the hosiery industry after 1929, and the automobile industry after 1937. As Sanford Jacoby (1986, 226) writes,

> most of our knowledge of early union grievance procedures is based on practices in the clothing industry. The industry's model for grievance resolution was the unsuccessful yet influential Protocol of Peace devised in 1910 by Louis Brandeis and others to settle a strike in the (New York City) women's garment industry.

The dispute resolution machinery involved joint labor-management shop committees, a Board of Grievances, and a Board of Arbitration that included a part-time, unpaid neutral chairman. Unresolved disputes had to pass through all levels before a strike or lockout could occur. Arbitration was binding on the parties (Nolan & Abrams, 1983a).[13]

While a 1916 strike in New York led employers to end the Protocol there, clothing centers in Chicago, New York, Boston, and Philadelphia copied it. In all cases, arbitration systems collapsed after a few years because they were less adept at handling interest impasses than they were resolving grievances (Nolan & Abrams, 1983a).

But it was in Chicago where the spirit of the Protocol thrived. As in New York, a strike precipitated negotiations on appropriate dispute resolution machinery between Hart, Schaffner and Marx (HSM) and the United Garment Workers. The HSM system was very successful owing to a number of factors: HSM was a large, prosperous company unlike many of New York's smaller and weaker firms; the parties were more cooperative; and the chairmen tended to be highly skilled advocates of the 'judicial model' of arbitration (Nolan & Abrams, 1983a).[14]

The millinery (1915) and hosiery (1929) industries adopted arbitration systems similar to men's clothing, but it thrived better in hosiery (Fleming, 1965; Jacoby, 1986).[15] Philadelphia's full-fashioned hosiery industry was localized, highly competitive and chaotic. Although partly unionized, the industry's skilled unionized workers exerted tremendous amounts of shop-floor power in establishing work rules and lucrative piece-rates. But higher labor costs and sporadic union militancy, including mass strikes, led a number of firms to migrate to rural areas of Pennsylvania and the South during the 1920s. A handful of surviving firms sought outside assistance in establishing dispute resolution procedures. The major institution was the impartial chairmanship, held for many years by university professor George W. Taylor. Nelson Lichtenstein (1993) calls Taylor the "founder of modern grievance arbitration," and notes,

> the key features of this new system . . . were employer recognition of union strength and permanency, a union commitment to industrial self-discipline, including a program of wage rationalization and moderation, and the establishment of a quasi-judicial umpire system that would resolve any outstanding disputes between the parties (117).

Taylor exercised broad powers in his role as the chairman and established key principles governing workplace disputes: progressive discipline, including just cause dismissal; the necessity for uninterrupted production; and the importance of seniority in personnel movement. In the place of the impersonal adjudicatory nature of the anthracite coal model, the hosiery model favored an informal, friendly atmosphere in which Taylor served as conciliator, friend, counselor, mediator, and arbitrator as last resort (Fleming 1965; Lichtenstein 1993).[16] Taylor's informal 'mediator model' competed with the more rigid 'judicial model' operating in coal and clothing.

The hosiery model was soon adopted and modified in heavy industry during the late 1930s and early 1940s, and was pushed by the War Labor Board. In 1937 General Motors and the United Auto Workers established a five-step grievance arbitration procedure based on the hosiery model, with some modification. GM executives wanted a more restricted chairmanship than the one in hosiery. After a few imperfect years, the 1940 contract called for the establishment of a permanent umpire, the first one being George W. Taylor. Instead of the freewheeling approach he was used to in Philadelphia, Taylor was limited to contract interpretations. No longer referred to as an 'impartial chairman', Taylor was now an 'umpire', merely calling 'balls and strikes' (Atleson, 1998; Lichtenstein, 1993). Still, the GM-UAW arbitration system was a remarkable innovation',

> for it represented the very first such permanent mechanism established in heavy industry, and as such, would go a long way in defining the character of the industrial jurisprudence that would evolve in the core sectors of the U.S. economy (Lichtenstein, 1993: 129).

This occurred with the encouragement of the War Labor Board. Jim Atleson (1998, 70) notes: "By war's end . . . the basic structure of today's common arbitral system was in place."

The automobile industry's arbitration model spread across the industrial landscape in subsequent years. In other sectors of the economy, mechanisms were also in place to resolve workplace conflicts. Yet, with the exception of some of the early experiences noted above in the literature reviews, not much is known about how these systems developed over time. In the sections that follow, the experience of the ITU will be discussed, followed by a case study of the Columbus Typographical Union.

THE INTERNATIONAL TYPOGRAPHICAL UNION

The International Typographical Union (ITU) formed in 1852 as the National Typographical Union, but changed its name to the ITU in 1869, after accepting Canadian subordinate locals to membership. Delegates present drew lots to establish local numbers. Columbus delegates drew lot number five, and their union became ITU No. 5 (Tracy, 1913).[17] The ITU took a conciliatory approach toward employers, advocating strikes only as a last resort (Barnett, 1909; Tracy, 1913). This attitude, similar to other skilled trade unions, had its roots in the printers' work culture where most journeymen were willing to work with masters to promote the trade. Until the 1880s, locals operated with a high degree of autonomy, the only mandatory program being control over 'tramp', or traveling, printers (Barnett, 1909).

According to Robert Max Jackson (1984, 247),

> (f)rom 1880 until 1920 the Typographical Union experienced a remarkably steady growth, due both to the growth of industry and the a progressive increase in the proportion of printers who were unionized.

The organization of printers increased from 25% in 1900 to 45% by 1920, with union density greater in cities than elsewhere (Jackson, 1984, 247). ITU membership experienced a steady upward trend, peaking in 1959 at 103,548).[18]

The ITU came to exert tremendous power at work by controlling hiring through union foremen and union-sponsored apprenticeships. This was possible owing to low labor substitutability, intense competition among employers, the lack of foreign competition, and the perishability of the daily newspaper (Marks, 1989). Union power manifested itself in the closed shop, ITU-determined and enforced laws governing job rights (including seniority), and union control of the grievance procedure. Control over labor market factors led Selig Perlman (1928) to point to the ITU as the epitome of business unionism in the United States.

Printers developed tight occupational communities that complemented workplace control.[19] According to Marks (1989: 152), their occupational community,

> institutionally based in the Chapel and expressed in their sense of exclusiveness, their occupational pride, and their relatively low rates of occupational mobility gave them the capacity to ... challenge capitalist innovation.[20]

Chapels governed every aspect of printers' working life and institutionalized democratic procedures for adjudicating personal and collective grievances. They also enforced a highly complex web of rules and regulations governing the quality and pace of work, giving printers considerable authority on the shop-floor (Marks, 1989; Wallock, 1984).

Economist George Barnett (1912: 15) referred to the chapel as a 'mass-meeting with an elected president', called the chairman.[21] The chair's role evolved over time to include presiding over trials, interpreting and enforcing price lists, and policing labor agreements and ITU General Laws. [22] Through direct vote, printers present at chapel meetings determined the outcome of their peers' grievance cases, a unique feature in American industrial relations.

ARBITRATION IN NEWSPAPERS AND COMMERCIAL PRINTING

During the 1890s, newspaper publishers began adopting mechanical typesetting machines in composing rooms. The most common machine, the linotype, could set between four and five times as much type as a hand compositor. The ITU feared massive job displacement from linotypes,[23] while many publishers found themselves engaged in intense competition with contiguous newspapers, some part of chains, as each sought to outdo the other by adding special features and new departments.[24]

Since a daily newspaper must be produced and consumed daily, labor unrest could lead to irreparable losses in profits and prestige. In 1901, when a number of ITU locals engaged in defensive strikes, progressive employers of the American Newspaper Publishers' Association (ANPA) and leaders of the ITU hatched the first of five national arbitration agreements.[25] Overall, the ITU's fears of widespread unemployment went unrealized (Barnett, 1909; Fagan, 1930; Zerker, 1982). Nonetheless, the deals were necessary to protect employers against strikes and boycotts, and printers against lockouts and sudden pay reductions (Nolan & Abrams, 1983a; Weiss, 1923).[26] At this time, only three fields employed national arbitration – stove molding, general foundry, and the machinists' trades (Loft, 1944).

However, as early as the 1870s, ITU locals in Washington and Chicago had agreed to the arbitration of wage disputes. The Chicago local also had concluded grievance arbitration agreements with publishers as early as 1892. These deals provided the model for the 1901 national arbitration agreement (Burns, 1942).

The arbitration agreement in 1901 established three-member tripartite local boards to resolve disputes over contract terms. Either party could appeal cases to a national board that consisted of the ANPA's labor commissioner, the ITU president, and a third person if the two could not agree. Before the pact expired, local boards were increased to five, while the national board grew to seven members. No strikes affected offices covered under the agreement during the first year, while seven newspaper strikes occurred elsewhere (Nolan & Abrams, 1983a; Weiss, 1923).

Over the four subsequent five-year arbitration agreements, the parties made continuing changes to the scope of arbitration, board composition and procedures. For example, working conditions and practices not covered by the union's internal laws, and interest disputes became arbitrable. The 1909 pact made an official distinction between grievance and interest disputes, such that interest disputes had to be heard first by local boards before being appealed to the national board, while grievance cases could be appealed directly to the national board.

After some tinkering with board composition, the 1917 agreement reinstated tripartite boards that resembled those from 1901. It also removed people unconnected to the industry as arbitrators, and rejected the idea of a permanent umpire as employed in anthracite coal and later in the needle trades and automobiles (Burns, 1942; Nolan & Abrams, 1983a).

These voluntary arbitration agreements succeeded in preventing work stoppages, improving labor relations, and in establishing more informal attempts at dispute resolution. Local arbitrators familiar with local conditions matched the decentralized industry structure and better served the parties. By the 1920s, argue Nolan and Abrams (1983a: 391), "the arbitration concept was firmly embedded in newspaper industry labor relations." Following the ITU example, photoengravers, pressmen and stereotypers signed similar arbitration deals with newspaper publishers once they established independent unions around the turn of the century.

However, tensions between the ITU and the ANPA over the union's refusal to subject its General Laws to arbitration, as well as the ANPA's opposition to shorter hours in commercial shops, led to the collapse of the international agreements by 1922 (Loft, 1944; NLRB, 1938; Weiss, 1923). But since the national deal was in effect supplemental to local arbitration agreements in existence in many cities, local arbitration agreements continued after 1922.[27] In 1929, the printing trades rivaled only the street railway industry in the extent of arbitration clauses. For example, of the 244 ITU contracts on file with the ANPA in 1929, 200 (82%) adopted arbitration; by 1940, 246 of the 263 agreements (93.5%) on file did. Only 17 ITU contracts excluded arbitration that year. Grievance arbitration predominated in ITU agreements, while interest arbitration was more common in pressmen and stereotyper contracts. In practice, however, the parties adhered closely to conciliation as the preferred method of dispute settlement (Loft, 1944: 234, 236, 249).

During the 1940s, local arbitration agreements continued to flourish, peaking at 1,125 in 1943. In 1945 the ITU barred locals from using unofficial international arbitration machinery that had survived the collapse of the last agreement in 1922 (Emery 1950: 180).[28] Emery (1950: 194) observes that, (d)espite the sound and fury, the tendency in daily newspaper labor relations policy was negotiatory, with an advocacy of collective bargaining, conciliation, and arbitration. A belligerent attitude toward the mechanical unions has been held by only a small minority.

In the commercial branch, competition was more intense and anti-union animus was more prevalent.

Arbitration in Commercial Printing

The commercial printing industry was more decentralized, fragmented and competitive than the newspaper industry which, over the course of the twentieth century, became more centralized and controlled by newspaper chains (Demers, 1994; Loft, 1944). Emily Clark Brown, a keen observer of the branch, described the industry in this way in 1942:

> This industry ranges all the way from the tiny old-fashioned 'bedroom shop' to the huge plant with two or three thousand employees, producing mail-order catalogues, telephone directories, or popular periodicals or books, by methods approaching mass production. A larger part of the products are the unstandardized, made-to-order, small-run jobs needed by local businesses. The typical printer is small (119).

There were other differences as well. For example, the perishability of the newspaper made good labor relations paramount, hence the ITU/ANPA arbitration agreements. Newspaper wages were only a small part of total production costs given the larger capital requirements. Commercial shop owners lived close to the edge financially. Excessive price and wage cutting occurred with a vengeance during slack times. Trade associations continually urged their members to install cost systems to prevent the downward spiraling of profits that followed price cuts.[29] Despite being better craftsmen than newspaper compositors, commercial printers worked in a more chaotic and less certain branch of the industry (Burns, 1942; Loft, 1944).[30]

The industry's major trade association, the United Typothetae of America (UTA) was founded in Chicago in 1887,

> for the purpose of devising plans for united action upon the recent demand of the International Typographical Union that nine hours shall constitute a day's labor (Powell, 1926).[31]

In contrast to business-related issues[32] that spurred the ANPA's founding in 1887, in Rochester, New York, the UTA was born to fight unions.[33]

Industry fragmentation, incomplete organization and varying attitudes toward unions among master printers and local associations made arbitration more tentative and less widespread. The ITU concluded a deal with the UTA's Closed Shop Division between 1917 and 1926, only to see it crippled when the union pushed for the 44-hour week in 1921 (Loft, 1944). Another short-lived agreement followed the pioneering ANPA/ITU agreements under the auspices of the International Joint Conference Council (IJCC), founded in 1919 with 10 charter members – 5 employer groups and 5 unions (Baker, 1957; Bonnett, 1922).[34]

The newspaper industry developed a more stable national arbitration system than that found in commercial printing. Because the number of arbitration cases heard in any year was small, the most appropriate to study the workings of grievance procedures is at the local level. As the Columbus case reveals, the history of grievance processing unfolded in four phases, with much continuity across the phases. Given the paucity of available information, it is uncertain whether or not the development of other ITU grievance procedures also occurred in four phases. However, sketchy evidence provided below suggests that, at least for the larger locals, the same four phases could be identified but with some modifications. For example, given differences in industry development and the degree of employer association activism, bigger locals in Chicago and New York engaged in formal collective bargaining earlier than in Columbus. As such, the start and length of particular phases varied by location.

THE COLUMBUS TYPOGRAPHICAL UNION NO. 5: A CASE STUDY IN THE DEVELOPMENT OF A CRAFT UNION GRIEVANCE PROCEDURE

The Columbus ITU's grievance procedure evolved over four distinct phases between 1859 and 1959. Yet, there also was much continuity over the years. For example, despite the increasing formality and structure, the process exhibited a high degree of conciliation, cooperation, peer review, and union control. ITU politics and industry-wide labor relations were more responsible for procedural changes than were wars and laws, or other external factors. And while forces outside Columbus impacted the grievance procedure, local traditions and preferences mitigated these effects for many years, thus preserving local autonomy.

A micro-level examination is the most appropriate way to study the grievance procedure since the workplace is the locus of grievances. While industry-level analyses of grievance procedures help to make broad generalizations, they tend to focus on the most challenging and symbolically important cases, leaving out the vast majority of cases. This study focuses on grievances at all levels in the process and, as such, is able to capture how all grievances are handled. Moreover, the long length of time covered permits us to notice both subtle and significant shifts in the grievance procedure.

Phase I: Grievance Settlement Before 1885: the rudiments of a grievance procedure

Columbus printers formed a protective society in 1850

> for the purpose of relief of its members in the time of sickness or distress, but soon the members saw the necessity of being identified with the National Typographical Union ... (1909 anniversary souvenir, Ohio Historical Society, mss 125, box 40, folder 13. Hereafter referred to by box and folder numbers).[35]

Economic distress forced the Columbus group to relinquish its charter in the late 1850s, much to the dismay of devout unionists and travelers who found no place to deposit their union cards. But on September 24, 1859, printers revived the old organization, and effective October 30, 1859 received a new charter with their old Local 5 designation.

From the beginning the Columbus local sought to cooperate with employers. Its constitution's preamble explicitly reveals this:

> We, the journeymen printers of Columbus, Ohio, believing that the formation of *union societies has a mutual tendency to promote the interests of the employer and the employed* (italics mine), and especially to secure the journeyman a just reward for his labor, as well as to protect the regular workingman from the encroachments of persons professing to be printers, without the least claim to that title, do hereby form ourselves into a Typographical Union, for these purposes, under the name of Columbus Typographical Union ... (minutes of first union meeting, 11/07/59; box 1, folder 1).

Beginning during the latter part of the nineteenth century, as the industry changed, relations between printers and employers became more strained, with each group having more distinct interests than before (Wallock, 1984). But in Columbus, labor peace prevailed. Only one strike took place during the local's first one hundred years; that occurred when the owner of the daily *Statesman* refused to comply with the union's price list in 1860.

In Columbus union's formative years, labor relations was conducted largely on an informal basis, while the grievance procedure was in an embryonic stage. The first recorded grievances occurred during the early months of 1861 and pertained to either the violation or interpretation of the union's rules.[36] For example, on March 2, union representatives visited the Harris & Hurd print shop to discuss with one of the proprietors, Colonel Harris, the matter of pressroom foremen receiving $9.00 per week, below union scale. Harris was unaware that the union held jurisdiction over pressroom employees and, after an amicable conversation with the union men, Harris raised wages (minutes, 3/3/61; box 1, folder 1). This was a typical grievance that the parties adjusted short of strike, lockout, third party intervention, or the union declaring the employer 'unfair'.

Before collective bargaining appeared in Columbus in 1902, the local employed a variety of means to resolve outstanding grievances. For example, in addition to an informal, personal approach, the union also established ad hoc committees.[37] During the summer of 1862, the local appointed a committee of three to investigate and report 'whether a foreman of rats and women is eligible to membership in this union'. Upon discovering women in the employ of the *Columbus Gazette*, the 'Committee of Rats and Women' dispatched a letter to the newspaper's proprietor notifying him that the union would not recognize any office that employed women.[38] Without explanation, the union rescinded its resolution prohibiting the employment of women in ITU shops. The best explanation is that the employer complied with the union's demands or changed the women's duties (minutes, 8/2, 9/6, and 12/6/62; box 1, folder 1).

The use of temporary committees between 1862 and 1870 marked a subtle change in the grievance procedure. These committees worked closely with the 'Father of the Chapel' (later called the chapel chairman) to settle disputes. For example, when rumors circulated at the *Gazette* in July 1865 and later in October 1870 that a violation of the price scale had occurred, the local instructed the Father to enforce the scale, while a committee of three made a thorough investigation (minutes, 8/5/65 & 11/5/70; box 1, folders 1 & 2).

The union also rewrote its constitution and by-laws and changed its price list to accommodate employers and solve problems.[39] In one case, member George Coffroth presented before the union proof of railroad advertisements for which a dispute had arisen between him and his foreman. A member vote of 20 to 3 ruled that the compositor had to measure the advertising matter and should not be paid by time. A fellow printer suggested the union revise its Scale of Prices to reflect the members' ruling (minutes, 10/1/70; box 1, folder 2). This case also reveals an early form of peer review that became more prominent after 1910.

At its regular June 6, 1868 meeting, the union created a standing committee of three, the first permanent local-wide body. Previous to this action, each chapel had its own committee (box 1, folder 1).[40] One advantage to this new structure was the uniform enforcement of union rules. Still, the use of temporary investigative bodies did not die. The new standing committee did not hear a grievance until September 1871, when it investigated an alleged violation of union rules in the news and book offices of the *Statesman* (minutes, 10/7/71; box 1, folder 2).[41]

The standing committee's activities worked in tandem with the local's grievance (organizing) committee. However, if employers failed to obey the union's established price list or work rules, the union declared the shop unfair and sent out its grievance committee to bring the shop back under its jurisdiction. The name of this committee suggests that the union's biggest disputes were over

The Evolution of an Alternative Grievance Procedure   89

recognition. Once the parties established an ongoing relationship, they resolved conflicts amicably.

Even with a permanent standing committee after 1871, the local convened temporary bodies to resolve grievances. For example, it created a 'Secret Committee of Five' to investigate an alleged scale violation by nine members at the Statesman in 1876. A similar problem had occurred there in 1873. Given the depressed economy, the men refused the union's request to quit work. Consequently, the union published and circulated a 'rat list' containing the nine names (minutes, special meeting, 9/8 and regular meeting, 11/4/76; box 1, folder 3). Boycotts were another tactic used to resolve outstanding grievances before 1900.[42]

Phase II: The Birth of the Executive Committee: 1885–1901
During this phase, both the ITU and the Columbus union were undergoing bureaucratization. This process affected the grievance procedure in Columbus and elsewhere. A significant outcome at the local level was the birth of the executive committee, a critical union body.

The ITU was highly decentralized before the1880s, but between 1880 and World War One, it became much more centralized and involved in local union affairs. This was caused by changes in the nature and scope of conflicts with employers along with internal union politics. The creation of a national strike fund, the appointment of paid union organizers to service locals, the centralization of death and pension benefits, the use of political referenda, and the increased application of union laws were mutually reinforcing and moved the ITU toward centralization (Jackson, 1984).

The Columbus union was not immune to these changes, but it did preserve much of its autonomy in a number of places, most notably in the workings of its grievance procedure. The birth of the local's executive committee in 1885 derived from the ITU's formalization around the same time. The establishment of the local executive committee did not upset the informal and cooperative relations between employers and the local union, however. But it added some structure to the grievance procedure.

In May 1885, the Columbus union established a local-wide, two-member executive committee that evolved from the standing committee. The executive committee's duties were first made explicit in a December 1888 constitutional revision. Upon a price scale or constitutional violation, members were expected to notify the chapel chairman. Failing to solve the dispute, the executive committee was entrusted to bring the matter to a close, subject to an appeal to the local union. When notified of an appeal, the local president called a special meeting to investigate the case. Only a two-thirds vote by members present could initiate a strike. Until the union concluded the case, 'the business of the office in which such dispute arises shall in no wise be clogged or retarded, but proceed as though no such difference had arisen' (minutes, 12/2/88; box 2, folder 1). This quote highlights the importance attached to both office efficiency and members' workplace rights, and closely resembles a modern day grievance procedure.

A second constitutional amendment in 1890 increased the committee's membership to five-members and required that at least two members come from the commercial branch. It also outlined the chapel chair's duties. For example, the chair was elected annually, had the power to adjust disputes between employers and journeymen, enforced ITU and local laws, and collected dues and other moneys. The chair's decision could only be reversed by the local union (minutes, 2/290; box 2, folder 1).

Even with the maturing executive committee taking on greater responsibilities, there were still a number of local bodies operating without clearly defined duties. For example, at a union meeting held October 1, 1899, members of the discipline committee (formerly the grievance committee) argued with executive committee representatives over proper jurisdiction. The local resolved that the discipline committee would handle organizing, while the executive committee would handle grievances and other duties. An arbitration (negotiations) committee of two managed Scale of Price changes (minutes, 8/4/73 & 10/1/99; box 1, folder 2 & box 2, folder 1).

The executive committee's first major grievances involved the use of plates, matrices, or the reproduction of matter (type) in 1886 and again in 1891.[43] The 1886 dispute also marked the beginning of ITU officer involvement in local grievance handling. For example, in a dispute at the *Columbus Daily Times* over the use of plates and the subsequent decline in the number of columns composed and printers needed, the ITU permitted publishers to transfer ads and news matter to the supplement at prevailing composition prices. The ITU did not object to plate matter. In fact, it recognized its permanency and 'respectfully ask(s) that the transfer of matter ('set-up' in the newsroom of that office) to the present plate supplement be allowed to the greatest extent'. The local then placed the entire matter in the hands of the *Times* chapel for proper adjustment (minutes, 6/6/86 and special meeting, 6/18/86; box 1, folder 3).

A 1891 plate dispute at the *Dispatch* warranted ITU president Plank's clarification on the proper steps to be followed in resolving the dispute that saw six printers discharged for redundancy. The details of the case are less important than its impact on the steps in the grievance procedure. An exchange of letters straightened out the uncertainties in the matter at hand, but created some confusion in the proper steps taken in resolving grievances. Whereas in 1886 the chapel chairman's decision could be appealed to the local union and then to the executive committee prior to ITU involvement, the 1891 dispute required

The Evolution of an Alternative Grievance Procedure 91

the grievant to appeal the chairman's decision to the executive committee *before* the local union handled it (minutes of 6/7/91; box 2, folder 1). This became the preferred sequence in subsequent years and made the role of the local executive committee more integral in the grievance procedure.

The most likely reason for the difference comes from a change made to the local's constitution in 1888 that required chapel members to report constitutional violations to the executive committee and then to the local union.

Even as the grievance procedure became more formalized, the union showed its willingness to work with employers on tricky issues. One early example occurred in May 1895 when the new proprietor at the *Press-Post*, G. P. Stephens, a former ITU man, asked the union to relax its adherence to its price list because

> to be compelled to pay composition on ... advertisements, would necessarily place us at a disadvantage. The *Dispatch,* our strongest competitors, employs a less number (sic) of men, all of them by the week, and pays less money for composition than does the *Press-Post*.

Stephens concluded, "Whatever your decision may be in the case, it will not alter the friendly relations of this office towards the Union." The union honored his request (minutes, 6/1/95; box 2, folder 1). This example reveals not only the cooperative relations formed from shared experiences, but also the union's power in the workplace.

As the twentieth century dawned, the grievance procedure became more structured owing to the establishment of the executive committee, local constitutional amendments applied to internal procedures, the ITU's centralized control over subordinate unions, and national arbitration. Although external events impinged upon ITU No. 5's labor relations and grievance process, local traditions moderated their effects. The operation of the grievance procedure between 1859 and 1901 reveals a high degree of informality and experimentation with different structures and procedures. The main grievance subjects dealt primarily with wages, hours, reproduction rules, the measurement of matter by hand compositors, and apprenticeship regulations. There were no differences between commercial and newspaper offices as the branches were not yet distinct.

In the next phase, the grievance procedure would become even more structured and formal owing to external factors such as industrial relations between the ITU and national employers associations, the establishment of a two-party political structure within the ITU, and the emergence of collective bargaining agreements in 1902. Together, these factors added new dimensions to the Columbus union's grievance procedure, including the creation of a 'dual grievance procedure'. Overall, the grievance procedure would remain almost exclusively in the control of the local union.

Phase III: Grievance Handling Under Collective Bargaining, 1902–1939
Collective bargaining reached its high point between 1898 and 1902, a period of economic prosperity and greater demand for skilled labor. National contracts between unions and employer groups ensured labor peace and industrial stability. In the printing industries, the ITU and the United Typothetae hatched a national pact in 1898, followed in 1901 by separate deals between the ITU, Printing Pressmen, Stereotypers and Electrotypers and the American Newspaper Publishers' Association in 1901(Van Tine, 1973). The Columbus ITU negotiated its first collective agreements with local newspaper and commercial employer associations in 1902 and 1903, respectively. Following the spirit of the national agreements, local contracts called for dispute resolution language that had the effect of creating a 'dual' grievance procedure.

Disputes dealing with union rules, and later ITU General Laws, were handled internally within the union hierarchy. Since all foremen were unionized, and almost always a party to the grievance, the ITU considered grievances to be strictly internal union affairs. Parties to the dispute had the right to appeal to the ITU Executive Board for adjudication. Under rare circumstances, outstanding grievances were settled on the ITU convention floor. This 'internal' grievance procedure had its roots in what David Feller (1973) calls the "trade agreement."

Through trade agreements, skilled craft unionists unilaterally established wages and work rules governing their employment. Employers either accepted or rejected the agreement as a whole. Members who violated its terms could be fined or expelled upon the conclusion of a formal hearing. The closed shop and union foremen ensured both member and employer compliance with the trade agreement.

Disputes that involved either contractual violations or interpretations required the involvement of both union and employer representatives as part of a multistep process. This 'external' grievance procedure, normally part of 'industrial agreements', was not controlled exclusively by the union (Jacoby, 1986).[44]

In Columbus throughout this period, the internal, union-controlled grievance procedure was much more formal and prominent than the external, joint labor-management standing committee. A key feature of the internal procedure was peer review, which was highly consistent with chapel procedures and ITU democratic traditions. Tacitly employed by printers, it was made explicit by a local constitutional revision in 1910. Among other things, the amendment stipulated that a chapel vote must precede an appeal to the local executive committee and union.[45] On the other hand, joint standing committees (JSCs) met infrequently, rarely left written records, and resolved all disputes by conciliation.

Outside influences continued to potentially impact the Columbus ITU's grievance procedure in this period. The ITU's push for shorter hours in the commercial branch between 1906 and 1923 and its internal political fights did alter labor relations and grievance procedures in a number of locations.[46] In Columbus, while grievance procedure contract language sometimes changed in response, the parties continued to adjust grievances largely through the union's hierarchy and, to a much lesser extent, jointly with employers. Reasons for this could be found in the make-up of both the commercial employers' association and Columbus employers in general.

Until 1919, Columbus's commercial employers were a loose-knit group, in and out of the UTA since 1887. But with the formation of Columbus Typothetae in 1919, the Columbus chapter became a permanent organization.[47] The lack of employer organization and hostility in Columbus may be attributed to a number of mutually reinforcing factors. For example, a tradition of cordial relations between printing employers and the ITU had existed for half a century by this time. This was coupled with inactive employer associations, which helped to nurture these cooperative labor relationships.

Moreover, Columbus was less industrial than Cleveland and Cincinnati and had a more diverse economic base, rooted in state politics, commerce and, only later, industry. Its population and workforce were largely native-born and relatively docile, leading the Columbus Chamber of Commerce in 1915 to boast that 'Columbus labor is American labor' (Blackford, 1984; Columbus Chamber, 1915; Garrett & Lentz, 1980; Hunker, 1958; Schneirov, 1993).[48]

Internal ITU politics also affected the Columbus union's procedure. From the strong democratic traditions of the chapel structure emerged a unique two-party political structure within the ITU by 1911. Informal and secretive factions had been operating since the first few decades of the nineteenth century in order to enable foremen to control the hiring of substitutes in the face of employer discrimination of union labor. Foreman control of 'sub-lists', however, led groups of regular printers to demand that they hire their own subs to prevent favoritism (Taft, 1944).[49] This conflict eventually led to the ITU's 1890 Priority Law, an important law governing chapel-based seniority and discharge (property) rights in newspaper offices (Loft, 1944; Porter 1954).[50]

Factions and cliques operated informally for a number of years until the ITU's first direct membership vote of officers took place in 1898. According to former ITU president A. Sandy Bevis (1978, 4),

> while the so-called 'Wahnetas' had existed as successors or continuations of previous (secret) societies – the first open international party in the ITU (the Progressive party) was formed in 1911.

The Progressives, however, were unable to unseat the more conservative Wahneta-Administration party in the 1912 election.[51]

The Wahnetas, in charge between 1900 and 1920, negotiated the industry-wide arbitration agreements with the ANPA. The Progressives (Progs) were more militant and opposed conciliation and arbitration. No single party came to dominate the Executive Council between 1920 and 1928 and from 1938 to 1944, but when a Prog captured the presidency in 1922, he ended the arbitration agreements (Lipset et al., 1956; Taft, 1944). The ideological battles also affected grievance procedures as a 1908 internal ITU case reveals.

The Denver Decision of 1908

The controversial *Denver Decision* was passed in 1908 under the conservative leadership of ITU president James Lynch. At the core of *Denver* was the publishers' opposition to certain aspects of the ITU's 1890 Priority Law that specified four reasons for discharge. Specifically, the ANPA protested the right of the discharged printer to be reinstated during the long appeals process. It complained that locals frequently resisted valid discharges, thus impairing the foreman's authority and causing composing room discipline problems. It was possible that discharged printers could continue to work almost a year before the union determined the legitimacy of the discharge.

The conciliatory Lynch and the international arbitration panel recognized the validity of publishers' complaints and ruled that, pending final settlement, employers did not have to comply with a local's order of reinstatement.[52] The chapel still retained the right to reinstate the discharged printer, but could no longer compel the union foreman to do so. If the foreman refused reinstatement, the chapel could appeal to the local union, where its ruling could be appealed (by either the foreman or printer) to the ITU Executive Council. Employers disliked having to pay for all lost time if the ITU returned the printer to work. In deciding this case, ITU officers tried to balance the authority of the foreman with the rights of ITU members:

> We agree that the authority of foremen as set forth in (ITU) law must be sustained, and the rights of chapels and members must also be sustained; and any attempt to evade the law on the part of a foreman, chapel or members is inimical to the peace and good fellowship now existing between the (ANPA) and the (ITU)(Bulletin, 1913, v.2, no.1, 6–7).

Conspicuously absent was the role of management, except through its surrogate, the foreman.

When the Progressive candidate won the presidency in 1922, he repealed *Denver* for being too concessionary and conservative. But when the conservative Lynch reclaimed the presidency in 1925, he reinstated *Denver*. One year

The Evolution of an Alternative Grievance Procedure 95

later, Lynch lost again and the Denver ruling was once again voided, except where locals, by contract, agreed to binding joint standing committee decisions (Loft, 1944).

As the ITU's political parties tossed around the *Denver* ruling as a political football, the ANPA had been working to reduce its members' financial risks. As a result, in 1912, the ITU recommended a change in local procedures such that now the employer had the option of submitting discharges to local joint standing committees, with appeal to arbitration, if necessary. After 1928, the ANPA insisted upon joint standing committee provisions in local contracts.$_{53}$ It clearly wanted input in discharge grievance cases. From only 11 such contracts in 1915, by 1940 69% (or roughly 175) of ANPA contracts stipulated joint committees (Burns, 1942; Loft, 1944). This number most likely increased after the passage of Taft-Hartley Act in 1947.

Despite discharge language appearing for the first time in the 1937 Columbus newspaper contract, local publishers did not demand input through the JSC until 1941, thus illustrating the power of local traditions and the union's control in the workplace.[54] Loft (1944) identifies and describes three types of discharge procedures in existence across the ITU's jurisdiction after 1928. One provided for joint committee involvement, with reinstatement only after a JSC vote; a second ignored *Denver* and provided immediate reinstatement, if necessary; and the third accepted *Denver*, such that a discharged printer could only be reinstated if the ITU supported it.

Emily Clark Brown studied dispute resolution in the commercial branch and noticed variations in procedures contingent upon city size and employer association activity. She argues that in smaller cities with inactive employer associations, JSC activity was minimal. Moreover, when a

> joint committee gets a dispute, it seldom issues a formal decision, interpreting the obligation of one or the other side . . . Sometimes the Association allows a discharge dispute to be decided through the union appeal machinery. Employers . . . in some cases . . . prefer to put the final decision up to the (ITU) executive council (Brown, 1942: 146).

Even in very large cities, JSC activity was light. The Columbus case supports her conclusions of very informal joint meetings and deference toward the union's internal procedure. For example, between 1903 and 1939, no commercial cases found their way to the JSC, while newspaper JSC meetings never concluded with formal decisions. Instead of formal 'external' arbitration proceedings involving labor and management, there emerged around the turn of the century a formal 'internal' arbitration procedure involving the ITU Executive Council as an arbitration panel. The Council served in a judicial capacity well before the Hart, Schaffner & Marx arbitration panel began operating in 1914.

The ITU Executive Council as Arbitration Panel

By the early 1900s the ITU's influence in subordinate union affairs was commonplace. Since the 1880s the ITU had helped to resolve local grievances when called upon by Columbus officers. By 1904, with the *McDonald v. ITU No. 5* discharge/priority decision, ITU No. 5's internal grievance procedure expanded to officially include the ITU Executive Council as an arbitration panel.

Between 1904 and 1939, 22 Columbus cases found their way to ITU Executive Council dockets.[55] The cases dealt exclusively with ITU laws and focused on three main issues: priority (seniority),[56] discharges, and overtime violations.[57] All cases originated in newspaper offices, mostly from the *Citizen* (14 cases). The *Dispatch* and *Journal* chapels each produced 4. Of the seven discharge cases, four dealt with intoxication; two sustained the foreman, one favored the grievant, and one was dismissed after the member died.

Over time, this internal arbitration system produced a common law that that governed ITU workplaces. Executive Council decisions were very detailed, given case numbers, and resembled court decisions, especially their use of precedent-setting cases.[58] Beginning in 1913, the ITU published Council decisions in its *Bulletin* and disseminated them to all local officers to assist them in interpreting union laws, developing equity and uniformity throughout its jurisdiction, and to reduce its caseload.

A few cases will help to illustrate how this process worked. The first Columbus case to incorporate a precedent from another local came in 1924 in *D. Johnson & Frank W. Willoth v. No. 5* (Case No. 3935-E, 1924). Referring to a 1917 Worcester, Massachusetts case, which cited a 1915 Indianapolis one, the Council sided with ITU No. 5 in an overtime cancellation case at the *Columbus Citizen* dating to Labor Day 1923 (Grievance Files, box 21, folder 6).

Another *Citizen* case is interesting because it makes use of three prior ITU Council rulings, and was the only Columbus case appealed to the convention floor. In this case, *W. W. Wever v. No. 5* (Case No. 5987-E, 1935), an advertising man charged foreman Wever with a priority violation and conduct unbecoming a union man. The local voted to fine Wever $100 and expelled him from the ITU. The ad man argued that, when the foreman switched operators to floor work during the bank holiday of 1933, he was deprived of work. The Executive Council found nothing "to justify the conclusion that switches were made to either discriminate against the original complainant or to invade his priority rights" and sustained the foreman.

The ad man appealed to the convention floor. In preparing an argument, Wever referred to similar cases from Tulsa, San Francisco, and Waco (Grievance Files, box 21, folder 6; minutes, 5/5/35 & 1/6/36, box 7, folders 1 & 2).[59] The supporting cases, as well as the one at issue, show how the ITU attempted to balance the rights of members under ITU law with the right of management to deploy labor efficiently. In a number of cases the ITU sided with management's desire to maintain efficient production. This meant upholding discharges as it did in two cases in 1933 and 1934.[60]

Of the 22 ITU Council appeals sent from Columbus, 4 were heard before 1920, six during the 1920s, and 12 during the1930s. All of these cases dealt either with discharges, priority or overtime violations, and involved either individual property rights (discharge and priority) or group property rights (cancellation of overtime).[61]

The Council's involvement in resolving grievances added a greater degree of formality to ITU No. 5's internal grievance procedure and, to some degree, directed it more in line with other locals through the development of a common law of typographical chapels. The external procedure, however, remained unchanged by this development.

The Joint Standing Committee

Newspaper and commercial JSCs were contractually stipulated local bodies comprised of four members each, two from the union and two from the employer groups. Either party could appeal JSC cases to neutral arbitrators.[62] As part of the external grievance procedure, they added another dimension to local grievance processing after 1902. Only six documented JSC meetings took place between 1903 and 1939, five of which pertained to wage and hour disputes; the other with resetting advertisements. As with ITU Council cases, all JSC activities occurred in the newspaper branch. The JSC sustained the union's position in 5 of 6 cases.[63] In two cases heard in 1935 and 1936, the JSC deferred to the local union's executive committee for final resolution (minutes, 1/5, 9/6 & 11/1/36, box 7, folder 2). Only three cases found their way to local arbitration proceedings between 1905 and 1912.[64] They involved the exchange of matrices at the *Press-Post* in 1905 and at the *Dispatch* in 1912, and fines for careless proofreaders at the *Press-Post* in 1906. All of the recorded cases, including the three that invoked arbitration proceedings, were settled by conciliation, without formal, written decisions (minutes, 2/5/05 & 4/1/06, box 4, folder 1; minutes, 2/4 & 4/3/12, box 5, folder 1). Not until 1957 would an arbitrator's formal ruling adjudicate a dispute.

Between 1903 and 1939 the most common disputes related to priority, discharge, overtime cancellation, and wage and hour violations. Priority and exchange of matrices affected newspaper offices, while the competitive commercial branch dealt more with wage and hour cases. Discharges cut across both branches, although the ITU Executive Council heard discharge grievances only from newspaper offices.

The union's control over the grievance procedure continued into the final period under study, 1940–1959, but there were a number of visible differences indicating greater employer input in the process.

Phase IV: Grievance Settlement, 1940–1959: joint grievance settlement emerges

Grievance handling after 1940 continued to reflect the practices of the previous period. Owing to economic changes in Columbus and the war, some noticeable changes occurred that pushed the grievance procedure inexorably toward an industrial union model, where joint labor-management resolution of disputes is the norm. The change was gradual and more marked after 1960, however, after industry consolidation and technological changes swept through the printing industries.

Columbus's economic make-up changed significantly during World War Two when the Federal government built the Curtiss-Wright aircraft plant in 1941. At its peak, the plant employed over 25,000 workers and expanded the city's semi-skilled labor pool. Before the war, there were 30,000 total workers engaged in manufacturing activities. Local labor relations changed when, in 1941, the United Auto Workers organized 12,000 Curtiss-Wright workers, 'at one stroke greatly increasing the numbers and political clout of the labor movement in Columbus' (Schneirov, 1993, 90). Through the 1950s, Columbus experienced a boom in manufacturing construction, erecting plants for the production of autos, refrigerators and parts supplied to heavy industry. Many of these workers organized into CIO unions (Hunker, 1958; Schneirov, 1993).

The grievance arbitration procedures governing these workers resembled the model advocated by the War Labor Board. Perhaps, as a result, the ITU No. 5's grievance procedure began to change to reflect this. Overall, the local grievance procedure remained under the union's control, even as the external procedure became more significant.

During this phase, grievances related to discharges and priority were the most common, followed by wage and hour and ITU overtime violations. Apprentice regulation grievances became prominent and emerged out of wartime labor shortages. Disputes over exchange of matrices, jurisdiction, improper hiring, illegal transfers, and sanitary conditions continued, but declined in absolute numbers. New issues such as vacation time and call-back pay emerged but were not frequent. Through 1959, as before, grievance activity remained light.

More grievances originated in the larger, more bureaucratically organized newspaper offices than in commercial shops, especially those that related to priority, discharge, matrices, ITU overtime, transfers, and vacations. Apprenticeship considerations, jurisdiction, and sanitation issues were more common in commercial plants. Wage and hour violations and illegal hiring affected both branches equally. Transfer of personnel violations occurred only in newspaper offices, while sanitation problems affected the shop of F. J. Heer exclusively.

The ITU Executive Council received more cases from Columbus after 1940. Whereas 26 cases reached ITU dockets before 1940, the Council decided 29 cases after 1940. Over twice as many cases per year were appealed to the ITU than in the previous period.[65] Of the 29 cases, 69% involved priority (12), discharges (4), and ITU overtime laws (4). These issues comprised 100% of all ITU appeals prior to 1940. The other 31% involved new issues such as vacation, call-back pay, discipline, and the authority of foremen.

For the first time, three appeals from commercial shops reached the ITU. More significantly, in two of them, commercial owners themselves filed the appeal.[66] In both cases union members prevailed. The written record is silent on why the owners appealed these cases. Within the newspaper branch, all cases either came from the *Citizen* or the *Dispatch* composing room, with more originating from the former.[67]

Local JSCs were more active after 1940 than before. For example, only 6 JSC cases arose between 1902 and 1939, while 20 cases required involvement after 1940. Although not large, the change is meaningful. For example, while only roughly 0.18 cases per year required JSC assistance before 1940, JSCs heard 1 case per year after 1940. Most of these cases came from newspaper offices with no single issue prominent. One discharge case, however, was significant in marking a change in the grievance procedure.

Finally, for the first time since formal procedures emerged in local contracts, an arbitration case was concluded with a formal decision. The increased activity coming from the external grievance procedure provides evidence that a new era in labor relations and grievance handling was dawning in Columbus.

Section 46: Discharge
The discharge of a *Citizen* compositor on November 29, 1940, for removing company property from the premises (neglect of duty), was not unusual. The printer appealed the discharge to the chapel which, by a 15 to 11 tally, voted to uphold his dismissal. The plaintiff appealed the chapel's ruling to the executive committee, which reversed the foreman's ruling. This decision enabled the compositor to return to his November 11, 1940 priority status. The foreman then lost an appeal at the local union level. At this point the case becomes more significant to the grievance procedure's history because the foreman demanded an appeal to the JSC.

For the first time in the union's history, and 4 years after the newspaper contract allowed for it, the employer wanted direct input in determining a discharge case. On March 7, 1941, two representatives from the publishers' group and two from the local union met to interpret Section 46 of the contract pertaining to proper procedures used to resolve discharge cases. The language read:

> Appeal may be taken from the action of the chapel to the Union, and then to the Joint Standing Committee for decision. Provided that nothing herein shall prevent appeal by either party to the International Typographical Union Executive Council (box 22, folder 1).

The controversy focused on whether or not the ITU was the final arbiter of the case. The employer argued that the JSC made the final determination, while the union argued for complete control. The two separate grievance procedures – internal and external – were possibly merging into one. Correspondence between the local and the ITU reveals that, at the time, a variety of procedures existed across the country. For example, ITU President Claud Baker wrote the following note to Secretary Bird of Columbus on January 8, 1941:

> It would . . . be a source of constant chaos and friction should a system be established whereby a local joint agency would first have jurisdiction over discharges and then appeal might be made from that jurisdiction to the Executive Council (box 22, folder 1).

But in a letter to Bird of the same date, ITU Secretary-Treasurer Woodruff argued a different opinion:

> Inasmuch as section 46 specifically retains jurisdiction for the International Typographical Union Executive Council, the last sentence of section 46 ('All decisions of the Standing Committee shall be final and binding on both parties'.) could not be operative as regards discharge cases. It is therefore my opinion that discharge cases under contract should go to the union and then to the Executive Council (box 22, folder 1).

The local union used Randolph's opinion to guide them, although they agreed to a March 7 JSC meeting, where the following compromise was reached:

> If petitioner . . . does *not* (italics added) elect to take appeal to the Joint Standing Committee, then nothing shall prevent appeal by petitioner to the (ITU) Executive (Council). It is further interpreted by the (JSC) that when appeal is taken to the (JSC) for decision, that decision shall be final and binding on both parties (box 22, folder 1).

Since *Citizen* management wished the case to be heard by the JSC, the joint agency agreed to convene a meeting by March 14, 1941 (Letter from Newspaper Joint Standing Committee to ITU and local union officers, 3/5/41; box 22, folder 1). This action sparked a protest by members who, at a special meeting of March 7, 1941, resolved by a 36:1 vote to prevent future JSC meetings regarding this case. President Baker overruled them, and directed the local to proceed with a JSC hearing.

Dissidents opposed to Baker's decision called another special meeting for March 16, at which they requested the ITU to withhold the JSC's decision pertaining to Section 46. They vehemently opposed the finality of JSC decisions, and argued that Section 46 entered the contract in 1937 under stressful bargaining.[68] Members argued they were unaware that Section 46 would have interfered with their rights to an ITU council hearing.

In the end, the ITU decided in favor of JSC resolution. On March 27, the Council, in *D. H. Burgoon v. No.5* (Case No. 7112-E), decided that "Since the decision of the joint committee, when rendered, will dispose of the issue herein involved, the appeal is dismissed . . ." (box 22, folder 1). Consistent with the use of precedents and the establishment of a common law across chapels, local traditions gave way to prevailing national practices (box 22, folder 1).[69]

This case is significant because it shows the diminution of the local's control over the grievance procedure relative to both the employer and the ITU. The intensity with which members debated and fought over this discharge case indicates that 'workers' control' was not anachronistic almost mid-way through the twentieth century. And though the union lost this case on both fronts, it still exerted tremendous shop-floor control.[70]

Additional evidence of management's desire to resolve grievances jointly came in a 1957 arbitration case involving a women proofreader who was no stranger to discharges. Between 1951 and 1959 she was involved in eight major incidents, mostly ending with her dismissal at either the *Dispatch* or the *Citizen*.[71] In the arbitration case, the company contended she was let go to reduce the force. The union argued that the foreman's actions stemmed from personal dislike, violations of a personnel transfer rule, and priority. Arbitrator and bankruptcy court referee Gail Butts upheld the company and found no contractual violation (Arbitration Proceedings, box 37, folder 62).[72]

The greater role played by employers in grievance settlement in Columbus was framed by the disruptions of the war and the consolidation of the local newspaper industry. In 1958, the *Ohio State Journal* and *Dispatch* composing rooms merged. One year later, the Citizen and the Ohio State Journal merged to create the *Citizen-Journal* (box 11, folders 1 and 2).[73] These events would set the tone for the post–1960 period, which witnessed a computer revolution in printing, a major shift in the balance of power in composing rooms, and further changes in the grievance procedure.

CONCLUSION AND IMPLICATIONS

This chapter traced the evolution of the Columbus Typographical Union No. 5's grievance procedure over its first one hundred years, 1859 to 1959, a period marked by steady union growth and industry stability. While four separate phases could be identified, there was much continuity over the years. For example, conciliation and cooperation between labor and management, rooted in the printing craft's work culture, typified the 'external' grievance procedure, while peer review and union control anchored the 'internal' grievance procedure. A number of events originating outside Columbus impacted the ITU No. 5's grievance procedure, but local traditions dictated how the process worked on a day-to-day basis. That is, new dispute resolution language was added but old ways prevailed for many years. Most of these external factors involved internal ITU political and administrative affairs, and labor relations between the ITU and the major industry trade associations and individual employers. These same factors, however, were more influential in other ITU workplaces.

Only after 1940, owing to more significant external factors, such as the industrialization and subsequent unionization of heavy industry in Columbus, national printing industry labor relations practices, and a general movement toward an industrial union model of workplace organization, did employers became more involved in grievance resolution. Despite the existence of arbitration language as early as 1902, the first arbitration case to require a formal decision occurred as late as 1957. But the winds of change were in the air by the early 1940s. It was not until the gale winds of computerized typesetting and industry restructuring swept through Columbus after 1960 that the grievance procedure would finally come to resemble the industrial model more closely.

This case study enhances our understanding of the historical development of grievance arbitration in the United States in a number of ways. First, unlike Nolan and Abrams (1983a) who refute the 'exaggerated autonomy' of the emergence of arbitration, the newspaper industry in general, and the Columbus case in particular, shows that the incorporation of arbitration procedures came about voluntarily, often without labor strife. Previous investigations showed how wars, laws and influential outsiders inaugurated arbitration in industries such as railroads, anthracite coal, the needle trades, and heavy industry. However, in this study, the key factors were more internal to the union and the industry: the ITU's centralization and political affairs, and labor relations between industry trade associations, employers and the ITU. Even the 1940 Section 46 discharge case that changed the employer's role in grievance handling was largely rooted in contemporary newspaper industry labor practices, although the timing also coincided with the rise of the industrial union grievance arbitration model.

Second, previous research highlights the period between the late 1930s and the 1940s as the era of the widespread adoption of grievance arbitration in heavy industry. When discussing the craft union model of grievance arbitration, heretofore overlooked, a different periodization may be required. Craft unions are older and had extensive work rules codified in trade agreements, including dispute resolution procedures. This study found that as early as the 1880s, a formal grievance procedure was taking shape. By the beginning of the twentieth century, a 'dual' grievance procedure emerged. In general, he 'internal' procedure was more formal and structured than the 'external' one, and was based on the 'judicial' model, later becoming widespread in heavy industry. Moreover, while Jacoby (1986) and Lichtenstein (1993) demonstrate how arbitrators deferred to the craft union model of job property rights when dealing with progressive discipline cases in the needle trades during and after the 1910s, ITU locals and the Executive Council had employed these principles in resolving grievances decades earlier.

Third, critical legal scholars such as Atleson (1998) argue that labor arbitration 'de-radicalized' workers and unions by removing conflict from the shop-floor and preserving the status quo until cases were decided at a later date.[74] While these scholars are generally correct in their assessment, the process of de-radicalization varied across and within unions. The Columbus ITU's 'radicalism' began to weaken by the early 1940s, decades later than many other ITU locals. For example, in spite of the 1908 *Denver* decision that gave publishers the right to discharge printers and remove them from their positions *until* reinstated either by a joint standing committee or arbitrator, the Columbus union maintained its ability to keep the printer at work *until* a higher body ruled otherwise. Through 1940, all higher bodies were strictly union ones.

Fourth, this case also shows the endurance of labor-management cooperation in highly competitive industries concerned with quality and cost. Thus, adversarialism is neither inevitable in labor relationships in general, nor in dispute resolution, in particular. Traditions and customs developed over long periods of time may be as equally important as economic factors in determining the labor relations climate. They may also be crucial to the success or failure of alternative dispute resolution techniques in union settings.

Fifth, the Columbus case reveals the existence of a viable system of peer review of grievances made possible by a constellation of factors, some unique to the printing trades. But in the context of more decentralized bargaining relationships since 1980, and in settings where employees work in team-based structures, peer review may become more widespread.[75] To work effectively, however, a strong, democratic union is required to safeguard members' rights, to prevent breakdowns in worker solidarity and protect against unilateral management actions.

Finally, as with Dorothy Sue Cobble's (1991) historical study of waitress 'occupational unionism', this study raises the possibility of extracting key features of an older craft union model to be melded with current conditions.[76]

For example, combining the use of teams and peer review in a unionized setting, with employer involvement at later steps in the grievance procedure could increase organizational flexibility without compromising workplace rights. This is the scenario that developed in Columbus after 1940.

NOTES

1. Since just about all grievance procedures end with arbitration as the final step, I will sometimes use grievance procedures synonymously with grievance arbitration.
2. Atleson (1998, 96) argues that grievance arbitration also had negative effects on industrial democracy. First, written agreements provide the only source of employee rights. And since contracts represent the outcome of power in the workplace, where employers dominate, they usually favor management. Second, arbitration removes the conflict from the workplace and the immediately affected workers. Finally, arbitration procedures reflect the hierarchical system in the plant, and the substantive rules indicate that only a limited participatory democracy is to be created. As a result, not all unions favor this system.
3. Because unions cannot strike over every issue, then and now, grievance arbitration helps to balance the power in the workplace.
4. Brody (1993) argues that signs of 'workplace contractualism' appeared before the CIO, the Wagner Act, and even before first contracts. He dates the rise of this workplace system to the mid-1930s.
5. The dependent measures included: grievance rate, step level of settlement, speed of settlement, arbitration rate, importance of issue, and equity of settlement. One of their findings revealed that many grievants and their supervisors experienced adverse consequences on measures such as performance ratings and promotions upon using the procedure.
6. See, for example, Lewin and Peterson (1988), Peterson (1992), Feuille and Hildebrand (1995) and Bemmels and Foley (1996) for literature reviews on contemporary grievance research and practice.
7. I am revising a sequel to this story that examines the changes in grievance handling and labor relations from 1960 to 1992, the final period of the Columbus union's history.
8. This case involved the meaning of Taft-Hartley's Section 301. The union sought to enforce an agreement to arbitrate, which was included in the collective agreement. The United States Supreme Court ruled that "the agreement to arbitrate grievance disputes is the *quid pro quo* for an agreement not to strike." The decision expressed a federal policy that federal courts should enforce collective agreements (Fleming, 1967: 22).
9. During the nineteenth and early twentieth centuries, arbitration referred to both interest and grievance (rights) arbitration.
10. Fleming (1965) argues that the distinction between grievance (rights) arbitration and interest arbitration occurred during World War Two.
11. Jim Atleson (1998) stresses the importance of the War Labor Board in convincing and sometimes pushing management to adopt grievance arbitration procedures as an indispensable tool to make collective bargaining work. Unions welcomed it since they gave up the right to strike during the war. Both Atleson and Nolan and Abrams (1983a) agree that by war's end the basic structure of contemporary arbitration was in place. This meant a rights-based dispute resolution procedure no longer based on tradition and custom.

12. They attribute a few major factors to arbitration's maturation. First, the War Labor Board greatly extended the use of arbitration, making it a universal system for dispute resolution. Second, the changing legal environment, from the Taft-Hartley Act to Supreme Court decisions, supported a system of private arbitration. The third impulse came from internal debates about arbitration: the proper roles of arbitrators, the relationship to external law, the efficiency of the process, the professionalization of practitioners, etc.

13. Brandeis advocated conciliation, but after the system almost collapsed in 1914, he resorted to a judicial model at the Grievance Board level, where a full-time impartial chairman held court.

14. Originally an arbitration board of three members heard all grievances until it soon became swamped with cases. In 1912, just a year after its birth, the HSM system established the Trade Board, an intervening body that handled cases before the Board of Arbitration. This greatly reduced the burden on the arbitrators (Fleming, 1965).

15. The millinery arbitration agreement lasted from 1915 to 1923, and was reestablished in 1932.

16. Both the Protocol and the HSM agreement asserted that it was the right of the employer to administer progressive discipline and discharge employees, but underlying this system was the worker's right to a job. Unlike the 'drive system' under which workers were terminable at-will, in the clothing industry workers could only be discharged for just cause. Job property rights were borrowed from craft union rules (Jacoby, 1986).

17. Columbus printers had formed a short-lived society as early as 1832.

18. The Columbus union's membership rose from 182 in 1892 to 305 in 1912, to 661 in 1959, also a peak year (Stanger, 1994: 404–407). ITU figures were taken from ITU annual reports, while ITU No. 5 data were extracted from membership roll books part of the manuscript collection. Data are missing for some years but there was a clear upward trend line.

19. See Lipset, Trow and Coleman's (1956) *Union Democracy* for a detailed cases study of the New York City local from a sociological and political perspective.

20. Each unionized typographical workplace organized into a chapel. Although weakened over the years, chapels still function today and had their roots during medieval times. They became more active in this country during the 1830s (Marks, 1989; Wallock, 1984).

21. The chairman was originally called the Father of the Chapel.

22. ITU General Laws and bylaws evolved over many decades beginning in the 1870s. Aspects of these laws will be discussed in later sections.

23. In the short run, thousands of union printers lost jobs to the more efficient machines. Over the long-run, a combination of union control over operating the machines, the relatively inelastic skills of ITU members which were needed to work the linotypes, and the growth of the industry negated job displacement effects.

24. Columbus newspapers introduced linotypes in 1894, but no disruptions occurred. The local's main concerns were over jurisdiction and pay form, rather than keeping out the new machines. On February 3, 1896, without any strikes, and after consultations with employers and two ratification votes, the union voted 33 to 4 to accept the new machine pay scale. Members ratified the first scale by a vote of 33 to 2, but employers demanded further modification, hence the second vote (minutes, 1/6/96, 2/3/96, 4/7/96, 5/5/96; box 2, folder 1). The major change was the shift from piece-rates to hourly pay rates for linotype operators, but not all shops could afford to install the machines. To protect its

members, the local amended its constitution in August 1896 to include fines for chapel chairs who did not uphold the new pay scale (minutes, 8/2/96; box 2, folder 1).

25. Emery (1950) notes that the first references to arbitration agreements with printing unions came as early as 1895. In 1900, the ANPA established a special standing committee on labor problems, headed by publishers from the larger metropolitan dailies.

26. The five agreements covered 1901, 1902–1907, 1907–1912, 1912–1917, and 1917–1922. The stereotypers, electrotypers, and photoengravers were part of the ITU in 1902 (Baker, 1957: 266).

27. The Columbus Typographical Union opposed the arbitration deals, but incorporated them into local contracts out of political expediency. Between 1901 and 1913, a few arbitration cases were begun but were settled short of arbitration (see Stanger 1994: 223–229 for a discussion on the local's reaction to the national arbitration pacts with the ANPA).

28. By the late 1950s, only the Pressmen's Union maintained national arbitration pacts, and only they were to expose their laws to arbitration (Baker, 1957). The agreement's longevity reveals no serious compromises to the union's laws, as the ITU had feared.

29. The Columbus Typothetae concentrated its efforts on business matters such as cost systems, advertising and the benefits to organization when seeking new members. Although some members negotiated contracts with the Columbus ITU, the Columbus Typothetae decided that 'the labor question be completely left out of the activities of the organization as it was one that might otherwise cause friction' (minutes, executive committee, 12/20/18, Printing Industries of Central Ohio).

30. Nancy Maradie's (1984) study of printer mobility in Columbus during the 1920s reveals greater job stability in the newspaper branch and more mobility with less job security in the commercial branch. Many printers left the city owing to a surplus of union printers in town. Many took jobs in the larger nonunion commercial sector.

31. The UTA lost the 9-hour day fight by 1898. The ITU pressed on for the 8-hour day almost immediately, eventually winning it in 1909. At that time, printers worked six days in a week.

32. Growing union power was a concern for newspaper publishers at this time, but they were more concerned with advertising-related issues. By the turn of the century, with competition growing, circulation rising fast, the size of newspapers doubling, technology becoming more complex, and labor costs on the rise, the ANPA became more interested in union issues and arbitration.

33. Despite its *raison d'etre*, not all UTA affiliates or commercial printers were hostile to organized labor.

34. Here too, the Pressmen's Union had the greatest success with arbitration for the longest time. After 1925, the IJCC's influence as a national organization waned. Moreover, the UTA's Closed Shop Division and the Printers' League dropped out of sight. In 1922 the UTA forbade its labor divisions to use the name Typothetae, and in 1928, it removed all constitutional provisions for labor divisions. Membership declines throughout the 1930s rendered the UTA ineffective. On July 12, 1945, it ceased to exist after 58 years. In its place, the Printing Industry of America was born with over 1,000 members in 19 affiliated associations (Baker, 1957).

35. An historical sketch of the union's early history comes from three anniversary souvenir booklets published in 1909, 1934, and 1959. Unfortunately, the later editions did not update the local's history.

36. In the early years grievances were placed into the minutes without subheading. In later years, after 1900, they were noted under a separate heading. Moreover, quanti-

fying grievances added very little to the understanding of the process. Only select and important ones will be discussed in this paper.

37. On January 19,1863 the union convened a special meeting "to take under consideration the action of the 'powers that be' in the *Statesman* office" for employing too many apprentices. A vote of 8:2 supported strike action but none took place. Instead, at the September 12 regular meeting, members voted to change the ratio of apprentices to journeymen to 1:4 (minutes,1/19 and 9/12/63; box 1, folder 1).

38. Ava Baron (1982, 1992) argues that male printers viewed their trade as manly and saw women as a threat to their skill, wage, and social standing. By excluding women for a number of years, the ITU actually made women more of a threat to them.

39. The union altered its apprentice regulations on 12/2/88 and 12/1/89 (box 2, folder 1; box 3, folder 1).

40. The union's December 5,1863 minutes indicate the announcement of standing committees at the *Statesman, Express, Crisis, State World, Gazette,* and *Ohio State Journal*. It was not until 1871 that they handled a grievance case.

41. In 1881, the standing committee's composition changed from three to two members (minutes, 1/1/81; box 1, folder 3)

42. When the *Columbus Daily Democrat* imported cheap labor, 'unworthy of association', the union declared the paper's actions as 'repugnant to the feelings of all workingmen, irrespective of (political) party'. So long as the paper remained unfair, the union pledged itself and all Columbus workingmen not to read the *Democrat*, and admonished merchants to withhold placing ads therein (minutes,1/4 & 9/7/79; box 1, folder 3).

43. By exchanging plates of made up advertisements and related matter, newspapers could save on composition costs. To the ITU, this meant less work for printers at the newspaper receiving made up plates. Loft (1944: 124) argues that "in the field of newspaper composition, perhaps the greatest outcry of the publishers, exceeding the protests raised over the union discipline of foremen or the priority law, was stimulated by the general I.T.U. shop rule requiring reproduction of purchased or borrowed matter."

In 1902, the ITU passed its 'reproduction' rule which allowed the use of matrices only if printers in each office reproduced the matrix. The ITU required that all locals include this clause in local agreements. The local had control over 'foreign' matrices, or those made up outside the city. While employers considered this to be 'make work', they did not fight the union too much over this issue because there was usually enough slack work during which reproductions could be done, and because the practice artificially raised advertising rates (Jackson, 1984; Loft, 1944).

44. With the exception of the ITU for many years, industrial agreements covered all workers in a bargaining unit, not just union members. Collective bargaining occurs over management's rules, not the union's. Federal labor policy since the Wagner Act of 1935 has supported the industrial agreement (Feller, 1973).

45. Section 11, By-Laws, stated that it "shall meet at least once a month, and, during the recess of the Union, shall decide all questions in dispute between employers and employes(sic), and take such steps as it may deem necessary (except ordering strikes) in all matters involving the interest of the craft and the good and welfare of the Union." Further, the committee "shall also decide on all matters referred to it by a vote of the Union and its decisions shall in all cases be binding upon the members . . . until reversed by a majority of the members present at any regular meeting."

Finally, the amendment required the committee to make sure all shops had a chapel organization, and to hold a meeting to decide upon "any matter referred to it by any member of a Chapel in good standing within forty-eight hours after an appeal in writing is presented to it. It should be the duty of the Executive Committee to report its action in all cases to this union for approval or rejection" (minutes,1/2/10; box 4, folder 2).

46. The ITU battled with the United Typothetae to reduce the 54-hour workweek it won in 1898. When the push for shorter hours ended, union printers won, first, the 48-hour week and, then, the 44-hour week by the early 1920s. Hostilities were at a minimum in Columbus, unlike many places around the country. The cooperative labor relations in Columbus yielded no strikes over shorter hours, even though the UTA urged local employers to be more aggressive against ITU #5. Local traditions of cooperation and conciliation, and contractual stipulations prevented labor unrest. Still, some bad blood did result, prompting the local union to discourage master printers from holding ITU cards in 1907. See Powell (1926) and Stanger (1994: 230–248) for more details on the shorter hours movement.

47. Present at the UTA's first meeting was Columbus delegate, L. D. Myers. Myers was one of the original members of the UTA's Committee on Permanent Organization (UTA Proceedings, October 1887) and co-owned one of the largest shops in Columbus, employing 50 people and doing $85,000 per annum in business (1870 Census of Columbus area, Schedule 4, Products of Industry).

48. Schneirov found cordial relations to thrive in Columbus's pipe trades.

49. In 1888 the ITU outlawed secret societies which sought to control hiring.

50. Commercial shops were smaller and did not extensive internal labor markets the way newspaper offices did.

51. The Wahnetas became the Administration Party in 1912 and the Independent Party in 1932 (Bevis, 1978).

52. The ITU did not publish this decision and make it widely available to locals until 1913 when it published the ruling in the *Bulletin* (v.2, no. 1: 6–7).

53. Loft (1944) indicates that not all disputes involving priority were categorized as discharge cases. Those that were not were processed through the union's internal grievance procedure.

54. The 1935 Columbus newspaper contract and the 1940 commercial pact included language related to discharges, but placed the resolution of these disputes solely within the auspices of the union. It was not until the 1949 newspaper contract and the 1955 commercial agreement that, for the first time, a separate discharge section appeared. Language permitted either party to appeal to the chapel, the local union, and the joint standing committee. Subsequent contracts specified time limits. Both of these contracts made explicit the reasons for discharge and the employee's right to challenge the fairness of the foreman's actions (labor agreements; box 19, folder 1).

55. Prior to 1920 all three members of the Executive Council wrote decisions. Thereafter, the secretary wrote all decisions.

56. The 1890 law was modified a number of times over the years. The law decreed that foremen could discharge workers for four reasons: (1) incompetency, (2) violation of office, chapel or union rules, (3) neglect of duty, and (4) reduction in force. (Jackson, 1984; Lipset et al., 1956). Priority reduced the foreman's power to hire and fire at will. Regular situation holders chose their own substitutes.

57. In 1890, the ITU prohibited members from working more than six days in one financial week, in order to spread the work to printers unable to secure regular situations. Only if a substitute could not be secured were members permitted to work on the seventh day. Failure to 'beg off' when a competent sub was ready to work led to a fine

of one day's pay. During the Great Depression, the ITU changed the mandatory workweek to five days (Porter, 1954).

58. The ITU attached a case number to each case around 1914. Decades later council cases were indexed by category and number. Prior to that, each edition of the *Bulletin* indexed cases by topic. This was a more labor intensive process of searching for cases to support one's argument.

59. The final outcome cannot be located.

60. *Wever v. No. 5* (Case No. 5534-E, 1933) at the *Citizen and Berry v. No. 5* (Case No. 5653-E, 1934) at the *Dispatch.*

61. See Porter's (1954) 'Job Property Rights' book for a detailed analysis of job property rights in the typographical union. He classifies the union's reproduction rule, control over substitutes, cancellation of overtime, and jurisdiction over new processes as group property rights, while discharge and priority are considered individual property rights (65).

62. The procedures for selecting the outside arbiter and the composition of the JSC varied over the years owing in part to changes in the ANPA/ITU arbitration agreements. See Stanger (1994: 251–257).

63. The *Journal* won a decision concerning overtime pay in the summer of 1927 (minutes, 7/3/27; box 6, folder 2).

64. Sketchy evidence from the local's records reveal individual arbitration agreements signed by the *Dispatch,* the *Ohio State Journal,* the *Press-Post,* and the *Monitor.* Only three *Dispatch* agreements have survived, although the minutes note a couple of cases involving the *Press-Post,* while the ITU's *Bulletin* in 1913 mentions agreements with the *Journal* and *Monitor.*

65. Between 1902 and 1939, there were 0.68 cases per year. From 1940–1959, however, there were 1.45 cases per year.

66. One case involved priority at the Carroll Press (*Carroll Press, Inc. v. No. 5,* Case No. 7023-E, 3/19/41; box 21, folder 21) and the other concerned jurisdiction at F. J. Heer (*Fred J. Heer Printing Company v. No. 5,* Case No. 7041-E, 3/19/41; box 21, folder 20).

67. The preponderance of ITU appeals from the *Citizen* office were caused by an imperious foreman.

68. Either party could appeal the JSC's ruling to outside arbitration if this panel could not settle the case.

69. Just before the JSC convened for the final time on April 11, the compositor who had been discharged left Columbus.

70. In May 1948, after an apprentice was dismissed for incompetence at the F. J. Heer Printing Company, a controversy erupted. Despite the 1941Section 46 case, Heer appealed the case to the JSC and the ITU. In the end the JSC worked out a compromise without the aid of the Council (box 37, folder 5). Given the less bureaucratic and more informal nature of commercial labor relations, past practices prevailed.

71. Union law dictated a six-month bar from the office if discharged. Printers could still work at other offices in town while the bar was in effect.

72. The plaintiff returned to the *Citizen* and soon found herself involved in yet another grievance after the foreman removed her name from the slipboard after she failed to show up for work. Although the chapel sided with the foreman, the executive committee reinstated her to her priority (minutes, 9/6/59; box 11, folder 2).

73. The Dispatch Printing Company produced the *Citizen-Journal* and the *Dispatch*, while Scripps-Howard maintained an editorial voice in the merged paper. This joint operation agreement lasted from 1959 to 1986 (Torry, 1985).

74. See a number of related chapters in Lichtenstein and Harris (1993).

75. Feuille and Chachere (1995: 35) conducted a survey of dispute resolution procedures in nonunion workplaces. Of the 111 firms that reported data, only 7 allow for peer review panels where the majority of the panel is nonsupervisory personnel. They argue that more talk of peer review and outside arbitration exists than actual practice.

76. This system was characterized by an emphasis on occupational identity, control over labor supply, portable rights and benefits, and peer responsibility for performance standards and discipline.

ACKNOWLEDGMENTS

Special thanks are in order to those people who gratefully helped to conceive, read and offer valuable comments, and assist in the archival research: Warren Van Tine and Stephen Mangum (dissertation advisors), Jim Atleson, David Bensman, John Delaney, Howard Foster, David Lewin, Bruce Kaufman, and the library staff of the Ohio State Historical Society. This study is in honor of the late Gus Gassman of the Columbus Typographical Union who socialized me to the lost world of the craft printer.

REFERENCES

Atleson, J. (1998). *Labor and the Wartime State: Labor Relations and Law During World War II.* Urbana: University of Illinois Press.

Baker, E. (1951). The Printing Foreman – Union Man: A Historical Sketch. *Industrial and Labor Relations Review*, (January), 223–235.

Baker, E. (1957). *Printers and Technology.* New York: Columbia University Press.

Barnett, G. (1909). *The Printers: A Sudy in American Trade Unionism.* Cambridge: American Economic Association.

Barnett, G. (1912). National and District Systems of Collective Bargaining in the United States. *Quarterly Journal of Economics, 26*, 425–443.

Baron, A. (1982). Women and the Making of the Working Class: A Study of the Proletarianism of Printers. *The Review of Radical Political Economics, 14*(3), 23–42.

Baron, A. (1992). Technology and the Crisis of Masculinity: The Gendering of Work and Skill in the US Printing Industry, 1850–1920. In: A. Sturdy, D. Knights, & H. Willmott (Eds.), *Skill and Consent: Contemporary Studies in the Labour Process,* (pp. 67–95). London: Routeledge.

Bemmels, B., & Foley, J. R.. (1996). Grievance Procedure Research: A Review and Theoretical Recommendations. *Journal of Management, 22*(3), 359–384.

Bensman, D. (1985). *The Practice of Solidarity: American Hat Finishers in the Nineteenth Century.* Urbana: University of Illinois Press.

Bevis, A S. (1978). ITU's Two-Party System Unique. *Typographical Journal, 4*, 28.

Blackford, M. (1982). *A Portrait Cast in Steel: Buckeye International and Columbus, Ohio, 1881–1980*. Westport, Conneticut: Greenwood Press.
Bonnett, C. E. (1922). *Employers' Associations in the United States: A Study of Typical Associations*. New York: The MacMillan Company.
Brody, D. (1993). Workplace Contractualism in Comparative Perspective. In: N. Lichtenstein & H. J. Harris (Eds.), *Industrial Democracy in America: The Ambiguous Promise*, (pp. 176–205). New York: Cambridge University Press.
Brown, E. C. (1942). Book and Job Printing. In: H. Millis (Ed.), *How Collective Bargaining Works*, (pp. 118–182). New York: The Twentieth Century Fund.
Bulletin. various dates. International Typographical Union.
Bureau of National Affairs. 1992. *Basic Patterns in Union Contracts*. Washington, D.C.
Burns, R. K. (1942). Daily Newspapers. In: H. Mills (Ed.), *How Collective Bargaining Works*, (pp. 31–117). New York: The Twentieth Century Fund.
Burns, R. K. (1949). Industrial Relations in Printing. In: C. E. Warne (Ed.), *Labor in Postwar America*, (pp. 419–428). Brooklyn, New York: Remsen Press.
Census of Franklin County/Columbus. 1870.
Cobble, D. S. (1991). Organizing the PostIndustrial Work Force: Lessons From the History of Waitress Unionism. *Industrial and Labor Relations Review, 44* (April). 419–436.
Columbus, Ohio: Industrially and Commercially. (1915). Columbus, OH: The Columbus Chamber of Commerce.
Columbus Typographical Union No. 5. Ohio Historical Society, Manuscript Collection 125. Columbus, Ohio.
Demers, D. P. (1994). Structural Pluralism, Intermedia Competition, and the Growth of the Corporate Newspaper in the United States. *Journalism Monographs*, 1–43.
Emery, E. (1950). *History of the American Newspaper Publishers Association*. Westport: Greenwood Press Publishers. 1970 reprint.
Fagan, H. B. (1930). *Industrial Relations in the Chicago Newspaper Industry*. Unpublished doctoral dissertation, University of Chicago, Chicago.
Feller, D. E. (1973). A General Theory of the Collective Bargaining Agreement. *California Law Review, 61*, 663–856.
Feuille, P. and D. Chachere. (1995). Looking Fair or Being Fair: Remedial Voice in Nonunion Workplacess. *Journal of Management, 21*(1), 27–42.
Feuille, P., & R. Hildebrand. (1995). Grievance Procedures and Dispute Resolution. In: G. R. Ferris, S. D. Rosen, & D. T. Barnum *Handbook of Human Resource Management*, (pp. 340–369). Cambridge, MA: Blackwell Publishers.
Fleming, R. W. (1965). *The Labor Arbitration Process*. Urbana, Illinois: University of Illinois Press.
Garrett, B. and E. R. Lentz. (1980). Columbus, America's Crossroads. Tulsa, OK: Continental Heritage Press.
Greenwald, M. S. (1987). Life After Death. *Presstime* (July), 12–17.
Hunker, H. (1958). *Industrial Evolution of Columbus*. Columbus, OH: Bureau of Business research, College of Commerce and Administration.
International Typographical Union. (1964). *A Study of the History of the International Typographical Union 1852–1963, (1)*. Colorado Springs, Colorado: The Executive Council of the International Typographical Union.
International Typographical Union. (1967). *A Study of the History of the International Typographical Union 1852–1966, (2)*. Colorado Springs, Colorado: The Executive Council of the International Typographical Union.
Jackson, R. M. (1984). *The Formation of Craft Labor Markets*. Orlando: Academic Press, Inc.

Jacoby, S. (1986). Progressive Discipline in American industry: Its Origins, Development and Consequences. *Advances in Industrial and Labor Relations, 3,* 213–260.

Kuhn, J. (1961). *Bargaining in Grievance Settlement.* New York: Columbia University Press.

Lewin, D., & Peterson, R. B. (1988). *The Modern Grievance Procedure in the United States.* New York: Quorum Books.

Lichtenstein, N. (1993). Great Expectations. In: N. Lichtenstein & H. J. Harris, (Eds.), *Industrial Democracy in America: The Ambiguous Promise,* (pp. 113–141). New York: Cambridge University Press.

Lichtenstein, N., & Harris, H. J. (1993). *Industrial Democracy in America: The Ambiguous Promise.* New York: Cambridge University Press.

Lipset, S. M. (1952). Democracy in Private Government: A case study of the International Typographical Union. *British Journal of Sociology, 3* (March), 47–65.

Lipset, S. M., Trow, M., & Coleman, J. (1956). *Union Democracy: The Internal Politics of the ITU.* Garden City, New York: Anchor Books, Doubleday and Company, Inc.

Loft, J. (1944). *The Printing Trades.* New York: Farrar and Rinehart, Inc.

Maradie, N. J. (1984). *A Mixed Review: Instability in the Midst of a Stable Union: Columbus, Ohio printers, 1919–1929.* Unpublished masters thesis, The Ohio State University, Columbus.

Marks, G. (1989). *Unions in Politics: Britain, Germany, and the United States in the Nineteenth and Early Twentieth Centuries.* Princeton: Princeton University Press.

Montgomery, D. (1979). *Workers' Control in America.* Cambridge: Cambridge University Press.

National Labor Relations Board. (1938). *Collective Bargaining in the Newspaper Industry: A Study of Newswriters' Organizations and Representative Unions in the Mechanical Trades and an Analysis of the Effects Upon Interstate Commerce of Industrial Conflict Within the Industry.* Washington, D. C.: Government Printing Office.

Nolan, D. R., & Abrams, R. I. (1983 a). American Labor Arbitration: The Early Years. *University of Florida Law Review, 35*(3), 373–421.

Nolan, D. R., & Abrams, R. I. (1983b). American Labor Arbitration: The Maturing Years. *University of Florida Law Review, 35* (4), 557–632.

Perlman, S.(1928). *A Theory of the Labor Movement.* New York: The MacMillan Company.

Peterson, R. B. (1992). The Union and Nonunion Grievance System. In: D. Lewin, O. E. Mitchell, & P. D. Sherer (Eds.), *Research Frontiers in Industrial Relations and Human Resources,* (pp. 131–162). Madison, WI: Industrial Relations Research Association Series.

Porter, A. R. Jr. (1954). *Job Property Rights: A Study of the Job Controls of the International Typographical Union.* New York: King's Crown Press.

Powell, L. M. (1926). *The History of the United Typothetae of America.* Chicago: The University of Chicago Press.

Printing Industry of Central Ohio. Private Collection. Westerville, Ohio.

Schneirov, R. (1993). Pride and Solidarity: *A History of the Pumbers and Pipefitters of Columbus, Ohio, 1889–1989.* Ithaca, New York: ILR Press.

Slichter, S., Healy, J., & Livernash, R. E. (1960). *The Impact of Collective Bargaining on Management.* Washington, D. C.: The Brookings Institute.

Stanger, H. R. (1994). *Cooperation, Conciliation, and Continuity: The Evolution of a Modern Grievance Procedure in the Columbus Typographical Union No. 5, 1859–1959.* Unpublished doctoral dissertation, The Ohio State University, Columbus.

Taft, P. (1944). Opposition to Union Officers in Elections. *Quarterly Journal of Economics, 58* (February), 246–264.

Torry, J. (1985). Goodbye, Columbus. *Columbus Citizen-Jounal,* December 31, 1.

Tracy, G. A. (1913). *A History of the Typographical Union.* Indianapolis: International Typographical Union.
Typographical Journal. various dates. Indianapolis, IN and Colorado Springs, CO.
United States Census. 12th census of 1900; 14th Census of 1920.
United Typothetae of America Proceedings. 1887–1927.
Van Tine, W. R. (1973). *The Making of a Labor Bureaucrat: Union Leadership in the United States, 1870–1920.* Amherst: University of Massachusetts Press.
Wallock, L. S. (1984). *Chapel, Custom, Craft: The Transformation of the Struggle to Control the Labor Process among the Journeymen Printers of Philadelphia, 1850–1886.* Unpublished doctoral dissertation, Columbia University, New York.
Weiss, D. (1923). History of Arbitration in American Newspaper Publishing Industry. *Monthly Labor Review, 17,* 15–33.
Witte, E. E. (1952). *Historical Survey of Labor Arbitration.* Philadelphia, PA: University of Pennsylvania Press.
Zerker, S. F. (1982). *The Rise and Fall of the Toronto Typographical Union, 1832–1972: A Case Study of Foreign Domination.* Toronto: University of Toronto Press.
Zieger, R. (1994). *American Workers, American Unions.* Baltimore: The Johns Hopkins University Press. Second edition.

CERTIFICATION OUTCOMES AND RETURNS TO SHAREHOLDERS IN CANADA

Felice Martinello, Robert Hanrahan
Joseph Kushner and Isidore Masse

ABSTRACT:

Event study methods are used to estimate the effects of union certification applications on the returns to shareholders in Canada. Two methods of inference are employed: a classical method, and a resampling method which makes no assumptions about the distributions of share returns. Certifications granted without a representation vote have virtually no effect on returns, whereas certifications granted after a vote have a negative impact. Dismissed applications that required a representation vote also have a negative effect. These results suggest that the certification process itself is important; providing another explanation for the difference in the experiences of the Canadian and U.S. labour movements.

INTRODUCTION

Over the past thirty years, American union density has declined to the point where the very relevance and viability of U.S. unions are seriously questioned (Kochan & Wever, 1991, Bronfenbrenner et al., 1998). An important reason for this decline is that union organizing has declined and fallen far short of replenishing the members lost each year (Rose & Chaison, 1996, Bronfenbrenner, 1998; Freeman, 1985, 1988). The Canadian labour movement, on the other hand, has been characterized as strong, vibrant and resilient (Kumar, 1993) with union density remaining roughly constant between 33.2 and 31.1 percent of total paid employment between 1967 and 1997 (Akyeampong, 1997). While Canadian organizing activity does appear to have declined over this period, the declines have been much smaller than those experienced in the U.S. (Martinello, 1996).

These differences are remarkable because the Canadian and U.S. economies, labour forces and labour movements are very similar, linked by extensive trade and subject to the same pressures and transitions (Kumar, 1993; Meltz, 1990; Verma & Thompson, 1989). In many cases, the same unions organize and negotiate on both sides of the border, often with the same firms. Moreover, the public policy framework governing industrial relations in Canada is modelled on the Wagner Act and contains the same basic provisions (Kumar, 1993; Meltz, 1990; Verma & Thompson, 1989). Only twenty five years ago, the Canadian industrial relations system was considered a part of a single North American system; so similar that comparative analysis was considered redundant (Rose & Chaison, 1996; Kumar 1993).

The divergence between Canada and the United States emerged in the mid-1960s and a literature has developed to attempt to explain it (Chaison & Rose, 1991; Kumar, 1993; Meltz, 1985, 1990; Riddell, 1993; Gottlieb Taras, 1997; Weiler, 1983 and the references therein).[1] This chapter contributes to the divergence literature in two ways: first, by demonstrating a cause for the divergence that has not been suggested previously and second, by providing empirical support for a commonly cited reason for the divergence (mandatory representation votes in certification applications in the U.S. but not in Canada).

In this work, we employ event study methods to estimate the effects of certification applications on the returns to shareholders of Canadian firms. Given the assumptions specified below, returns to shareholders are a measure of the expected profitability of the firm. We find that certifications granted without a representation vote have no effect on shareholder returns and, therefore, the expected profitability of the firm. This contrasts sharply with the estimates for U.S firms, where union certification is associated with large decreases in profitability and returns to shareholders (Belman, 1992). It is widely argued that this reduced profitability is an important cause of the decline of organized labour in the United States because competition forces the lower profit unionized firms or plants out of the marketplace; thereby eliminating union jobs and reducing union density (Hirsch, 1991; Belman, 1992; Lineman & Watcher, 1986; Becker, & Olson, 1987). Since certification without a vote was by far the most common type of certification in Canada, our results suggest that the union movement remained much more robust in Canada because it did not have the same negative impact on profitability that it had in the United States.

The literature's most common explanation for the Canada U.S. divergence is that Canadian legislation is more supportive of unions, and that Labour Relations Boards in Canada enforce the legislation more rigorously and expeditiously. Faced with stricter constraints on its behaviour, Canadian management does not oppose unions as vigorously as its U.S. counterpart. Instead, Canadian management is more accepting of unions and willing to work within the collective bargaining system (Kumar, 1993; Verma & Thompson, 1989; Kochan & Verma, 1992).[2] The literature stresses that this is especially true during organizing drives where the ability to win certification solely with signed union cards and no representation vote limits management's opportunity to oppose the application. Verma and Thompson (1989, p. 263) go on to suggest that the constraints on Canadian management provide a 'positive feedback cycle' that may stabilize the industrial relations system. The absence of a negative impact on shareholder returns in certifications granted without a vote provides empirical support for this hypothesis. We find that certification procedures that limit management's opportunity to oppose union organizing are not associated with large decreases in shareholder returns. This, in turn, should reduce management's incentive to oppose the union and reduces market pressures for deunionization, thereby helping to maintain union density.

The empirical support for the 'positive feedback cycle' is strengthened by showing that the opposite occurs when management has an opportunity to oppose certification through a representation vote. In Canada, some certification applications are decided by representation votes. We employ the same event study method to estimate the effects of certification applications granted or dismissed after a representation vote, and find that both types of applications are associated with large decreases in shareholder returns. Virtually all U.S. certification applications are decided by representation votes. Thus, when Canadian jurisdictions use certification procedures that are similar to those employed in the U.S., the estimated effects of certification applications are similar to those reported for the United States.

CERTIFICATION IN CANADA

All the certification applications in the samples were filed with the Ontario, British Columbia or Canadian Labour Relations Boards which administer the legislation concerning unions. The Canadian Labour Relations Board covers crown corporation employees and private sector employees in the transportation, communications, broadcasting, banking, uranium mining and grain elevator industries. The Ontario and British Columbia Labour Relations Boards cover most of the private sector employees in the other industries in their respective provinces. Coverage of public sector employees and the definitions of who is in the public sector varied across jurisdictions and over time, but these are irrelevant for this chapter since all of the firms in the sample are in the private sector with shares listed and traded on the Toronto Stock Exchange.[3]

Certification procedures were very similar in all three jurisdictions over the period of the sample. If 55% of the employees in the bargaining unit (50% in the Federal jurisdiction) signed union cards, the Board would certify the union without a representation vote. This gave the firm little opportunity to contest the application since most of the cards were usually signed before the application was filed and the firm may not have even known that a signup was occurring (Weiler, 1983). If 45 to 55% of the employees signed union cards (35 to 50% in the Federal jurisdiction and in British Columbia prior to 1978), the Board would order a representation vote. The period between the filing of the application and the vote gave the firm an opportunity to contest the application, and the incentive to do so since the firm could affect the outcome by influencing employees. The vote also lengthened the process which allowed management more time to oppose the application. If the number of signed union cards was insufficient, the Board would dismiss the application with no vote.

In Ontario, the union could also request a pre-hearing representation vote if at least 35% of the workers had signed cards at the time of the application. The pre-hearing vote would be held soon after the application was filed and would determine the outcome of the application.

In British Columbia, representation votes were mandatory from 1984 to 1993 in all certification applications except the construction industry. From 1987 to 1993, the votes had to be held within ten days of the filing of the application. Only two of the twenty 'granted with a vote' applications and, coincidentally, two of the twenty 'dismissed with a vote' applications were covered by this provision. These applications are retained in the samples even though the process was different because the votes did take place and management was given the extra opportunity to oppose the application.

DATA

The data consist of certification applications filed from 1975 to 1992. The applications were sorted by outcome into three samples: applications granted without a representation vote, applications granted after a representation vote, and applications dismissed after a representation vote. Each sample was analysed separately. Raid or displacement applications were excluded so the applications cover only employees who were not already represented by a union. The dates of the applications, final decisions, type (raid or non-raid), method (vote or no vote) and size of the bargaining unit were obtained directly from the Labour Relations Boards.

Applications were excluded if the proposed bargaining unit represented less than 1 percent of the firm's employment.[4] Applications were also excluded if the firm was subject to continuing attempts at certification (often at different plants or for different bargaining units) or if applications with different outcomes or processes overlapped.

All of the firms involved in the applications were incorporated, publicly held, and listed on the Toronto Stock Exchange (TSE). Monthly closing stock prices and dividends were obtained from the Canadian Financial Markets Research Centre. The firm's most junior share was used, but if it did not trade regularly, a more senior share that did trade was used. Monthly returns from holding a firm's shares were calculated using the formula:

$$R_{it} = \ln(P_{it} + D_{it}) - \ln(P_{it-1})$$

where R_{it} is the return on the firm's stock, P_{it} is the stock's closing price at the end of month, D_{it} is the regular dividend in the ex-dividend month, i indexes the application, and t indexes the month. Monthly closing prices of the shares were adjusted for stock splits and recapitalizations of equity. In a few cases, a month was deleted if there were no trades in that month. In that case returns were calculated from the previous to the most recent trade closing prices. Returns were then divided by the square root of the number of months between the trades to adjust for heteroscedasticity in the returns.[5]

Table 1 presents descriptive statistics for the three samples. They consist of 54 certification applications granted with no representation vote, 20 applications granted after a vote and 20 applications dismissed after a vote. The majority of applications are filed with the Ontario Board in all three samples and almost half of the applications come from the single digit SIC manufacturing industry. Within manufacturing, the applications are spread fairly evenly over two digit SIC manufacturing industries. Communications and transportation are the second and third most common single digit industries and, the other applications are spread fairly evenly across other single digit industries. The firms are fairly large compared to an average firm in the economy, but small compared to other firms listed and trading on the TSE. The percentage of the firm's employees covered by the application is small, with most of the applications covering fewer than ten percent of the employees. In the samples with representation votes, there is a fairly even distribution between prehearing and posthearing votes. Table 1 shows that there are no substantial differences between the three samples that would account for the different results reported below.

METHODOLOGY

Event study methodology assumes the semi-strong form of efficiency of stock markets. This means that there is sufficient well-informed and inexpensive arbitrage trading to make a firm's share price equal the expected present value of its future profits. This also means that the market correctly uses all publicly available information to estimate the expected profitability of the firm. An event occurs when new information, relevant to the expected future profitability of the firm, becomes available. If the new information suggests higher (lower) profitability, then the firm's share price and shareholder returns increase (decrease) accordingly. Event studies estimate the effect of new information on the firm's expected future profitability by estimating the change or abnormal return to the share, conditional upon the overall performance of the stock market.

The event date is the date that the new information becomes available. Specifying the event date for certifications is difficult because the process is spread over several months and there is no way of knowing when information concerning the application becomes available. The application process starts when employees contact a union, or a union agent approaches the workers, and the market may or may not know that an organizing drive has started. The union collects signed union cards and files an application when it believes it has sufficient support; thereby making the organizing drive public knowledge. The Labour Relations Board notifies the firm, the employees and other relevant parties and schedules the required meetings and hearings. At this point, the market definitely knows about the application but not its outcome. The Board publicly announces its decision within a few months of the application; but even after the Board's decision, there is still uncertainty as to when a new collective agreement would be signed, how difficult or disruptive the bargaining will be, and the new terms of the agreement.

Since stock prices adjust to information about the application as it becomes available, one would expect market adjustments before the application is filed,

Table 1. Descriptive Statistics

	Granted Without a Vote	Granted after a Vote	Dismissed after a Vote
Number of Applications	54	20	20
Number of Applications by Jurisdiction			
Ontario	29	13	11
Federal	22	4	6
British Columbia	3	3	3
Number of Applications by Industry			
Manufacturing	22	11	9
Food	3		
Leather and allied products	2		
Textiles	2		
Paper and allied Products	2	3	
Fabricated Metal Products	2	2	2
Machinery	1		1
Transportation Equipment	1	1	1
Electrical Products		2	
Non-Metalic Mineral Products	2	2	
Chemical	3	1	2
Other	4		3
Transportation	7	2	4
Communications	11	2	3
Wholesale Trade	6		
Mining	3	3	2
Other	5	2	
Average percentage of employees covered	7.6 %	8.2 %	11.7 %
Average number of employees in firms	2864	3574	8177
Number of Applications with Pre-hearing vote		10	7
Number of Applications with Post-hearing vote		10	13

during the adjudication process, and after the final decision; as information about the application and its ultimate effect on the firm become available.[6] To capture all of these potential adjustments, we estimate abnormal returns for a period starting three months prior to the application and ending six months after the decision is announced. This period is called the event window.

For presentation purposes, the months in the event window are labeled as follows:

app0 = the month that the application is filed
app1, app2, app3 = the three months before the application
dec0 = the month of the final decision
dec1, dec2, ..., dec6 = the six months following the final decision
interf = the first month between the application and final decision
interl = the last month between the application and final decision
interm = any months between interf and interl.

Different events have different combinations of the interf, interl, and interm months depending on the number of months between the application and final decision. If there is only one month between the application and final decision, it is specified as interl.

Let $dvapp0_{it}$ be a dummy variable that equals one if the month is app0 (i.e. if application i is filed in month t), and zero otherwise. Dummy variables for the other months with the prefix `dv', are similarly defined. The following market model regression equation is specified

$$R_{it} = \alpha_i + \beta_i R_{mt} + \sum_{j=0}^{3} \gamma_{ij}^a \, dvappj_{it} + \sum_{j=f,m,l} \gamma_{ij}^l \, dvinterj_{it} + \sum_{j=0}^{6} \gamma_{ij}^d \, dvdecj_{it} + \varepsilon_{it} \quad (1)$$

where R_{mt} is the total return on the TSE 300 market index, ε_{it} is a random error term with zero mean, i indexes the applications, t indexes months and j indexes the month in the event window. Equation (1) is estimated using OLS on data consisting of the event window and the 60 months before the event window. In some cases, where sufficient data before the event are not available, 60 months after the event period are used. In a few cases, data before and after the event window are pooled for the regression. A minimum of 48 observations outside the event window are included.

The coefficients on the dummy variables (the gammas) provide estimates of the monthly abnormal returns which are interpreted as the market reaction to the event in that month. The estimated standard errors are calculated in the usual manner. Cumulative abnormal returns are the sum of the event's monthly abnormal returns from the beginning of the event window. Since cumulative abnormal returns are a linear combination of monthly returns, estimates of their variances are obtained from the quadratic form made up of the linear relationship vector and the estimated variance-covariance matrix of the monthly abnormal returns.

In most cases there is only one certification application for a firm and equation (1) is estimated separately for each of those applications. Since each of these regressions involves a different firm and a different time period, each regression yields independent estimates of the abnormal returns. In some cases, however, firms are involved in more than one application.[7] Applications involving the same firm are considered independent (and therefore included in a sample) as long as their regression periods do not overlap. If the event windows for two applications with the same firm and outcome overlap, then their event windows are combined and the average effects of the applications are estimated.[8] If averaging multiple events causes ambiguity as to the classification of a month in the event window, then that month is excluded. If the final decision for an application occurs in the same month that the application is filed, then that month is considered to be the decision month and no application month is specified.

The average and median monthly and cumulative abnormal returns are calculated for each month over the events in the sample. A classical method and a distribution free method are then used to estimate sampling distributions and determine the statistical significance of the estimates.

Classical Method of Inference

ε_{it} is assumed to be distributed iid normal with zero mean and variance σ_i^2. Under the null hypothesis of no abnormal return, the estimated abnormal return divided by its estimated standard error is distributed as a student's t with τ_i degrees of freedom, where τ_i is the degrees of freedom from regression 1. In equation form:

$$t_{ij}^a = \hat{\gamma}_{ij}^a / s_{ij}^a \quad \sim t_{(\tau_i)} \tag{2}$$

where s_{ij}^a is the estimated standard error of the $\hat{\gamma}_{ij}^a$ coefficients from equation (1). Similar t statistics are calculated for the inter ($\hat{\gamma}_{ij}^I$) and decision ($\hat{\gamma}_{ij}^d$) estimates and all of the cumulative abnormal return estimates. Under the null hypothesis, t_{ij}^a has zero mean and variance $\tau_i/(\tau_i-2)$, and is distributed independently for each application (i) in the sample. Average t_{ij}^a over the n_j applications on that month in the sample and the central limit theorem implies

$$\bar{t}_j^a \sim N[0, ((1/n_j^2)\sum_{i=1}^{n_j} \tau_i/(\tau_i-2))] \tag{3}$$

under the null hypothesis. As above, equation (3) holds for the inter, decision and cumulative estimates as well. The average t statistic calculated from the sample is compared to the distribution shown in equation (3) to test the hypothesis of zero average abnormal returns. For brevity, we report only the *p*-values for the one-tailed hypothesis test of zero average abnormal returns.

Distribution Free Method of Inference

A large literature suggests that the strong assumptions made about the distribution of the error terms in the classical method of inference do not hold for stock returns. For monthly returns, skewness is generally not believed to be a severe problem, but there is wide agreement that returns are not normally distributed and exhibit excess kurtosis. Pagan (1996) shows that the excess kurtosis is not simply a matter of 'fat tails'. Instead, long thin tails caused by outliers account for the excess kurtosis, while the peak of the distribution is actually much higher and tighter than a normal distribution. There is also considerable evidence of heteroscedastic returns.[9] All of these problems mean that the standard errors calculated with the classical method will be incorrect, as will any inferences based on them. Thus there is good reason to employ a distribution free or nonparametric method of inference.

Accordingly, equation (1) is estimated using OLS, assuming only that the error term has zero mean, for each event in the sample. The mean of the estimated abnormal returns is then bootstrapped or resampled to calculate confidence intervals for the estimated mean and p-values for the one tailed hypothesis test of zero mean abnormal returns. The bootstrapping procedure is outlined in the appendix. Resampling has been shown to generate accurate confidence intervals when the data do not conform to the usual parametric assumptions.[10] Note that the bootstrap inference may reject the null hypothesis of zero abnormal return more or less often than the classical method. For example, if the error term in equation (1) is distributed with fatter tails than the normal or is heteroscedastic, the OLS standard errors will be too small and the classical method will reject the null hypothesis too often. If, however, the error term is skewed or has a high peak and long thin tails as suggested by Pagan (1996), the OLS standard errors will be too large and the null hypothesis will not be rejected often enough.

Another advantage of the bootstrap is that it can be used to generate confidence intervals for other measures of central tendency such as the median. Since the distributions of abnormal returns are often skewed with long thin tails due to outliers, we also report the median abnormal returns and test the hypothesis that they equal zero. The median abnormal returns are bootstrapped to generate p-values for the one-tailed hypothesis that they equal zero.

RESULTS

Figure 1 shows the monthly and cumulative abnormal returns for the three samples. The mean and median abnormal returns are plotted for each month in

Certification Outcomes and Returns to Shareholders in Canada

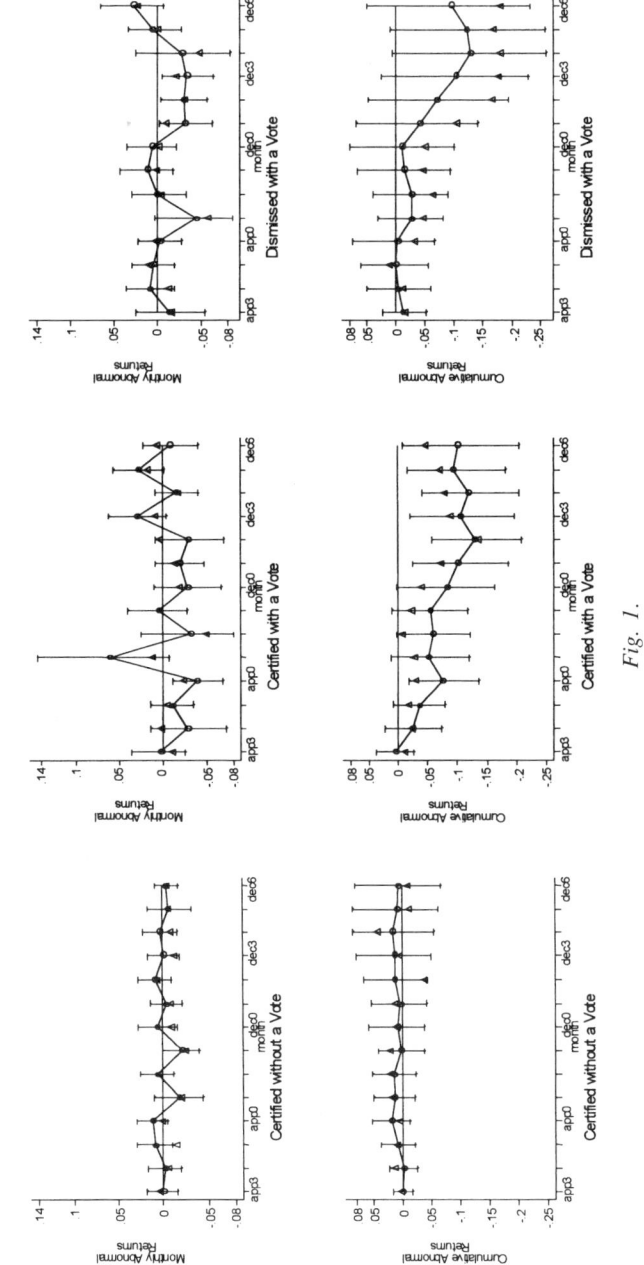

Fig. 1.

Table 2. Certification Applications Granted without a Vote

Month	Mean	Normal p-value	Bootstrap p-value	Median	Bootstrap p-value	PropPos	Number
Monthly Abnormal Returns							
app3	0.0006	0.4663	0.4610	0.0037	0.3195	0.5283	53
app2	-0.0013	0.4022	0.4420	-0.0046	0.3375	0.4630	54
app1	0.0096	0.2541	0.2075	-0.0138	0.0745	0.4074	54
app0	0.0118	0.2395	0.1355	0.0014	0.4540	0.5000	50
interf	-0.0176	0.1772	0.1415	-0.0200	0.1455	0.3889	18
interm	0.0059	0.2722	0.3110	0.0042	0.4140	0.5000	12
interl	-0.0205	0.0702	0.0605	-0.0242	0.0190*	0.3226	31
dec0	0.0056	0.3675	0.3230	-0.0086	0.2515	0.4528	53
dec1	-0.0035	0.4768	0.3765	-0.0080	0.3365	0.4808	52
dec2	0.0085	0.1885	0.2130	0.0080	0.1915	0.5577	52
dec3	-0.0004	0.4387	0.5015	-0.0112	0.2475	0.4423	52
dec4	0.0031	0.4570	0.3980	-0.0074	0.2110	0.4423	52
dec5	-0.0064	0.3063	0.3225	-0.0052	0.3450	0.4717	53
dec6	-0.0031	0.4506	0.3375	-0.0032	0.4465	0.4902	51
Cumulative Abnormal Returns							
app3	0.0006	0.4663	0.4665	0.0037	0.3345	0.5283	53
app2	-0.0008	0.3786	0.4955	0.0150	0.1855	0.5556	54
app1	0.0088	0.4398	0.3265	0.0093	0.3795	0.5185	54
app0	0.0197	0.2923	0.1550	0.0076	0.3765	0.5185	54
interf	0.0138	0.3702	0.2550	0.0175	0.2260	0.5556	54
interm	0.0151	0.3443	0.2615	0.0227	0.1670	0.5741	54
interl	0.0034	0.4869	0.4495	0.0227	0.2210	0.5556	54
dec0	0.0089	0.4986	0.3860	0.0108	0.3610	0.5185	54
dec1	0.0055	0.4941	0.4150	0.0133	0.3095	0.5370	54
dec2	0.0137	0.3722	0.3560	-0.0373	0.3310	0.4815	54
dec3	0.0134	0.3911	0.3745	0.0076	0.4465	0.5000	54
dec4	0.0163	0.3836	0.3480	0.0429	0.3250	0.5370	54
dec5	0.0101	0.4295	0.4130	-0.0116	0.2725	0.4630	54
dec6	0.0072	0.4283	0.4605	-0.0088	0.3280	0.4630	54

* indicates significantly different from zero at the 5% level in a one tailed hypothesis test.

Table 3. Certification Applications Granted after a Vote

Month	Mean	Normal p-value	Bootstrap p-value	Median	Bootstrap p-value	PropPos	Number
Monthly Abnormal Returns							
app3	0.0030	0.4754	0.4565	-0.0111	0.2285	0.4000	20
app2	-0.0276	0.0826	0.1445	0.0025	0.4325	0.5000	20
app1	-0.0110	0.3568	0.2220	-0.0044	0.1585	0.4000	20
app0	-0.0396	0.0482*	0.0065*	-0.0230	0.0085*	0.2500*	20
interf	0.0600	0.0185*	0.0950	0.0109	0.4265	0.5000	8
interm	-0.0318	0.0656	0.1740	-0.0493	0.0595	0.2000	5
interl	0.0043	0.4354	0.3955	0.0030	0.3960	0.5000	16
dec0	-0.0276	0.0865	0.1095	-0.0196	0.1480	0.4000	20
dec1	-0.0190	0.1938	0.1240	-0.0134	0.0960	0.3500	20
dec2	-0.0294	0.1399	0.1040	0.0026	0.4590	0.5000	20
dec3	0.0292	0.0583	0.0725	0.0090	0.2350	0.6111	18
dec4	-0.0159	0.0919	0.1320	-0.0177	0.0420*	0.3158	19
dec5	0.0270	0.0816	0.0580	0.0166	0.0115*	0.7368	19
dec6	-0.0088	0.4474	0.3050	0.0063	0.4325	0.5263	19
Cumulative Abnormal Returns							
app3	0.0030	0.4754	0.4565	-0.0111	0.2410	0.4000	20
app2	-0.0246	0.1789	0.1950	-0.0238	0.2865	0.4500	20
app1	-0.0356	0.1669	0.1000	-0.0173	0.1595	0.4000	20
app0	-0.0752	0.0486*	0.0155*	-0.0295	0.2300	0.4000	20
interf	-0.0512	0.1430	0.0950	-0.0265	0.3190	0.4500	20
interm	-0.0592	0.1021	0.0545	-0.0064	0.4450	0.5000	20
interl	-0.0557	0.0998	0.0820	-0.0218	0.3000	0.4500	20
dec0	-0.0834	0.0494*	0.0525	-0.0388	0.0450*	0.3000	20
dec1	-0.1023	0.0377*	0.0170*	-0.0712	0.0410*	0.3000	20
dec2	-0.1317	0.0240*	0.0010*	-0.1345	0.0310*	0.3000	20
dec3	-0.1054	0.0792	0.0230*	-0.0876	0.0495*	0.3000	20
dec4	-0.1205	0.0461*	0.0070*	-0.0781	0.0360*	0.3000	20
dec5	-0.0949	0.1126	0.0235*	-0.0697	0.1030	0.3500	20
dec6	-0.1032	0.1190	0.0305*	-0.0457	0.1490	0.4000	20

* indicates significantly different from zero at the 5% level in a one tailed hypothesis test.

the event window, together with 90 percent confidence intervals for the mean, calculated from the bootstrap.

Tables 2, 3 and 4 report the numerical estimates showing: (i) the mean abnormal return and the p-value for the one tailed hypothesis test that the mean equals zero, calculated from the classical method (Normal p-value) and the bootstrap (Bootstrap p-value), (ii) the median abnormal return and the p-value for the one tailed hypothesis that the median equals zero calculated from the bootstrap, (iii) the proportion of estimated abnormal returns in the sample that are positive (PropPos), and (iv) the number of observations for that month in the sample. p-values less than 0.05 are marked with an asterisk.

Certification Applications Granted without a Vote

Certification applications granted without a representation vote have virtually no effect on the returns to shareholders. Almost all the estimated mean and median effects are small and statistically insignificant. The only estimate that is close to significant is a negative monthly abnormal return of about 2% in the month before the final decision. All of the estimated cumulative effects are close to zero and are insignificant. This suggests that a certification granted without a vote has no discernible impact on the expected profitability of the firm.

Certification Applications Granted after a Vote

Certifications granted after a representation vote generate a very different market reaction. The average and median abnormal returns in the application month are negative, large, and statistically significant according to every measure. This suggests a large decrease in the expected profitability of the firm when the application is filed, as evaluated by the stock market. Negative average returns also occur in the decision month and the two months following, but the means and medians are not significantly different from zero.[11] The expected profitability of the firms improves towards the end of the event window. Three and five months after the decision the abnormal returns are positive and either statistically significant or close to it. However, the negative cumulative abnormal return shows that this improvement is small compared to the original decreases in expected profitability.

The cumulative abnormal returns show a striking decline starting two months before the application is filed and declining to a minimum of −13% two months after the final decision. Most of the average and median cumulative returns following the decision are significantly different from zero. As noted above,

Table 4. Certification Applications Dismissed after a Vote

Month	Mean	Normal p-value	Bootstrap p-value	Median	Bootstrap p-value	PropPos	Number
Monthly Abnormal Returns							
app3	-0.0126	0.2721	0.3260	-0.0148	0.2390	0.4211	19
app2	0.0086	0.4990	0.3205	-0.0119	0.0530	0.3158	19
app1	0.0049	0.4971	0.3665	0.0110	0.3975	0.5263	19
app0	-0.0030	0.3000	0.4180	0.0028	0.4085	0.5263	19
interf	-0.0434	0.0403*	0.0660	-0.0565	0.0540	0.2727	11
interm	-0.0004	0.4128	0.4755	-0.0036	0.3280	0.4286	7
interl	0.0121	0.4328	0.2745	0.0011	0.2325	0.5882	17
dec0	0.0057	0.4434	0.4150	-0.0008	0.4450	0.5000	20
dec1	-0.0313	0.0388*	0.0295*	-0.0103	0.2145	0.4000	20
dec2	-0.0296	0.0263*	0.0305*	-0.0309	0.0225*	0.3000	20
dec3	-0.0337	0.0534	0.0230*	-0.0201	0.0425*	0.3000	20
dec4	-0.0268	0.0541	0.2080	-0.0474	0.1190	0.3684	19
dec5	0.0057	0.2433	0.3690	0.0001	0.4690	0.5000	20
dec6	0.0285	0.0562	0.0945	0.0231	0.0465*	0.7000	20
Cumulative Abnormal Returns							
app3	-0.0126	0.2721	0.2955	-0.0148	0.2245	0.4211	19
app2	-0.0040	0.3472	0.4465	-0.0111	0.3960	0.4737	19
app1	0.0009	0.3878	0.4935	0.0119	0.3960	0.5263	19
app0	-0.0021	0.2981	0.4790	-0.0321	0.2510	0.4211	19
interf	-0.0272	0.1250	0.2220	-0.0465	0.2325	0.4211	19
interm	-0.0273	0.1186	0.2265	-0.0639	0.1185	0.3684	19
interl	-0.0156	0.1645	0.3685	-0.0452	0.3325	0.4500	20
dec0	-0.0099	0.1826	0.4085	-0.0497	0.2680	0.4500	20
dec1	-0.0413	0.0641	0.2525	-0.1038	0.2085	0.4000	20
dec2	-0.0709	0.0232*	0.1595	-0.1650	0.1390	0.4000	20
dec3	-0.1046	0.0091*	0.0940	-0.1767	0.2140	0.4000	20
dec4	-0.1300	0.0035*	0.0565	-0.1797	0.1100	0.3500	20
dec5	-0.1243	0.0090*	0.0620	-0.1683	0.1435	0.4000	20
dec6	-0.0958	0.0306*	0.1285	-0.1790	0.0940	0.3500	20

* indicates significantly different from zero at the 5% level in a one tailed hypothesis test.

the negative returns recover somewhat three months after the final decision. The recovery is not surprising since a 13% decline is excessive in view of the results reported in the literature and the size of the bargaining units in our sample. Thus it appears that the market initially overreacts and then moderates its estimate of the impact of the certification. However, the basic message is clear. The market expects a significant decrease in the expected profitability of the firm when certifications are granted after a representation vote.

Certification Applications Dismissed after a Vote

Further evidence of the effect of the process is obtained by examining applications that were not granted but required a vote. Negative abnormal returns are also estimated for this type of application even though the application is dismissed. The estimated abnormal returns are very small in the decision month, the application month and the months preceding the application. There are, however, large negative abnormal returns in each of the four months after the decision and the first three are statistically significant according to most of the measures used. As with certifications granted with a vote, the firms' prospects improve at the end of the event window; with a positive abnormal return whose median is statistically significant in the last month.

The cumulative abnormal returns are negative in the application month, decline sharply in each of the four months after the final decision and then recover slightly in the fifth and sixth months. The classical method shows that the cumulative returns are significantly different from zero for months two through six after the decision, whereas most of the bootstrap confidence intervals for the mean are huge. The fourth and fifth months are, however, very close to being significant. The estimated median cumulative returns are also negative and large but not statistically significant. Overall, certification applications dismissed after a representation vote do appear to have a negative impact on expected profitability, but the results are not as strong statistically as in the granted after a vote sample.

DISCUSSION

The absence of negative returns for certifications granted without a vote is contrary to a large literature (surveyed in Belman, 1992) showing that unionization decreases the profitability of firms. One possible explanation for this result is that unionism is less costly to Canadian employers because the union nonunion wage differential is smaller. Riddell (1993) considers this question and concludes that union nonunion wage differentials are very similar in Canada and the United States. Thus differences in wage differentials cannot account for the results presented above.

Another possible explanation for the conflicting result is that the bargaining units in the sample are simply too small relative to the size of the firm for any negative impact to be observed. However, the average percentage of employees covered in the granted after a vote sample is only slightly larger than in the no vote sample and substantial negative impacts on shareholder returns are evident in the former.

A third possible explanation for the absence of a profitability effect in the certification without a vote sample, is that shareholders anticipated the certification and had already discounted share prices accordingly. This expectation of unionization seems reasonable because most of the firms in the sample were already partially unionized and in industries with high union density. Again, however, the firms in the vote samples were also partially organized and in the same highly unionized industries, so there is no reason why the same expectations should not hold for those firms. This makes the negative returns associated with representation votes all the more striking and unexpected, and as with the earlier explanation, suggests that the certification process makes a substantial difference.

It is important to attempt to identify the mechanism through which the representation vote may affect the expected profitability of the firm. Although we have no further information about what occurred in each application and, therefore, no direct evidence about the process or mechanism involved, the industrial relations literature does provide a plausible explanation. First, the divergence literature cited above argues overwhelmingly that representation votes lengthen the certification process, provide management with the opportunity and incentive to oppose the application, and yield a more contentious process. Second, another large literature argues that the industrial relations climate or the quality of the employer – union relationship affects the performance of the firm (see Belman, 1992 and Kochan & Katz, 1988 for surveys). Thus it seems reasonable that the more contentious environment brought by the extended election campaign and the representation vote can account for the difference in shareholder returns.

The references cited in footnote 2 make it clear that Canadian management, like its American counterpart, prefers to remain non-unionized; although they are less aggressive in their opposition because they are constrained by the stricter Canadian legislation. If representation votes have such large negative effects on expected profitability, the question arises as to why management opposes certification applications at all. Why does management not grant voluntary recognition, without any vote, to avoid the lower returns? In spite of the results presented above, management opposition may still be in the best interests of the firm. Management opposes certification applications in an attempt to get the application dismissed or withdrawn without a vote, and to signal to the unions and employees that they prefer to remain nonunion.[12] In general, management opposition is important because the same results would likely not occur if management ceased their opposition to unionism. The estimates presented above only show that returns are higher when there is no election campaign and vote; i.e. when the union and management are both pursuing their best interests, but with fewer opportunities for direct conflict. This does not imply that the higher returns would accrue if management accepted unionism voluntarily.

A further explanation for management opposition is that management is simply pursuing management's best interests. Freeman and Kliener (1990) and Clark (1980) report that unionization has a serious negative impact on the careers of managers and that they face strong incentives to oppose unionization.

Finally, there is other evidence that the effect of unions on profitability may be different in the Canadian economy. Laporta and Jenkins (1996) examine 1987 data on Canadian three digit industries and report that returns on sales are positively related to union density in some industries.

CONCLUSION

The results presented above provide new evidence as to why union density has declined drastically in the United States but not in Canada. We find that certification applications granted without a representation vote have no discernable impact on returns to shareholders while certification applications granted or dismissed after a vote are associated with large decreases in returns to shareholders. Since certification without a vote has been the norm in Canada, while representation votes have been mandatory in the United States, the results suggest that the profitability costs of a certification have been lower in Canada. A lower cost of certification implies less management resistance to unionization and weaker market pressures for deunionization, which has certainly been the case in Canada over the past thirty years. The results also provide empirical support for the Verma and Thompson (1989) suggestion that the constraints on management opposition imposed by a card based process provide a positive feedback cycle that helps to stabilize the industrial relations system.

Weiler (1983, 1990) examined U.S. certification procedures and compared them to the Canadian card based system with the intention of recommending reforms to the U.S. system. He argued that allowing certifications with only signed union cards and no representation vote would reduce levels of conflict and employee intimidation, and allow employees' preferences for unionization (if any) to be realized. To the extent that our results are applicable to the U.S., they support this argument. In addition to making certification easier and reducing the opportunity for management opposition, allowing certification without a vote would reduce the profitability cost of certification and thereby lessen management's incentive to oppose the application and reduce market pressures against unionization.

Weiler (1983, 1990) did not, however, recommend certification without representation votes. Instead, he recognized the symbolic value of a vote and recommended a compromise of `instant' representation votes held soon (e.g. within five days) after the application is filed. The reasoning is that quick elections provide little opportunity for management opposition and therefore avoid the worst aspects of long election campaigns. While quick elections may help to limit management opposition, our results suggest that they do not eliminate the large negative impact on shareholder returns. Table 1 shows that roughly half the cases where a certification vote was held had prehearing votes which took place soon after the application was filed. Further, separate examination of the prehearing and posthearing cases shows that the estimated negative impact on shareholder returns is actually larger in the former. Thus the compromise solution of a quick vote does not solve the problem of a large negative impact on profitability and the consequences which follow.

Certification without a representation vote is controversial in Canada. The provincial jurisdictions of Alberta, Newfoundland, Nova Scotia, and more recently Ontario have legislated mandatory representation votes for most certification applications. All these jurisdictions require prehearing or quick votes in an attempt to avoid the negative effects of election campaigns identified by Weiler (1983, 1990). However, as noted above, our results suggest that quick votes do not avoid the large decreases in shareholder returns so these jurisdictions can expect the problems associated with the mandatory vote process. The recent switch to mandatory representation votes in Ontario, Canada's largest jurisdiction by far, suggests that Canada may yet imitate the U.S. experience.

NOTES

1. There is some debate about the extent to which Canadian union density has remained stable and diverged from the U.S. experience (Troy, 1990; Chaison & Rose, 1991; Kumar, 1993; Meltz, 1985, 1990; Riddell, 1993). This debate centres mainly on how union density data should be adjusted for differences in the composition of the economies (especially public sector versus private sector differences) and the labour forces. The general conclusion, however, is that after adjusting for these differences the Canadian experience is still very different from the American (Riddell, 1993; Kumar, 1993; Rose & Chaison, 1996).

2. Surveys show that Canadian management has the same attitudes towards unions as American management and the same desire to remain non-union (Chaison & Rose, 1991; Kumar, 1993). In Canada, however, management is constrained by legislation to be more accepting of unions and collective bargaining. For example, Thompson (1995, p. 113) writes "The manager of one American-owned firm that is almost entirely non-union in the United States but about 35% organized in Canada declared 'We play by the rules where we operate. In the United States, there are no rules. Here rules exist and we follow them'." This is not to deny the importance of strategic choice by management. The stricter rules in Canada make less resistance the rational choice for management in Canada.

3. Wiles (1984) and the references cited therein provide more detailed descriptions of the jurisdictions of each board.

4. Two exceptions were made in the certified after a vote sample where the bargaining units represented 0.9% of the firm's employment. Total employment in the firm was obtained from sources such as the Survey of Industrials and Dun and Bradstreet.

5. Heteroscedasticity occurs because the variance of returns increases with the length of the period covered by the return. See Maynes and Rumsey (1993) for a discussion and comparison of techniques for dealing with periods where there are no trades.

6. Even if the first collective agreement simply codifies existing practice and the substantive terms of employment (wages, benefits, etc.) remain the same, there are certainly large procedural changes after a union is certified.

7. Five firms are used twice in the certified without a vote sample, one firm twice in the certified with a vote sample, and two firms twice in the dismissed with a vote sample. The sample period stretches from 1975 to 1993, so in many cases the applications are many years apart.

8. There are seven averaged events in the certified without a vote sample, one in those certified with a vote and four in those dismissed with a vote. The number of employees affected and the firm sizes are also averaged in these cases for the calculation of the proportion of employees covered.

9. Bollerslev, Chou and Kroner (1992) report similar findings with respect to skewness and kurtosis and argue that there is also conditional heteroscedasticity in stock market returns. deJong, Kemna and Kloek (1992) also report conditional heteroscedasticity and non-normality of returns. Further, Boehmer, Musumeci and Poulsen (1991) argue that event induced increases in variance result in incorrect standard errors. Finally, Fowler, Rorke and Jog (1979) show that thin trading on the TSE causes heteroscedasticity in returns and incorrect OLS standard errors.

10. See Efron and Tibshirani (1993) and Mooney and Duval (1993) for more details and references on resampling methods.

11. The large positive mean abnormal return in the first month after the application is due mostly to one firm with a 40% return caused by a take-over bid. This observation dominates the average since there are only eight observations for that interim month.

12. Unreported estimates show that if a certification application is dismissed or withdrawn without a vote, there is a small but positive effect on the expected profitability of the firm. However there are only 15 to 17 observations for these estimates. The small estimated effect and the small number of observations means that the estimates are far from statistically significant.

ACKNOWLEDGMENTS

The authors thank Sean Clancy, Ron Lebi, Richard MacDowell and Sandy Sabbarwal of the Ontario Labour Relations Board; Jim Callon of the Canadian Labour Relations Board; and Jacki Johnson and Stan Lanyon of the British Columbia Labour Relations Board for their assistance with the collection of the certification data. The authors also thank Rob Martin, Paul Michaud, Jeff Pelletier and Hannah Stanwick for excellent research assistance. Research support from SSHRCC Grant No. 410-94-0608 is gratefully acknowledged.

REFERENCES

Akyeampong, E. (1997). A Statistical Portrait of the Trade Union Movement. *Perspectives on Labour and Income, 9,* 45–54.

Becker, B. E., & Olson, C. A. (1987). Labor Relations and Firm Performance. In: M. Kleiner, R. Block, M. Roomkin, & S. Salsburg, (Eds.), *Human Resources and the Performance of the Firm* (pp. 43–85). Madison WI: Industrial Relations Research Association.

Belman, D. (1992). Unions, the Quality of Labour Relations, and Firm Performance. In: L.Mishel & P. B. Voos (Eds.), *Unions and Economic Competitiveness* (pp. 41–107). Armonk NY: M. E. Sharpe.

Boehmer, E., Musumeci, J., & Poulsen, A. (1991). Event-Study Methodology under Conditions of Event Induced Variance. *Journal of Financial Economics, 30,* 253–72.

Bollerslev, T., Chou, R., & Kroner K. (1992). ARCH Modelling in Finance. *Journal of Econometrics, 52,* 5–59.

Bronfenbrenner, K., Friedman, S., Hurd, R., Oswald, R., & Seeber, R. (1998). Introduction. In: K. Bronfenbrenner, S. Friedman, R. Hurd, R. Oswald & R. Seeber (Eds.), *Organizing to Win* (pp. 1–16). Ithaca NY: ILR Press.

Chaison, G. N., & Rose, J. B. (1991). Continental Divide: The Direction and Fate of North American Unions. In: D. Sockwell, D. Lewin & D. B. Lipsky (Eds.), *Advances in Industrial and Labor Relations* (pp. 169–205). Greenwick CT: JAI Press.

Clark, K. B. (1980). The Impact of Unnionization on Productivity: A Case Study. *Industrial and Labor Relations Review, 34,* 451–468.

de Jong, F., Kemna, A., & Kloek, T. (1992). A Contribution to Event Study Methodology with an Application to the Dutch Stock Market. *Journal of Banking and Finance, 16,* 11–36.

Dun and Bradstreet of Canada (Various Years). *Reference Book of Dun and Bradstreet of Canada.* Calgary, Alberta: Dun and Bradstreet.

Efron, B., & Tibshirani, R. (1993). *An Introduction to the Bootstrap Monographs on Statistics and Applied Probability* No. 57. New York: Chapman & Hall.

Financial Post Corporation Service (Various Years). *Survey of Industrials.* Toronto Ontario: Financial Post Information Services.

Fowler, D., Rorke, C. H., & Jog, V. (1979). Heteroscedasticity, R^2 and Thin Trading on the Toronto Stock Exchange. *Journal of Finance, 34,* 1201–1210.

Freeman, R. B. (1985). Why are Unions Faring Poorly in NLRB Representation Elections?. In: T. Kochan, (Ed.), *Challenges and Choices Facing American Labor* (pp. 45–64). Cambridge MA: MIT Press.

Freeman, R. B. (1988). Contraction and Expansion: The Divergence of Private Sector and Public Sector Unionism in the United States. *Journal of Economic Perspectives, 2,* 63–88.

Freeman, R. B., & Kliener, M. (1990). Employer Behavior in the Face of Union Organizing Drives. *Industrial and Labor Relations Review, 43,* 351–366.

Hirsch, B. T. (1991). *Labor Unions and the Economic Performance of Firms.* Kalamazoo Michigan: W. E. Upjohn Institute.

Gottlieb Taras, D. (1997). Collective Bargaining Regulation in Canada and the United States: Divergent Cultures, Divergent Outcomes. In: B. Kaufman (Ed.), *Government Regulation of the Employment Relationship* (pp. 295–342). Madison WI: Industrial Relations Research Association.

Karier, T. (1985). Unions and Monopoly Profits. *Review of Economics and Statistics, 62,* 34–42.

Kochan, T. & Katz, H. (1988). Collective Bargaining and Industrial Relations. Homewood IL: Irwin.

Kochan, T., & Wever, K. (1991). American Unions and the Future of Worker Representation. In: G. Strauss, D.Gallagher, & J. Fiorito (Eds.), *The State of the Unions* (pp. 363–86). Madison WI: Industrial Relations Research Association.

Kochan, T., & Verma, A. (1992). A Comparative View of United States and Canadian Industrial Relations: A Strategic Choice Perspective. In: A. Gladstone (Ed.), *Labour Relations in a Changing Environment* (pp. 186–201). New York NY: Walter de Gruyter.

Kumar, P. (1993). *From Uniformity to Divergence.* Kingston Ontario: IRC Press.

Laporta, P., & Jenkins, A. W. (1996). Unionisation and Profitability in the Canadian Manufacturing Sector. *Relations Industrielles Industrial Relations, 51,* 756–777.

Linneman, P., & Watcher, M. (1986). Rising Union Premiums and the Declining Boundaries Among Noncompeting Groups. *American Economic Review, 76,* 103–108.

Martinello, F., Hanrahan, R., Kushner, J., & Masse, I. (1995). Union Certification in Ontario: Its Effect on the Value of the Firm. *Canadian Journal of Economics, 28,* 1077–1096.

Martinello, F. (1996). *Certification and Decertification Activity in Canadian Jurisdictions.* Kingston Ontario: IRC Press.

Maynes, E., & Rumsey, J. (1993). Conducting Event Studies with Thinly Traded Stocks. *Journal of Banking and Finance, 17,* 145–157.

Meltz, N. M. (1985). Labor Movements in Canada and the United States. In: T. Kochan (Ed.), *Challenges and Choices Facing American Labor* (pp. 315–334). Cambridge MA: MIT Press.

Meltz, N. M. (1990). Unionism in Canada, U.S.: On Parallel treadmills?. *Forum for Applied Research and Public Policy, 5,* 46–52.

Mooney, C., & Duval, R. (1993). *Bootstrapping: A Non-Parametric Approach to Statistical Inference Quantitative applications in the Social Sciences* No. 95. New York NY: Sage.

Pagan, A. (1996). The Econometrics of Financial Markets. *Journal of Empirical Finance, 3,* 15–102.

Riddell W. C. (1993). Unionization in Canada and the United States: A Tale of Two Countries. In: D. Card & R. B. Freeman (Eds.), *Small Differences that Matter* (pp. 149–190). Chicago IL: University of Chicago Press.

Rose, J., & Chaison, G. (1996). Linking Union Density and Union Effectiveness: The North American Experience. *Industrial Relations, 35,* 78–105.

Thompson, M. (1995). The Management of Industrial Relations. In: M. Gunderson & A. Ponak (Eds.), *Union-Management Relations in Canada* (pp. 105–130). Don Mills Ontario: Addison-Wesley.

Troy, L. (1990). Is the U.S. Unique in the Decline of Private Sector Unionism?. *Journal of Labour Research, 11,* 111–143.

Verma, A., & Thompson M. (1989). Managerial Strategies in Canada and the U.S. in the 1980s. In: B. Dennis (Ed.), *Proceedings of the Forty First Annual Meeting* (pp. 257–265). Madison WI: Industrial Relations Research Association.

Weiler, P. C. (1983). Promises to Keep: Securing Workers' Rights to Self-Organisation Under the NLRA. *Harvard Law Review, 96*, 1769–1827.
Weiler, P. C. (1990). *Governing the Workplace.* Cambridge MA: Harvard University Press.
Wiles, J. (1984). *Contemporary Canadian Labour Relations.* Toronto Ontario: McGraw-Hill Ryerson.

APPENDIX

THE BOOTSTRAP PROCEDURE

The following procedure was used to generate 90% confidence intervals for the estimated average abnormal returns and p-values for the one tailed hypothesis of zero mean or median abnormal returns.

(1) The sample of estimated abnormal returns is resampled with replacement. This means, for example, that the estimated abnormal return for the first application could be chosen two or three times while the estimated abnormal return for the second application may not even be included in the resample.
(2) The mean estimated abnormal return for the resample is calculated and saved.
(3) Steps one and two are repeated 2000 times to generate an empirical bootstrap distribution of the mean of the abnormal return consisting of 2000 observations.
(4) The 5th and 95th percentiles of the empirical bootstrap distribution are calculated to give the bounds of a 90 percent confidence interval for the mean abnormal return. The upper and lower bounds may be different distances from the mean of the original sample because the bootstrap empirical distribution may not be symmetrical. In fact, in many cases it was far from symmetrical.
(5) The percentile of zero in the empirical bootstrap distribution is calculated. This provides an estimate of the p-value for the one-tailed hypothesis test that the mean abnormal return equals zero.
(6) Steps one to five are repeated for each monthly abnormal return, each cumulative abnormal return and their medians.

HR/IR PROFESSIONALS' EDUCATIONAL NEEDS AND MASTER'S PROGRAM CURRICULA

PHILIP K. WAY

INTRODUCTION

The related questions of what future HR/IR professionals need to learn and what education HR/IR Master's programs offer have been of growing concern, not only for academic program administrators, but also for scholars. Over recent years, there have been noteworthy attempts to probe the demand side of the labor market for HR/IR professionals in order to unveil the knowledge, skills, and competencies needed in HR/IR positions. At the risk of over-generalization, the main conclusions have been threefold. First, HR knowledge is increasingly important relative to IR knowledge (Cappelli, 1991; Van Eynde & Tucker, 1997). Second, knowledge of business is important: it has been advocated that students should have a solid grasp of the fundamentals of the business (Lawson, 1990; Lawson & Limbrick, 1996; Ulrich et al., 1995), be educated concerning functions such as finance, accounting, and operations, and that HR courses should have a more strategic orientation (Kaufman, 1994, 1996). Third, HR competencies need to be developed. They may include goal and action management, functional and organizational leadership, and influence management (Lawson & Limbrick, 1996);

change management skills, especially relationship influence, innovation/transformation, and role influence (Ulrich et al., 1995); and job skills, especially writing, active listening, oral communication, initiative, and analytical skills (Hansen et al., 1996; Hansen, 2000).

While informative and intriguing, the literature still has shortcomings. First, opinions differ concerning which HR fields, skills, and types of business knowledge are most relevant for professionals. Second, although some have recognized that the relative importance may vary according to whether positions are generalist or specialist jobs (Yeung et al., 1996), the variation between positions at different levels of the profession is rarely explicitly addressed. Indeed, most studies focus on one level or another, such as relatively senior executives (Lawson & Limbrick, 1996; Ulrich et al., 1995) or entry-level professionals (Hansen et al., 1996; Van Eynde & Tucker, 1997). Third, prior research has tended to depend mainly on the views of persons other than the HR/IR incumbent, such as CEOs (Lawson & Limbrick, 1996), senior HR executives (Kaufman 1994; Van Eynde & Tucker, 1997), and associates of HR/IR professionals (Ulrich et al., 1995).

Complementing the demand-side studies, there have been periodic analyses of the curricula of IR/HR programs that heavily influence the IR/HR knowledge, competencies, and business awareness of individuals who supply their labor to the market for HR/IR professionals. The literature indicates that while innovations are occurring and curricula are becoming more oriented to HR, there still remains a significant IR emphasis (for example, Way, 1996).

The aim of this chapter is to examine whether and in what ways there is a disjunction between the HR/IR knowledge, competencies, and business awareness demanded in IR/HR positions and the curricula of HR/IR programs at the Master's level. The issue is important. Both program administrators and students need to be aware of any demand-supply gap. Faced with limited resources, increased competition in the market for HR/IR education, program review and assessment, and pressures for relevance, program administrators are increasingly concerned to offer courses that are most valuable to students. They are also cognizant of the need to structure programs optimally, with appropriate required courses and tracks. Students need more precise guidance because they too have limited funds and wish to make their educational investment wisely. The ultimate intent of the study is to derive the implications for program design so that the goals of program administrators and students are attained.

The main contribution of this work is that it analyzes both the demand side and the supply side, rather than simply one or the other. Further, on the demand side, its conception of the knowledge, skills, and abilities required in HR/IR positions (knowledge in HR/IR, competencies, and business awareness) is more encompassing than in most previous analyses. The study also has the advantage of providing quantitative valuations of the importance of various kinds of knowledge, skills, and abilities. It differs from most previous studies in that it relies on the views of incumbents, rather than associates or upper management. Finally, its attention to variations in educational needs across different levels and specialties of HR/IR is also of interest. On the supply side, the chapter provides a more current snapshot of the curricula of Master's programs in the United States.

The study first describes the research design, the research methods, and the data used. The results are then presented for the demand and supply sides. Finally, the implications for HR/IR programs are drawn out in the light of the demand-supply gap.

RESEARCH DESIGN, METHODS, AND DATA

The research task was to discover, first, the knowledge, skills, and abilities required in HR/IR positions and, second, the curricular content of Master's programs. On the demand side, the approach involved four complementary analyses. First, what HR/IR professionals do in their jobs was determined in order to deduce what substantive HR/IR knowledge is relevant. Second, the perceived importance of various business issues facing the organizations employing the professionals was ascertained. Third, the importance of different general business and HR competencies was investigated. Fourth, input was obtained concerning which courses would be most relevant to a position.

The research method was to survey HR/IR professionals to elicit perceptions of the importance of various job duties, environmental business factors, competencies and courses in their current positions, as well as descriptive information concerning their job title, the industry in which they worked, and the size of their organization and department. The justification for surveying incumbents (rather than only senior management for example) was that the current jobholders arguably had the most accurate and current information. The survey questions appear in Appendix 1.

First, regarding job duties, respondents were asked to specify the percentage of their average workweek they spent doing each of 19 job functions (including 'other duties' which they were encouraged to list). In designing the survey, it was recognized that HR/IR professionals might work in a variety of organizational structures, such as HR departments, other staff units (for example, medical departments, accounting or finance, and quality), and line management. Hence the job functions in the survey included some outside or on the periphery of HR/IR (such as accounting, total quality management, payroll, and EAP management), as well as more conventional HR/IR duties.

Second, the respondents were also asked to rate the importance of 16 business issues for their organizations on a 7-point scale where 1 represented 'extremely important' and 7 indicated 'extremely unimportant'. The issues included four external market and regulatory issues, six strategic emphases, and six relating to change in the organization. Respondents also rated the importance of three types of business information for job performance. In order to ensure the likely relevance of the issues and competencies, and hence the productiveness of the study, the issues and competencies were drawn from a previous study of senior HR executive competencies conducted for the Society for Human Resource Management (SHRM) by Lawson (1990).

Third, in the same way, respondents were requested to rate 15 general business and HR competencies in terms of their importance in helping incumbents perform well in their jobs. The competencies related to goal and action management, functional and organizational leadership, and influence management. They were also drawn from Lawson (1990).

Finally, the respondents also rated the importance of 34 courses for a new incumbent with no prior relevant education or experience. Given the insistence of the prior literature that not only HR/IR education, but also business education is important, the courses included 10 broad HR/IR courses relating to the main functional areas of the profession, 12 more specialized or focused HR/IR courses, and 12 business courses. The choice of academic subjects was based on the curricular implications of previous studies conducted by Kaufman (1994 and 1996), Ulrich et al. (1995), Lawson and Limbrick (1996), and Hansen (1996). The subjects of public sector IR and HR were added to rectify the bias of the studies toward the private sector. The precise course titles were generated from a survey of commonly-used titles in the catalogs of 34 IR/HR Master's programs in the United States. The programs whose catalogs were surveyed are listed in Appendix 2.

The survey was mailed to the 600 members of a professional human resource association in the Midwest. Of these, 113 questionnaires were returned. This is a response rate of 19%, which is reasonable in survey research. Most surveys provided information regarding each item. Table 1 summarizes the positions of the respondents, the industries in which they worked, and the sizes of their organizations. In common with every other study of this kind, it is not known how representative this sample was due to the lack of knowledge of the distribution of HR professionals in the area. That said, approximately three-quarters of the sample were generalists, and the majority of these were HR managers, as opposed to junior or senior HR professionals. Two-fifths were employed in manufacturing industries, the remainder in service industries. Organizations were typically of small and medium size. HR departments employed six people on average, excluding secretarial staff.

Table 1. Characteristics of Respondents to Survey

	Percentage of Respondents
Position in HR	
Generalists	
Senior	9.7
Manager	46.9
Junior	15.0
Specialists	
Employment	8.9
Compensation	4.4
Training & Development	3.5
Employee Relations	2.7
Line Management	6.2
Other and unknown	2.6
Industry	
Manufacturing	40.7
Services (general)	23.0
Distribution	8.9
Health Care	8.0
Finance	6.2
Insurance	4.4
Other	8.0
Unknown	0.9
Firm size (Average 736.4)	
1–100	19.5
101–500	43.4
501–2500	29.2
>2500	5.3
Unknown	2.6

On the supply side, the approach was to analyze the curricula of Master's programs in HR/IR. Since the study was designed to contrast the educational needs of HR professionals and the education offered by HR/IR programs, other types of programs (such as MBAs, those in human resource development, and at the undergraduate level) were excluded. The list of programs surveyed is in Appendix 2. It is believed to include most, if not all, the major U.S. HR/IR Master's programs.

The research method was to establish the incidence of courses concerning different subjects. The course subjects not only included those investigated in the demand-side analysis, but also others that were offered by programs. The content of the courses was determined by studying course titles and descriptions. The data were obtained from program catalogs and program web sites.

RESULTS

The purpose of this section is to report, first, the perceptions of HR/IR professionals regarding their job duties, important business issues, relevant HR competencies, and important courses; and, second, the courses offered in Master's programs in HR/IR. The following section discusses the degree of fit between the demand and supply sides and the implications for administrators of Master's programs and for current and prospective students.

The Demand Side: Job Duties, Business Issues, Competencies, and Courses

HR/IR Duties

Table 2 shows that survey respondents spent more than 5% of their time on average in six activities: employee relations, recruitment and selection, benefits, supervision, wage and salary administration, and training. Although the numbers of specialists and relatively senior and junior HR generalists were small compared to the number of HR managers, it is clear that job duties varied by function and level. For senior professionals, staffing and training were less important than for respondents as a whole, but employee relations, benefits and supervision took more time, and corporate strategy emerged as an activity that took more than 5% of the workweek. For managers, HR strategy and health and safety also consumed more than 5% of the workweek. Junior professionals spent much less time than the average respondent on supervision and wage and salary administration, but more on EEO/affirmative action, labor relations, and HRIS.

Predictably, for specialists, the predominant activities reflected their function. Employment specialists spent close to half their workweek on recruitment and selection and EEO/AA, but also more than 5% of their time on supervision, employee relations, and HR strategy. Compensation specialists were largely consumed with wage and salary administration and benefits, but also spent 5% or more of their workweek in supervision and HRIS. Training and development specialists devoted over two-thirds of their workweek to training and TQM, but also spent more than 5% of their time on employee relations, recruitment and selection, research, and corporate strategy. Those professionals in

Table 2. Percentage of Average Workweek of HR Professionals Spent Fulfilling Various Functions

Functions	All	HR Generalists			HR Specialists				
		Senior Managers	Managers	Junior Managers	Empl	Comp	Training & Dev.	Emp. Rels.	Line Mgt.
Employee Relations	17.6	22.5	17.4	25.9	8.1	2.0	17.5	55.7	6.6
Recruitment/ Selection	13.4	7.7	12.1	12.5	38.5	0.0	10.0	1.7	12.6
Benefits	8.7	16.8	8.6	7.2	3.2	34.0	1.2	1.7	1.4
Supervision	7.4	12.5	5.9	1.6	13.0	7.0	1.2	11.7	13.9
Wage and Salary Administration	7.3	7.7	7.9	3.5	2.7	44.0	0.0	0.3	1.3
Training	7.0	4.3	6.6	7.2	1.8	1.0	41.2	1.6	1.9
HR Strategy	4.9	2.8	6.6	2.5	6.3	2.0	7.5	0.0	2.7
TQM	4.5	3.0	3.0	2.8	2.5	1.0	27.5	3.3	3.1
EEO/AA	4.5	3.4	3.0	9.8	9.9	0.0	2.5	8.3	0.9
Health & Safety	4.3	2.9	5.1	4.4	0.5	0.0	0.0	0.0	15.3
Labor relations	4.2	2.5	4.3	8.8	1.5	1.0	2.5	9.0	2.4
Corporate Strategy	3.5	5.7	4.4	0.5	0.2	1.0	5.0	0.0	8.6
Career Development	2.7	2.3	2.7	1.7	4.0	0.0	3.8	2.0	0.0
HRIS	2.6	0.2	2.6	5.3	1.7	5.0	0.0	3.3	0.9
Payroll	2.6	1.4	4.4	0.9	0.0	2.0	0.0	0.0	2.0
Other	2.0	0.0	2.3	1.2	3.0	0.0	0.0	1.1	0.4
Research	1.9	2.3	1.4	3.7	1.3	1.0	5.0	3.3	0.7
Accounting	1.4	0.3	0.8	0.2	0.0	0.0	0.0	0.0	15.3
EAPs	1.1	0.8	1.9	0.6	0.1	0.0	0.0	1.6	0.1

Table 3. Determinants of the Percentage of Average Workweek of HR Professionals Spent Fulfilling Various Functions

Independent Variables	Dependent Variables Percentage Workweek Spent Fulfilling Function				
	Employee Relations	Recruitment & Selection	Benefits	Wage & Salary Administration	Training
		Coefficients (Standard Errors)			
Constant	14.641 (4.522)	9.233* (5.131)	7.840 (3.601)	3.966 (3.017)	10.880 (2.582)****
Organizational Size	0.005**** (0.001)	0.001 (0.001)	−0.001 (0.001)	0.000 (0.000)	−0.001 (0.001)
HR Manager	−0.903 (4.104)	1.532 (4.657)	1.213 (3.268)	4.636* (2.738)	−2.750 (2.343)
Senior HR	3.762 (5.498)	−2.250 (6.239)	9.427** (4.379)	4.369 (3.668)	−5.239* (3.140)
Specialists:					
Employment	−14.177** (5.499)	26.867**** (6.240)	−3.487 (4.380)	−0.464 (3.669)	−3.896 (3.140)
Compensation	−18.444** (7.086)	−9.861 (8.041)	26.632**** (5.643)	40.789**** (4.727)	−8.496** (4.046)
Training & Development	1.971 (8.753)	−3.085 (9.932)	−6.167 (6.970)	−3.329 (5.839)	21.764**** (4.998)
Employee Relations	27.393*** (8.980)	−14.793 (10.190)	−2.928 (7.151)	−3.059 (5.991)	−5.526 (5.128)
Line Management	−9.594 (6.722)	3.318 (7.628)	−6.394 (5.353)	−2.500 (4.484)	−8.816** (3.838)
Other	−10.156 (10.587)	20.086* (12.014)	−7.339 (8.431)	1.032 (7.063)	−7.735 (6.045)
N	108	108	108	108	108
F-statistic	4.836****	3.004****	3.389****	7.174****	2.997****
Adj. R-squared	0.32	0.19	0.22	0.43	0.19

Notes: ****$p < 0.001$. ***$p < 0.01$. **$p < 0.05$. *$p < 0.10$. (2–tailed tests)
Industry dummy variables omitted from table.

employee relations were preoccupied with employee relations, supervision, labor relations, and EEO/AA. Finally, the HR professionals with line management job titles spent sizeable amounts of time on health and safety, accounting, supervision, recruitment and selection, and corporate strategy.

Some of these differences were statistically significant. Ordinary least squares regression analyzes were performed with the percentage of time spent performing a particular duty as the dependent variable, and company size, HR position dummy variables (senior HR generalist, HR manager, and specialists in employment, compensation, training and development, IR/employee relations, line management, and other), and industry dummy variables (for manufacturing, finance, health care and distribution) as the independent variables. The reference HR position was junior HR generalist, while the reference industry was general and other services.

Table 3 shows the results for the five main HR duties: employee relations, recruitment and selection, benefits, wage and salary administration, and training. As the industry variables were insignificant, they are omitted from the table. It is evident that senior HR personnel were significantly more likely than junior HR professionals to spend time on benefits. HR managers devoted a significantly greater proportion of their time to wage and salary administration. Not surprisingly, specialists spent significantly more time in their areas of responsibility. Employment specialists were significantly more likely to work on recruitment and selection, but significantly less on employee relations. Compensation specialists were significantly more preoccupied with wage and salary administration and benefits, but significantly less with employee relations and training. Training specialists expended significantly more time on training. Employee relations specialists devoted significantly more time to employee relations. Line managers spent significantly less time training.

Business Issues
Table 4 shows that most business issues were at least of some importance for respondents' organizations on average. The ones that were closer to very or extremely important were the external factors of 'competition for market share' and 'governmental regulations'; the business strategies of 'price competition/cost control', 'need for sales growth', 'need to increase productivity', and 'product development'; and the internal environmental changes in technology, organizational and management structures, and management style.

When asked to consider the importance of business issues for job performance, HR professionals had mixed views (also Table 4). Organizational awareness, (including understanding the business, organizational issues, plans, and culture), was rated as very important. An understanding of the industry

Table 4. Importance of Business Issues for the Organization and for Job Performance

Business Issue	Rating of Importance	
	For Organization	For Job Performance
Competition for market share	1.9	
Price competition/price control	1.9	
Governmental regulations	1.9	
Need for sales growth	2.1	
Need to increase productivity	2.1	
Technological change	2.2	
Product development	2.4	
Change in organizational/management structures	2.4	
Change in management style	2.5	
Change in skill requirements	2.6	
Changing workforce demographics	2.7	
Managing rapid growth/business expansion	2.8	
Differentiation	3.2	
Global competition	4.0	
Acquisitions	4.4	
Organizational awareness		1.9
Understanding of the industry		2.6
General knowledge of finance, sales, marketing, corporate law and information systems		2.8

Note: 1 = extremely important
2 = very important
3 = somewhat important
4 = neither important nor unimportant
5 = somewhat unimportant
6 = very unimportant
7 = extremely unimportant

(including suppliers, product/service substitutes, buyers and potential entrants), and general knowledge of finance, sales, marketing, corporate law and information systems, were rated lower, slightly closer to 'somewhat important' than 'very important'.

Overall, the more senior generalists, and to a lesser extent the HR managers, were more likely than junior professionals to rate business issues as important. However, the differences in average ratings were not statistically significant. It is not possible to determine whether there were any significant differences in the importance attached to individual business issues among HR professionals (holding everything else constant) because the relatively small sample size

Table 5. Importance of Competencies to Job Performance

Competencies	Rating of Importance
Integrity	1.2
Ability to work effectively with others outside HR	1.4
Communication process skills	1.5
Proactivity (prevention of problem situations)	1.7
Ability to approach problems with a clear perception of organizational and political reality	1.7
Negotiation skills	1.9
Decisiveness	2.0
Sensitivity and consciousness about image	2.0
Communicating HR department's role, services, and capability to the rest of the organization	2.2
A value-added perspective	2.2
Group management skills	2.2
Developing other staff	2.3
Efficiency orientation	2.3
Strategic focus	2.4
Leading and mobilizing others with a vision	2.5

Notes: 1. Appendix 1 contains fuller descriptions of competencies.

2. 1 = extremely important
   2 = very important
   3 = somewhat important
   4 = neither important nor unimportant
   5 = somewhat unimportant
   6 = very unimportant
   7 = extremely unimportant

prevented the performance of ordered probit regressions of individual issues on relevant organizational, positional, and industry variables.

Competencies

The views of incumbents concerning the importance of job competencies are indicated in Table 5. Every competency was rated as at least midway between somewhat and very important on average. There was a considerable degree of agreement between incumbents in various HR positions: there were no statistically significant differences in average ratings. Again, the relatively small sample size prevented an ordered probit analysis of differences in ratings between different types of HR professionals, everything else being equal.

Overall, eight competencies were rated at least very if not extremely important: integrity (involving being open and candid, maintaining confidentiality, and being fair and ethical); an ability to work effectively with others in the organization outside HR; communication process skills; proactivity (involving the prevention of problem situations); an ability to approach problems with a clear perception of organizational and political reality; negotiation skills; decisiveness; and a sensitivity to the image of oneself and the HR function. It should be noted that six of these competencies were rated as or more important than the top-rated business-knowledge factor of organizational awareness in Table 4.

Important Courses

Table 6 shows the importance of the broad and focused HR/IR courses and the business courses for the HR professionals in general. The statistical significance of any differences between different HR levels and specialties, controlling for other factors, could not be investigated in view of the relatively small sample size.

Of the broad HR/IR courses, all but the international HR course were viewed as at least somewhat important. The courses that were rated closer to very important or higher were HRM, employment law, staffing, benefits, compensation, and training and development. It should be noted that these corresponded closely to the key job duties of professionals in the sample.

The focused HR/IR courses were not generally rated as highly as the broader courses. Two industrial relations courses and the two public sector courses were actually rated on the unimportant half of the scale. The major exception was a course on employee selection. Courses in dispute resolution, negotiations, and diversity had ratings close to that for training and development.

Likewise, in general, the business courses were not believed to be as important as the broad HR courses. However, there were three that ranked as high as benefits, compensation and training: they were motivation, communication in organizations, and persuasion. The ratings of these courses were consistent with the importance of employee relations in the workweek of the professionals and four of the top six competencies, namely working effectively with others in the organization, communication skills, approaching problems with a sense of organizational reality, and negotiation skills. Had ethics been offered as a course for respondent appraisal, it is hypothesized that it would have been highly rated, given the overwhelming importance of integrity as a competence for professionals.

Courses relating to organizations (psychology, development, behavior, and design) were rated between somewhat and very important. Perhaps it was felt that such courses could make students more organizationally aware. Again, consistent with the respondents' attitudes toward business issues, courses in marketing, accounting, and finance were ranked lowest, not even earning a 'somewhat important' rating.

Table 6. Importance of Educational Courses For Novices

Course Titles	Rating of Importance
Broad HR/IR courses	
HRM	1.7
Employment law	1.8
Staffing	1.9
Benefits	2.0
Compensation	2.1
Training & development	2.3
Labor relations	2.7
HRIS	2.9
Health and safety	3.0
International HRM	4.7
Focused HR/IR courses	
Employee selection	1.7
Dispute resolution	2.5
Negotiations	2.6
Diversity	2.6
Costing HR	2.8
IR law	2.8
Strategic HR	2.9
IR theory	3.5
Contemporary unions	4.0
History of IR	4.2
Public sector IR	4.6
Public sector personnel management	4.7
Business courses	
Motivation	2.0
Communication in organizations	2.2
Persuasion	2.3
Organizational psychology	2.6
Organizational development	2.6
Organizational behavior	2.7
Organizational design	2.7
Business law	3.0
Business policy	3.0
Financial analysis	3.4
Accounting	3.5
Marketing	3.6

Note: 1 = extremely important
        2 = very important
        3 = somewhat important
        4 = neither important nor unimportant
        5 = somewhat unimportant
        6 = very unimportant
        7 = extremely unimportant

Discussion

The general conclusion is that the educational needs of HR/IR professionals as perceived by incumbents are broad, encompassing functional knowledge, business awareness and competencies. Having said that, there are priorities, and these may vary according to the level or specialty of the professional.

Specifically, the results relating to job duties and appropriate courses indicate that the primary HR/IR knowledge needed by professionals concerns employee relations (which would include general HRM and employment law), staffing (with emphases on selection and diversity), benefits, compensation, training and development, and supervision. Secondary needs lie in dispute resolution, negotiation, labor relations, HRIS, health and safety, labor law, costing HR and strategic HR. Since different specialties and levels involve different job duties, the knowledge needs of professionals are likely to vary.

The HR/IR knowledge not accorded great importance concerns international HR, public sector industrial relations and personnel management, and contemporary unions and labor history. However, it is important to reiterate that this study was conducted in the Midwest region of the U.S. (where global competition is perhaps not as important as in the West or East coasts), in an area with low rates of unionization, and largely in private sector organizations. Therefore, these HR/IR subjects may be more relevant in different regions and sectors.

Since businesses are facing tough competition and are responding through aggressive business strategies, professionals also need a keen awareness of the business and organizational issues, plans and culture. While education cannot teach the specifics of an organization's internal and external environment, a general familiarity with the key dimensions of the environment could be gained through an appropriate course on organizations. However, according to the respondents in this study, there is no need for courses in marketing, finance and accounting. The latter finding is at odds with some studies that have found the opposite (Ulrich 1995; Kaufman 1996). It may be explained by the source of the data: in this study, the views of HR incumbents were sought, whereas, in the others, the opinions of associates and HR executives were tapped. It implies that internal customers' expectations of HR/IR professionals' qualities may be different from what professionals believe are relevant to their job.

Finally, professionals need to possess a wide variety of competencies. Skills could be honed through courses the professionals rated highly, such as ethics, motivation, organizational communication, and persuasion. In addition, the pedagogy of courses could be designed so that students are given the opportunity to develop relevant competencies. It would be easiest to build in opportunities to cultivate communication skills and negotiation skills, but case studies in a variety of courses could develop integrity, proactive behavior, and a sense of organizational reality.

The Supply Side: The Curricula of IR/HR Master's Programs

The incidence of courses in the 34 HR/IR Master's programs surveyed appears in Table 7. The courses listed are all those which were implied by the literature to be important and which appeared in the survey administered to the professionals (see Table 6), as well as those in HR/IR or business that were offered by at least five programs. It should be noted that the data refer to courses offered, but do not indicate students' course-taking patterns.

No courses were taught universally, although industrial relations/collective bargaining came close. In addition, over two-thirds of programs offered courses in compensation, employment law and staffing. Approximately half included courses in HRM, training and development, organizational behavior, strategic HRM, and dispute resolution, while slightly fewer offered organizational development or change, benefits, HRIS, and labor law. Approximately one-quarter to one-third offered courses in comparative IR, international HR, current issues in IR, public sector IR, labor history, negotiation, current issues in HR, and motivation. Other types of courses were seen in very small proportions of programs.

THE DEMAND-SUPPLY GAP AND ITS IMPLICATIONS

A significant demand-supply gap exists between the courses likely to be needed by HR/IR professionals and the courses offered by Master's programs. The primary HR/IR knowledge needs of HRM, employment law, staffing, and compensation, were covered by courses in a majority of, but not all, programs. However, benefits and supervision were not, unless they were covered in compensation and organizational behavior courses. Motivation (or performance management) courses, which would be useful to develop supervisory skills, were comparatively infrequent. Hence, overall, the supply of primary courses appeared inadequate. Not only did some programs not offer these courses, but also those that did often did not require them.

Most secondary HR/IR knowledge needs – dispute resolution, negotiation, labor relations, health and safety, labor law, costing HR, and strategic HR – were met by one-third to one-half of programs. Of these, the labor relations courses and strategic HR were much more common, while negotiation, health

Table 7. Course Offerings in HR/IR Master's Programs

Course Title	Percentage of Programs With Course
Broad HR/IR Courses	
IR/Collective Bargaining	91
Compensation	79
Employment Law	71
Staffing	68
Training & Development	53
HRM	53
Benefits	41
HRIS	38
International HR	29
Health & Safety	18
Focused HR/IR Courses	
Strategic HR	47
Dispute Resolution	47
Labor Law	38
Comparative IR	32
Current Issues in IR	29
Public Sector IR	26
Labor History	26
Negotiating	26
Current Issues in HR	24
Public Personnel Management	18
Contemporary Unions	18
Diversity	12
Costing HR	9
IR Theory	9
Employee Selection	6
Business Courses	
Organizational Behavior	50
Organizational Development/Change	44
Motivation	24
Organizational Psychology	24
Business Policy/Strategy	18
Organizational Design	15
Accounting	12
Communication	12
Financial Management	9
Marketing	6
Persuasion	3
Business Law	0

and safety, costing HR, and specialized staffing and diversity courses were much more rare. Therefore, in a large proportion of programs the secondary educational needs of professionals were not satisfied. At the same time, some courses were more common than might be expected given the needs of future professionals, especially courses in comparative IR, international HR, public sector IR and personnel management, and contemporary unions.

Business awareness may have been provided in organizational behavior and change courses that were each offered in approximately half of programs. However, again, a large proportion of programs did not offer or require such courses.

While it is difficult to assess whether the competencies were adequately covered by programs because they may have been infused in other courses, it is clear that few courses were offered in ethics, communication in organizations, persuasion, and motivation.

Most programs allowed students freedom to choose electives that suited their educational needs and preferences, but a few were very regimented, affording little scope for students to adjust their curriculum according to their career track. Of course, whether the students in flexible programs made appropriate choices was unknown.

In conclusion, if programs are attempting to educate students so that they are able to perform effectively in HR positions like those held by respondents in this survey, administrators should heed what incumbents perceive as important knowledge, business issues, competencies, and courses in this study, as well as the views of other stakeholders as revealed in other studies. Insofar as this study of incumbent views is concerned, many program administrators need to amend their curricula. Some courses may need to be added, and even made compulsory, while others could be eliminated. There may not be a net resource cost. In addition, program administrators need to recognize the need to provide opportunities for students to develop business awareness and various competencies. These may be taught through new courses or refined pedagogies in existing courses. Beyond curricula, there is a need for more informed advising concerning which courses would be most appropriate to take given the needs of the student.

The implications for students are that they should look carefully at the HR/IR knowledge, business awareness, and competencies demanded by organizations and positions in which they wish to work. They should then research alternative programs in order to choose an appropriate curriculum. In the process, they will help bring the demand and the supply sides of the market into balance.

ACKNOWLEDGMENTS

The author would like to thank the anonymous referees for their helpful comments.

REFERENCES

Cappelli, P. (1991). Is There a Future for the Field of Industrial Relations in the United States? In: R. D. Lansbury (Ed.), *Industrial Relations Teaching and Research: International Trends.* (pp. 3–40). Sydney: ACIRRT.

Hansen, W. L., Berkley, R. A., Kaplan, D. M., Yu, Q-S., Craig, C. J., Fitzpatrick, J. A., Seiler, M. R., Denby, D. R., Gheis, P., Ruelle, D. J., & Voss, L. A. (1996). Needed Skills for Human Resource Professionals: A Pilot Study. *Labor Law Journal, 47,* 524–534.

Hansen, W. L. (2000). Developing New Proficiencies for Human Resource and Industrial Relations Professionals. In: D. Lewin & B. E. Kaufman (Eds), *Advances in Industrial and Labor Relations,* (pp. 209-233). 10.

Kaufman, B. E. (1994). What Companies Are Looking For in Graduates of University HR Programs. *Labor Law Journal, 45,* 503–510.

Kaufman, B. E. (1996). Transformation of the Corporate HR/IR Function: Implications for University Programs. *Labor Law Journal, 47,* 540–548.

Lawson, T. (1990). *The Competency Initiative: Studies for Excellence for Human Resource Executives.* Minneapolis, MN: Golles & Holmes Custom education (in conjunction with the SHRM Foundation).

Lawson, T. E., & Limbrick, V. (1996). Critical Competencies and Developmental Experiences for Top HR Executives. *Human Resource Management, 35*(1), 67–85.

Ulrich, D., Brockbank, W., Yeung, A. K., & Lake, D. G. (1995). Human Resource Competencies: An Empirical Assessment. *Human Resource Management, 34,* 473–495.

Van Eynde, D. F., & Tucker, S. L. (1997). A Quality Human Resource Curriculum: Recommendations From Leading Senior HR Executives. *Human Resource Management, 36*(4), 397–408.

Way, P. K. (1996). A Survey of Curricula of IR/HR Master's Programs: Common Features, New Directions. *Labor Law Journal, 47,* 535–539.

Yeung, A., Woolcock, P., & Sullivan, J. (1996). Identifying and Developing HR Competencies For The Future: Keys To Sustaining The Transformation of HR Functions. *Human Resource Planning. 19*(4), 48–58.

APPENDIX 1

Survey Questions

Business Issues
Rate the importance of the following issues for your organization, as you perceive the situation. Use the following scale:

    1 = extremely important
    2 = very important
    3 = somewhat important
    4 = neither important nor unimportant
    5 = somewhat unimportant
    6 = very unimportant
    7 = extremely unimportant

Acquisitions
Global competition
Establishing and maintaining differentiation
Price competition/cost control
Governmental regulations
Changing workforce demographics
Product development
Need for sales growth
Competition for market share
Technological change
Deregulated environment
Need to increase productivity
Managing rapid growth/ business expansion
Change in organizational/management structures
Change in management styles
Change in skill requirements

Human Resource Duties
Please specify what percentage of your average workweek is spent doing each of the following functions:

Corporate strategy
Wage and salary administration
Payroll
Employee relations

Health and safety
EEO/AA
Research
Recruitment/selection
Total quality management
HR strategy
Benefits
Training
Labor relations
Employee assistance programs
Career development
HR information systems
Accounting
Supervision
Other: please specify

Human Resource Competencies
Please rate the competencies below in terms of their importance in helping you perform well in your job using the 7-point scale above:

Organizational awareness (including understanding the business, organizational issues, plans, and culture)

Understanding of the industry (including suppliers, product/service substitutes, buyers and potential entrants)

General knowledge of finance, sales, marketing, corporate law, and information systems

Efficiency orientation (involves cost-effective, superior, job performance; realistic goals; quick error correction; sufficient delegation)

Proactivity (prevention of problem situations)

Sensitivity and consciousness about one's professional image and that of the HR function

Decisiveness even when the data are limited or solutions are unpleasant

Developing, or arranging for the development of, other staff

Group management skills (e.g. team building skills)

Communicating the HR department's role, services, and capabilities to the rest of the organization

Leading and mobilizing others with a vision of the direction for the HR function

Integrity (involves being open and candid, maintaining confidentiality, and being fair and ethical)

Ability to approach problems with a clear perception of organizational and political reality
Ability to work effectively with others in the organization outside HR
Communication process skills (including effective use of written material, oral presentations, verbal interchange, and non-verbal cues, using appropriate channels)
Negotiation skills (including recognizing confrontational situations and persuading others)
Strategic focus (involving maintaining an awareness of the forces affecting the organization)
A value-added perspective (involving perceiving opportunities for HR to deliver services and programs that add value; providing ingenuity, innovation, and creativity)

Relevant Education and Training
Using the 7-point scale above please indicate the importance for your position of the following educational courses in preparing a person with no prior relevant education or experience.

Human Resource Management
Compensation
Training and Development
Employment Law
HR Information Systems
Dispute Resolution
International HRM
Public Sector Personnel
Contemporary Unionism
Employee Selection
Organizational Design
Organizational Development
Persuasion
Industrial Relations Theory
Business Law
Business Policy/Strategy
Marketing
Benefits
Staffing
Labor Relations

Labor Relations Law
Health and Safety
Strategic HRM
Negotiation
Public Sector Industrial Relations
Diversity
Organizational Behavior
Accounting
Communication in Organizations
Costing HRM
History of Industrial Relations
Financial Analysis
Organizational Psychology
Motivation

APPENDIX 2

HR/IR Master's Programs Surveyed

Appalachian State University
Cleveland State University
Cornell University
Georgia State University
Indiana University Pennsylvania
Loyola University (2 programs)
Marquette University
Michigan State University (2 programs)
Nova Southeastern University
Ohio State University
Pennsylvania State University
Purdue University
Rutgers University (2 programs)
St. Francis University
Texas A&M University
University of Alabama
University of Cincinnati
University of Illinois
University of Massachusetts-Amherst
University of Minnesota

University of North Florida
University of North Texas
University of Rhode Island
University of South Carolina
University of Texas-Arlington
University of West Virginia
University of Wisconsin – Madison
University of Wisconsin – Milwaukee
Utah State University
Wayne State University
Widener University

ARE WE PROPERLY TRAINING FUTURE HR/IR PRACTITIONERS? A REVIEW OF THE CURRICULA

C. Douglas Johnson and James King

INTRODUCTION

It is always prudent to monitor the degree to which education for a profession prepares students for that profession. It becomes more critical to do so when the profession has experienced or is undergoing significant change. For that reason Human Resources/Industrial Relations (HR/IR) seems to warrant particular attention to discern the degree to which the educational training continues to be appropriate preparation for practice.

Changes within businesses, as well as changes within the general environment that businesses operate, have spurred change in the practice of HR/IR. Ulrich (1997b; 1998) has suggested that the role, or agenda, of human resource practitioners has expanded beyond the traditional functions of personnel management, such as staffing, benefits, and compensation, to include such tasks as strategic planning and continuous improvement. This is particularly true in larger, Fortune 500-like companies (Kaufman, 1999). Leading companies, such as General Electric and Amoco, seek entry-level human resource/industrial relations practitioners who have the capacity to become strategic business partners and align themselves with the other functions to ensure organizational success. Specifically, those who seek admittance to General Electric's prestigious human resource management development program must possess a graduate degree or bachelor's degree from a reputable human resource/industrial relations (HR/IR) program (Keller & Campbell, 1992; Stockman, 1999). In addition to a specialized, professional degree, employers are expecting HR/IR practitioners to have accompanying skills (Kaufman, 1994). If indeed the expectations are different, or changing, then those training future HR/IR practitioners must ensure that the necessary adjustments are made to the curricula. For the purposes of this study, industrial relations (IR) is defined as the field of study involving not only union-management relations, but all aspects of the employment relationship (Strauss & Whitfield, 1998). On the other hand, human resources (HR) management is a series of integrated decisions about the employment relationship that influence the effectiveness of the organization and its employees (Milkovich & Boudreau, 1997). These definitions reflect the overlap and possible convergence of these two fields of study.

A basic step in assuring preparation is to determine whether existing programs adequately develop functional and strategic business partnering competencies. The purpose of the current study is to: (1) review the literature and practitioner sources to determine which skills or competencies are needed to be successful HR/IR practitioners in the future, and (2) evaluate the HR/IR curricula to ensure that these skills/competencies are being adequately addressed. The study is important in that it evaluates whether a gap exists between organizations' expectations of what an entry-level HR/IR practitioner should have learned and what is actually being addressed (e.g., taught in coursework, special seminars/guest speakers) at institutions. This was achieved by reviewing the literature and interviewing HR/IR practitioners to identify competencies, and evaluating program catalogs/brochures and responses to a questionnaire by program directors. The study combines and expands the methodologies employed in previous research (e.g., Hansen et al., 1996; Way, 1996) by including multiple programs and types of degree offerings, involving both practitioners and academicians in competency identification, and evaluating instructional methods utilized.

METHOD

The procedure employed in the current study involved reviewing the HR/IR literature to identify competencies, interviewing HR/IR practitioners to augment the literature review, content analyzing program catalogues/curricula, and surveying program directors. A description of each step in the process follows below.

Literature Review to Identify Competencies

Initially, three computerized databases (i.e., ERIC, ABI Inform, PsycINFO) were reviewed to identify scholarly work related to HR/IR competencies. The databases were searched using key words such as human resources curriculum, industrial relations curriculum, and human resource trends. To supplement the computerized search, six scholarly journals in the human resources and industrial relations domains were manually reviewed. These journals included *Human Resource Management, Human Resource Development Quarterly, Journal of Human Resources, Industrial Relations Journal, Industrial & Labor Relations,* and *Industrial Relations.* Each journal was manually reviewed for the period 1990–1998 in order to identify any articles that discussed HR/IR curricula, competencies, or trends in either of these two areas. This period was chosen because the primary interest of this step was to identify any new, or non-traditional, competencies that future HR/IR practitioners should possess upon entering a professional position. Once articles were identified and reviewed from these primary sources, the authors ascertained additional citations from the respective reference sections. Other key references were Ulrich's (1997b) book, *Human Resource Champions,* and the August 1996 special issue of the *Labor Law Journal,* highlighting papers from the 1st Innovative Teaching in Human Resources and Industrial Relations Conference.

Interviews with HR/IR Practitioners to Augment Literature Review

Interviews were conducted with middle to senior level HR/IR practitioners to obtain ratings of the importance of the competencies identified via the literature review. Respondents were given the option of completing a telephone interview or responding to the survey via fax or e-mail, with most opting to submit replies electronically. The HR/IR practitioners ($n = 12$) were representatives of companies from various industries, such as telecommunications, banking, and consulting, and have been acknowledged for having exceptional HR/IR development programs/departments. Five of the twelve HR/IR practitioners have substantial experience in a unionized environment. Therefore, we felt these companies adequately represented those organizations that were likely to employ future HR/IR practitioners, and had a vested interest in providing candid responses and feedback as a stakeholder in program/curricula evaluation.

Using a 5-point Likert scale (1 = not at all; 5 = very important), each respondent rated how important it was for entry-level, future HR/IR practitioners to possess each competency at the point of hiring. Additionally, the respondent was asked to provide any competencies (s)he felt essential that were not included in the survey.

Program Catalogue/Curricula Review

A generic letter was sent to each of the 90 programs included on the IRRA's listing of 'Industrial Relations and Human Resource Degree Programs in the U.S., Canada, and Australia', as of May 1998 (see http://www.irra.uiuc.edu), requesting that information on HR/IR programs offered be sent to the first author. Initially, 46 programs sent information. A follow-up telephone call was made to all programs that had not responded, which resulted in another 17 programs submitting brochures/catalogs. A response rate would be misleading in that some universities/colleges offer multiple programs and submitted multiple catalogs that were included in the review. Furthermore, some programs that responded were deemed inappropriate for use in the content analyses for various reasons (e.g., doctoral programs, brochures written in foreign language, catalog did not mention HR/IR specialization or concentration).

Kaufman (1996) asserted that an MBA is becoming the degree-of-choice for HR/IR practitioners who wish to acquire business skills. Weiss (1997) also suggested that the MBA is more important than specialized programs in developing HR professionals that are viewed as credible business partners by line management. So an effort was made to include MBA programs that offered a concentration/specialization in HR, IR, or HR/IR in this study. Three sources were utilized in identifying programs that offered a concentration in HR, IR, or HR/IR: (1) the 1999 *U.S. News & World Report*'s top business schools listing (Exclusive rankings, 1999); (2) *BusinessWeek*'s most recent listing of the best business schools (Reingold, 1998); and (3) the *Peterson's MBA Programs* reference (1998).

For each of the 71 programs included in the current review (HR, IR, and MBA), the program's catalog/curriculum was evaluated to determine whether the identified competencies were addressed. The content analysis involved reading the information and determining whether a course or other vehicle (e.g., outside seminars/conferences, guest speakers) was in place to ensure that the competency was developed. Each competency was coded either 0 (not covered) or 1 (covered).

Program Director Survey

A cover letter and survey was mailed to the program director of each program previously identified. If the listing included multiple degree offerings (e.g., BS, MS, MBA), a separate survey was sent for each of the degrees offered. If a specific contact person was listed, the survey was sent directly to that individual, otherwise it was sent to the general program address. The cover letter requested that the survey(s) be distributed to the appropriate person(s) and returned by a specified deadline.

In addition to asking for the degree program type, the four-page survey sought coverage ratings of the HR/IR competencies, as well as information pertaining to instructional methods and accessibility to relevant professional organizations. The respondents were not asked to identify themselves or their program in an effort to minimize response bias and obtain more candid, accurate responses.

RESULTS AND DISCUSSION

Literature Review Results

The changing nature of HR/IR and the competencies needed to effectively respond to those changes have received considerable attention in the scholarly literature. For instance, the *Human Resource Management* journal has had special issues discussing the future direction of HR from the perspective of academicians, executives and consultants (Ulrich, 1997a), and on HR competencies (Kochanski, 1996). There has been less attention given to IR competencies. This could be due to the trend to include discussions traditionally framed in the domain of IR as part of the constantly growing HR domain (e.g., Lewin & Kaufman, 1999). HR/IR competencies refer to an individual's demonstrated knowledge, skills, and abilities (KSAs) (Ulrich, Brockbank, Yeung & Lake, 1995). HR/IR competencies were reviewed rather than HR skills (enablers of knowledge or how the work is accomplished; Hansen et al., 1996) due to the breadth of coverage (i.e., HR/IR competencies broader than HR/IR skills).

Several models/categorizations were identified in the literature that focused specifically on HR competencies; however, no general consensus has been reached on the totality and/or validity of the HR/IR categorizations. Four of the most recent categorizations are described next. Ulrich and colleagues (1995) conducted what is purported to be the largest HR competency study involving almost 13,000 co-workers of HR professionals. In summary, the results of this study indicated that these co-workers perceived HR professionals who demonstrate competencies in business knowledge, delivery of HR, and management of change, as more effective. Keller and Campbell (1992) discussed the four competency areas that GE focuses on in developing its HR/IR capability: functional competencies (e.g., global HR, talent assessment); business competencies (e.g., organizational development, business and financial measured); personal competencies (e.g., career development, leadership style effectiveness); and organizational competencies (e.g., valuing diversity, facilitation/consulting). The Society of Human Resource Management (SHRM) identified leadership, management, functional and personal HR competencies as the core competencies essential for success in HR, as well as level- and role-specific competencies (Schoonover, 1998). Further, Heneman (1999) discussed the new curriculum for HR/IR in terms of 'classical IR', 'traditional HR', and 'new HR'.

Given that the purpose of the present study was to determine whether the HR/IR program curricula were adequately preparing future HR/IR practitioners, Heneman's (1999) categorization scheme seemed most appropriate to utilize as it reflects the trend occuring in the HR/IR field, and generally focused on an educational setting, which substantially increases its face validity. In addition, personal competencies, as discussed in both Keller and Campbell's (1992) and SHRM's (Schoonover, 1998) listing of essential competencies, were included. The listing of competencies generated from the approximately 100 references involved in the literature review (contact the first author for complete listing) are presented in Table 1.

Table 1. Essential Competencies for Future HR/IR Practitioners

Classical IR	*New HR*
Collective Bargaining	Business Process Reengineering
Discipline	Changing Nature of Employment Contracts
Labor Economics	Downsizing
Labor Relations	Employee Involvement
Laws/Legal Issues Affecting HR/IR	Ethics
	Evaluating HRM Function
	Facilitation/Internal Consulting
Traditional HR	General Business Management
Benefits/Health Care	Global HRM
Career Planning	HR Information Systems
Communications	Managing Change
Compensation	Managing Diversity/Cultural Diversity
Counseling/Employee Assistance Programs	Organizational Assessment
Employee Safety and Health	Quality of Worklife
HR Planning	Strategic Role of HRM
Job Analysis	Team Building
Job Design	Union Avoidance
Management Development	Work and Family Issues
Motivation	Workteams
Performance Appraisal/Management	
Recruitment	*Personal HR Competencies*
Selection	Formal Communications
Separation Process/Organization Exit	Interpersonal Communication
Succession Planning	Integrity
Training	Managing Relationships
	Problem Solving
	Technological Ability

The 47 competencies are presented in the following categories: Classical IR, Traditional HR, New HR, and Personal HR/IR competencies. Recognizing that it is beyond the scope of this article to include all possible competencies needed by future HR/IR practitioners, the competencies included represent those most frequently mentioned in the scholarly literature reviewed, and based on the authors' collective 20+ years of HR/IR-related applied and research experience. The authors independently assigned the competencies to one of the four categories, and agreed on 44 of the 47 competencies (93.61%). Total agreement/consensus was reached after discussion about the appropriate categorization of the three discrepant competencies.

HR/IR Practitioner Interview Results

Table 2 summarizes the results of the HR/IR practitioner interviews. Twelve HR/IR practitioners participated in the interviews.

The results suggest that those HR/IR practitioners responding generally concur with the competencies referenced in the scholarly literature by providing a rating of 3 or higher, and believed the listing was representative of the critical competencies needed by new HR/IR practitioners. Seven of those competencies were rated low in importance (less than 3.0 on a 5-point Likert scale): benefits/health care, business process reengineering, collective bargaining, employee safety and health, job analysis, labor economics, and union avoidance. This is consistent with the general trend of emphasizing HR and de-emphasizing IR (Lewin & Kaufman, 1999; Way, 1996), outsourcing of certain administrative HR functions, and organizations providing company-specific training rather than expecting entry-level HR/IR practitioners to already be proficient in certain areas upon hiring. The descending rank ordering of the importance current HR/IR practitioners placed on each competency suggests that personal competencies are among the most important. This might partially explain the alleged gap between what is covered in academic programs and what is desired/expected by businesses. Academic programs tend to focus on functional HR/IR competencies, while some organizations want new hires in HR/IR to possess certain personal HR/IR competencies and the organization can provide training (internal or external) where some functional deficiencies may exist (e.g., Gonzales, Ellis, Riffel & Yager, 1999; Stockman, 1999).

Content Analysis Results of Program Catalog/Curricula and Program Director Survey Results

The total number of programs included in the program catalog/curricula review was 71. Of those programs, 23 (32.4%) offered bachelor's degrees, 32 (45.1%)

Table 2. Results of HR/IR Practitioner Interviews ($n = 12$)

HR/IR Competency	Competency Type	Mean	SD
Integrity	Personal	4.92	0.29
Interpersonal Communication	Personal	4.75	0.45
Managing Relationships	Personal	4.58	0.67
Recruitment	Traditional HR	4.58	0.51
Managing Change	New HR	4.50	0.80
Problem Solving	Personal	4.50	0.67
Communications	Traditional HR	4.42	0.79
General Business Management	New HR	4.33	0.98
Laws/Legal Issues Affecting HR	Classical IR	4.33	0.78
Selection	Traditional HR	4.33	0.65
Strategic Role of HRM	New HR	4.25	1.14
Managing Diversity/Cultural Diversity	New HR	4.17	0.94
Team Building	New HR	4.08	0.79
Management Development	Traditional HR	4.00	0.85
Performance Appraisal/Management	Traditional HR	4.00	0.74
Motivation	New HR	3.92	1.38
Ethics	New HR	3.92	1.08
Quality of Worklife	New HR	3.83	1.19
Facilitation/Internal Consulting	New HR	3.83	1.11
Work and Family Issues	New HR	3.83	1.03
Technological Abilities	Personal	3.83	0.83
Organizational Assessment	New HR	3.67	0.89
Training	Traditional HR	3.67	0.65
Evaluating HRM Function	New HR	3.58	1.31
Downsizing	New HR	3.58	1.08
HR Planning	Traditional HR	3.58	1.00
Employee Involvement	New HR	3.58	0.79
Discipline	Classical IR	3.50	1.00
Separation Process/Organization Exit	Traditional HR	3.50	1.00
Compensation	Traditional HR	3.50	0.90
Formal Communications	Personal	3.50	0.90
Workteams	New HR	3.50	0.52
Succession Planning	Traditional HR	3.33	1.37
Career Planning	Traditional HR	3.33	1.30
Global HRM	New HR	3.33	1.23
Changing Employment Contracts	New HR	3.33	1.15
Counseling//EAPs	Traditional HR	3.25	0.75
Labor Relations	Classical IR	3.08	0.67
HR Information Systems	New HR	3.00	1.21
Job Design	Traditional HR	3.00	1.04
Job Analysis	Traditional HR	2.92	0.79
Union Avoidance	New HR	2.75	0.97
Employee Safety and Health	Classical IR	2.58	1.31
Labor Economics	Classical IR	2.50	1.09
Business Process Reengineering	New HR	2.42	1.08
Collective Bargaining	Classical IR	2.42	0.79
Benefits/Health Care	Traditional HR	2.33	0.98

offered master's, and 16 (22.5%) offered MBAs with a concentration in HR/IR. The MBA and master's degree were evaluated separately based on the fact that the MBA is a general, professional degree, while the masters is a specialized degree. Based on the title of the program, the types of program offered were 39 (54.9%) HR, 18 (25.4%) IR, and 14 (19.7%) HR/IR combination or other title. Although, several doctoral programs offer HR/IR specialties, these were excluded from the present review because the primary objective of most HR/IR doctoral programs is to develop academicians (e.g., teachers, researchers) rather than practitioners.

The 41 program directors responding to the survey represented a range of program and degree types. In summary, 11 offered bachelor's degrees, 19 offered masters, 8 offered MBAs with HR/IR concentrations, 2 did not indicate type of degree, and 1 reported both bachelor and masters. The type of program offerings were 15 HR, 18 IR, 6 offered either both HR and IR, or an HR/IR combination, and 2 did not report type of program offered. The results are presented in aggregate due to the sample size.

Table 3 provides a summary of the catalog/curricula review and program director survey results for the classical IR, traditional HR, and new HR competencies. The personal HR/IR competencies are summarized in Table 4 due to the different questions asked regarding competency evaluation versus coverage. Specifically, the program directors were asked if the program evaluated (actually assessed) the future HR/IR practitioner on the personal competencies versus covered the competency via lecture, classroom discussion, etc. The results for the catalog/curricula review and program director survey are presented together to provide an accurate picture of competency coverage. In some cases, the brochure/catalog may not have been explicit enough to determine whether the competency was covered. As previously mentioned, the authors primarily relied on information in the program catalog (e.g., course titles and descriptions, descriptions of topics covered in speakers series) to determine whether a competency was covered. Programs should attempt to clearly articulate in their respective brochures/catalogs what competencies are covered for purposes of recruiting new students, as well as showcasing their program to prospective employers. This may curtail some of the allegations that HR/IR program offerings are not meeting industry needs. What follows is a discussion of the results for each category of competencies.

Of the five Classical IR competencies, the program director surveys revealed that most programs did cover the competencies. The competencies were not necessarily required courses or electives, which would explain why the results were inconsistent between the survey and the catalog review. For example, only one program catalog explicitly stated a course on Discipline was offered.

Table 3. Results of Program Brochure/Catalog Review and Program Director Survey

	Overall Coverage	Program Brochure/Catalog Review							Reqd. Course	Program Director Response Frequency				
		Program Type*			Degree Type*					Elective	Covered in Reqd.	Covered Elective	Other	Not Covered
		HR	IR	HR/IR	BS/BA	Masters	MBA							
Classical IR														
Collective Bargaining	40 (56%)	14	16	10	12	25	3		19	15	7	4	0	1
Discipline	1 (1%)	1	0	0	0	0	1		4	2	25	11	0	1
Labor Economics	31 (44%)	7	13	11	4	24	3		17	11	2	6	0	3
Labor Relations	50 (70%)	26	13	11	17	26	7		18	13	6	5	0	2
Laws/Legal Issues Affecting HR	54 (76%)	26	16	12	15	28	11		17	13	11	5	0	0
Traditional HR														
Benefits/Health Care	22 (31%)	9	4	9	3	16	3		4	13	16	9	1	2
Career Planning	12 (17%)	7	3	2	3	7	2		2	3	17	12	2	7
Communications	11 (16%)	9	1	1	5	4	2		6	5	15	11	0	7
Compensation	51 (72%)	26	12	13	16	25	10		18	20	7	2	0	0
Counseling/EAPs	3 (4%)	2	0	1	0	2	1		1	6	17	12	0	5
Employee Safety and Health	16 (23%)	5	7	4	5	9	2		4	9	18	8	0	4
HR Planning	16 (23%)	5	5	6	4	9	3		5	7	24	7	0	2
Job Analysis	5 (7%)	3	2	0	2	2	1		3	2	27	11	0	1
Job Design	4 (6%)	2	1	1	0	3	1		2	1	29	10	0	2

Are We Properly Training Future HR/IR Practitioners? A Review of the Curricula   173

Table 3. (Continued)

	Overall Coverage	Program Brochure/Catalog Review							Reqd. Course	Program Director			Response Frequency		
		Program Type*			Degree Type*										
		HR	IR	HR/IR	BS/BA	Masters	MBA			Elective	Covered in Reqd.	Covered Elective	Other	Not Covered	
Classical IR															
Management Development	31 (44%)	19	5	7	11	14	6		7	6	16	12	1	3	
Motivation	15 (21%)	7	2	6	4	6	5		1	7	26	10	2	0	
Performance Appraisal/Management	17 (24%)	9	4	4	6	8	3		7	6	24	11	1	0	
Recruitment	32 (45%)	19	6	7	9	16	7		9	3	26	11	0	0	
Selection	27 (38%)	16	5	6	9	14	4		10	6	21	10	1	0	
Separation Process/Organization Exit	0 (0%)	0	0	0	0	0	0		2	1	24	12	1	4	
Succession Planning	1 (1%)	0	1	0	1	0	0		2	1	20	13	0	6	
Training	31 (44%)	14	8	9	8	19	4		3	15	14	9	0	2	
New HR															
Business Process Reengineering	0 (0%)	0	0	0	0	0	0		1	2	11	8	1	19	
Changing Employment Contracts	0 (0%)	0	0	0	0	0	0		1	2	30	8	0	2	
Downsizing	0 (0%)	0	0	0	0	0	0		2	1	27	10	0	4	
Employee Involvement	4 (6%)	2	1	1	0	3	1		2	4	29	8	0	0	
Ethics	14 (20%)	10	3	1	3	6	5		5	6	20	10	1	2	
Evaluating HRM Function	8 (11%)	3	2	3	0	7	1		5	2	24	9	0	1	

Classical IR	Overall Coverage	Program Type*			Degree Type*			Reqd. Course	Elective	Program Director Covered in Reqd.	Response Frequency Covered Elective	Other	Not Covered
		HR	IR	HR/IR	BS/BA	Masters	MBA						
Facilitation/Internal Consulting	9 (13%)	8	0	1	1	8	0	3	5	8	11	1	12
General Business Management	38 (54%)	25	7	6	18	12	8	16	2	7	3	0	11
Global HRM	23 (68%)	10	5	8	4	16	3	5	16	16	8	1	0
HR Information Systems	15 (21%)	2	6	7	3	11	1	5	13	10	8	0	6
Managing Change	25 (35%)	14	4	7	4	14	7	3	6	22	9	0	2
Managing Diversity/Cultural Diversity	29 (41%)	13	7	9	6	19	4	0	10	26	9	0	2
Organizational Assessment	10 (14%)	6	0	4	2	6	2	3	2	15	11	0	6
Quality of Worklife	5 (7%)	0	2	3	1	3	1	2	7	24	8	0	2
Strategic Role of HRM	25 (35%)	16	4	5	5	15	5	7	8	23	8	1	0
Team Building	5 (7%)	2	1	2	1	2	2	4	7	20	12	0	0
Union Avoidance	1 (1%)	1	0	0	1	0	0	0	1	11	8	0	22
Work and Family Issues	1 (1%)	0	0	1	0	1	0	4	1	23	17	0	0
Workteams	23 (32%)	11	6	6	3	12	8	3	6	22	14	0	0

*Total programs in Brochure/Catalog Review: $N = 71$.
Programs by Program Type: HR ($N = 39$), IR ($N = 18$), HR/IR ($N = 14$).
Programs by Degree Type: Bachelor ($N = 23$), Masters ($N = 32$), MBA ($N = 16$).
Total programs completing the Program Director Survey: $N = 41$. Total responses for each competency may exceed 41 due to respondents selecting multiple response options (e.g., a required course and covered in an elective).

On the other hand, only one program indicated on their survey that discipline was not covered in either a required course or elective. This example demonstrates that a gap exists between what is marketed in the program catalog and what is actually covered in the programs.

Of the 17 Traditional HR competencies, the program catalogs suggested that only six were covered by at least 25% of the program catalogs reviewed and only one (i.e., compensation) of those was covered by at least 50% of the programs. During the catalog review, covered was defined as a specific course mentioned in the brochure, and not specific topics covered within a course. The survey administered to the program directors sought information at the topic level. As shown in Table 3, the program director surveys indicated that certain programs did not cover 12 of the 17 competencies at all. Two of the traditional HR competencies (i.e., career planning and communications) were not covered by seven of the 41 programs (17%), while six programs (15%) did not address succession planning. It did appear that the majority of the competencies were at least a topic discussed in a required course.

The New HR competencies were infrequently mentioned in the catalogs, with only two of the 19 competencies (i.e., general business management and global HRM) being mentioned in more than 50% of the catalogs. Business process reengineering, changing nature of employment contracts, and downsizing were not mentioned in any of the catalogs. These competencies may be covered in business schools, given AACSB requirements regarding a core set of business knowledge, but were not specifically mentioned in the program catalog/brochure. Thirteen of the 19 competencies were not being covered by at least one program as indicated by the program director. The three most often cited as not being covered were union avoidance, not covered by 22 programs, facilitation/internal consulting (not covered by 12 programs), and general business management (11 programs). Again, most of these competencies are covered as part of a required course rather than an entire course dedicated to the topic.

Unfortunately, the six personal HR competencies are not receiving much attention based on review of the program catalogs and the program directors. Technological abilities (e.g., use of spreadsheets, e-mail) and formal communication (e.g., presentations, written) received the greatest coverage as determined by the content analysis of the catalogs, yet, were covered by less than 40% of the programs. The other four personal HR competencies are covered by less than 10% of the programs reviewed. Survey respondents indicated that integrity and managing relationships were frequently evaluated as part of course; however, most programs did not evaluate the majority of the personal HR competencies. Different criteria were used in assessing the competencies covered in the program catalog, which meant a specific course mentioned in

Table 4. Results of Program Brochure/Catalog and Program Director Survey for Personal Competencies

Personal HR/IR Competencies	Program Brochure/Catalog Review						Program Director Response Frequency				
	Overall Coverage	Program Type*			Degree Type*		Competency Evaluated in …				Not Evaluated
		HR	IR	HR/IR	Bachelors	Masters	MBA	Course	Seminar	Other	
Formal Communications	15 (21%)	12	1	2	7	4	4	4	0	8	30
Interpersonal Communication	3 (4%)	3	0	0	1	1	1	10	0	4	27
Integrity	0 (0%)	0	0	0	0	0	0	26	0	0	7
Managing Relationships	6 (9%)	4	1	1	3	2	1	20	0	0	14
Problem Solving	2 (3%)	0	2	0	0	2	0	7	0	5	29
Technological Abilities	27 (38%)	19	3	5	7	10	10	12	0	3	23

*Total programs in Brochure/Catalog Review: $N = 71$. Programs by Program Type: HR ($N = 39$), IR ($N = 18$), HR/IR ($N = 14$). Programs by Degree Type: Bachelor ($N=23$), Masters ($N=32$), MBA ($N=16$). Total programs completing the Program Director Survey: $N = 41$.

brochure, while evaluate in the program director survey was defined as an assessment conducted on the student's competency rather than a discussion of the competency. The limited coverage was disappointing given that these personal competencies complement the functional HR/IR competencies needed to yield success in the profession. These findings, however, are consistent with previous research that suggests programs are more content focused than skills focused (Hansen et al., 1996).

There were some findings that warrant particular attention. There were two New HR competencies that were not a required course in any program: managing diversity/cultural diversity and union avoidance. Given the demographic shift in the workplace (e.g., more women, older workers, more persons of color) (James, 1997) and the need for future HR/IR practitioners to develop/modify systems to address the concerns of a changing workforce, one might expect such a required course included in the curriculum. Further, several of the new HR competencies (e. g., facilitation/internal consulting) were not covered by a large number of programs. This was also surprising given the requirements of many HR/IR roles as revealed in the literature review on HR/IR competencies and based on the importance given these competencies by the HR/IR practitioners (see Tables 1 and 2). Academic programs may be reluctant to address 'soft skills' and are more comfortable teaching functional, 'hard skills' in their areas of expertise. As indicated by the program director's response to items on the survey, programs also do not seem to utilize other strategies (e.g., offering special seminars, encouraging students to pursue courses outside program) to ensure competencies are developed by future HR/IR practitioners (see Table 4).

The types of instructional methods employed in the programs were included in Section III of the survey. Lecture was used, on average, 48%, while case study and group projects were employed 22% and 25%, respectively. The remaining 5% of the time instructors utilized various instructional methods such as class discussions, simulations, role play, presentations, etc. Although lecture is the leading instructional method, it is encouraging to see instructors broadening their approach and facilitating the development of cooperative learning and team skills (Magney, 1996). The use of the Internet was not specifically mentioned by any of the respondents, but is an excellent resource for instructors. Hannah (1996) discussed potential HR/IR teaching applications on the Internet and listed over 30 Internet discussion listservs that would allow students to 'experience' the real, day-to-day issues facing HR/IR practitioners. Instructors may be reluctant to 'venturing into this unfamiliar domain' (Hannah, 1996, p. 516), such as the World Wide Web and other technological advances (e.g., listservs, on-line discussion groups), in the classroom due to their comfort with traditional techniques and are uncertain about the effects the Internet may have on learning and teaching quality.

Thirty-four of the 41 programs indicated that internships were available, however, only two stated that internships were a program requirement. This tends to support the previous research in this area by Way (1996), who suggested that requiring internships is a downward trend with most programs making it optional. This consistency was found with the sample size and diversity of programs responding.

The majority of the respondents (23 of the 41) indicated that they had revised their curriculum since 1998. Further, all programs responding with the exception of two had updated their curriculum within the last five years. The reasons given for curriculum revisions ranged from program consolidations to addressing professional demands to developing strategic competencies, from matching faculty interests to accreditation purposes and semester conversions. Adler and Lawler (1999) present an excellent case study regarding the offering of a strategic human resource management MBA concentration at the University of Southern California. Also, Heneman (1999) describes Ohio State University's MLHR program and its shift toward emphasizing analytical skills. As revisions to the curricula are made, some consideration should be given to the 'customers' of the program to ensure that stakeholder concerns are incorporated in the decision making process.

The final section asked for accessibility to professional organizations. Consistent with previous research (Way, 1996), the Society of Human Resource Management (SHRM) was the most often reported for having a student (35 of 41 respondents) and local (33 of 41) professional chapters available to the students. Accessibility to such organizations is important for future HR/IR practitioners to increase his or her social capital (e.g., Nahapiet & Ghoshal, 1998) by beginning to network, developing or enhancing professionalism and relationship skills, and remaining current on issues facing organizations that may not be covered within their respective programs.

CONCLUSION

If the majority of the programs were addressing the vast majority of the HR/IR competencies, the conclusion of this study would be that HR/IR programs are doing an excellent job of training future HR/IR practitioners. On the other hand, if only a few programs were developing a few of the competencies, we would conclude that future HR/IR practitioners were being inadequately prepared for their roles. Based on the results of this study neither of these extremes tends to be the case. The results of this study suggest that HR/IR programs are doing an adequate job at developing certain HR/IR competencies, however, they could place more emphasis on personal HR/IR competencies.

Based on the programs included in this review, Classical IR competencies, although limited in number due to an emphasis on HR topics and a de-emphasis on IR topics in HR/IR programs (e.g., Lewin & Kaufman, 1999), are being addressed sufficiently. This was clearly supported by both review of the catalog/curricula and survey responses from the program directors.

According to the program directors, and to a lesser extent the catalog/curricula review, Traditional HR competencies are covered by the majority of the programs. Some competencies (e.g., career planning, succession planning) may be emphasized less due to the dynamic business environment and the paradigm shift in the careers literature (e.g., Arthur & Rousseau, 1996) that suggests that individuals are assuming greater responsibility for their career management rather than relying on organizations.

Most of the New HR competencies are covered as part of a required course as highlighted by the program director survey. However, some of these increasingly important competencies (e.g., facilitation/internal consulting, general business management) are not covered by several programs. Organizations, particularly large ones, expect new HR/IR practitioners to perform traditional tasks and serve in the capacity of a strategic business partner to assist the organization in achieving its goals and objectives.

Although the Personal HR/IR competencies were among the most important competencies current HR/IR practitioners thought future HR/IR practitioners should possess, these competencies were rarely evaluated by programs included in this review. This is not surprising given academe's traditional focus on functional competencies (e.g., Hansen et al., 1996). However, programs may better serve its constituencies (e.g., students, organizations, society) by placing more emphasis on the development of Personal HR/IR competencies.

The present study has some limitations. A greater number of program responses in terms of the catalog/brochure review and program director survey could have yielded additional insights. Many programs are referring applicants to Internet web pages rather than mailing information, so this could have affected our response rate. Future researchers should also evaluate program information on the World Wide Web. Also, the quality of the catalogs and/or lack of course listings/descriptions hampered our ability to objectively state whether the competency was addressed or not. As previously mentioned, programs should ensure their collateral, or printed materials, accurately reflect the competencies emphasized and the unique aspects of their program offerings. Program directors may have been reluctant to participate in the study, or were not available during the time the survey was administered. It may have been useful to attempt to include more IR competencies in the listing of competencies reviewed such as arbitration, alternative dispute/ conflict resolution and negotiation. These were frequently mentioned in the program catalogs reviewed, but were mentioned infrequently in the scholarly literature reviewed to identify HR/IR competencies. In order to gain greater support for the competencies reviewed a larger number of HR/IR practitioners should have been interviewed.

Limitations not withstanding, the current study further substantiates previous research (e.g., Hansen et al., 1996; Way, 1996) and shows that the HR/IR programs are, at best, training future HR/IR practitioners in an adequate manner. The programs could still be more progressive in ensuring that the non-traditional, functional HR competencies, and especially the personal HR competencies, are developed. Future researchers should continue to assess the effectiveness of these programs, and consider employing longitudinal methodologies to identify trends within specific programs. Also, future research should attempt to minimize the limitations noted in this and other prior research.

REFERENCES

Adler, P. S., & Lawler, E. E., III (1999). Who needs MBAs in HR? USC's strategic human resource management MBA concentration. *Human Resource Management, 38,* 125–130.

Arthur, M. B., & Rousseau, D. M. (1996). *The boundaryless career: A new employment principle for a new organizational era.* New York: Oxford University Press.

Exclusive rankings: Schools of business (1999, March 29). *U.S. News & World Report, 86.*

Gonzales, B., Ellis, Y. M., Riffel, P. J., & Yager, D. (1999). Training at IBM's human resource service center: Linking people, technology, and HR processes. *Human Resource Management, 38,* 135–142.

Hannah, R. L. (1996). Teaching resources and patterns of association on the net. *Labor Law Journal, 47,* 516–523.

Hansen, W. L., Berkley, R. A., Kaplan, D. M., Qiang-Sheng, Y., Craig, C. J., Fitzpatrick, J. A., Seiler, M. R., Denby, D. A., Gheis, P., Ruelle, D. J., & Voss, L. A. (1996). Needed skills for human resource professionals: A pilot study. *Labor Law Journal, 47,* 524–534.

Heneman, R. L. (1999). Emphasizing analytical skills in HR graduate education: The Ohio State University MLHR program. *Human Resource Management, 38,* 131–134.

James, R. (1997). Human resource megatrends. *Human Resource Management, 36,* 453–463.

Kaufman, B. E. (1994). What companies want from HR graduates. *HRMagazine, 39*(9), 84–86.

Kaufman, B. E. (1996). Transformation of the corporate HR/IR function: Implications for university programs. *Labor Law Journal, 47,* 540–548.

Kaufman, B. E. (1999). Evolution and current status of university HR programs. *Human Resource Management, 38,* 103–110.

Keller, D. A., & Campbell, J. F. (1992). Building human resource capability. *Human Resource Management, 31,* 109–126.

Kochanski, J. T. (Special Guest Ed.) (1996). Human resource competencies [Special issue]. *Human Resource Management, 35*(1).

Lewin, D., & Kaufman, B. E. (1999). The HR/IR teaching conference. *Human Resource Management, 38,* 165–170.

Magney, J. (1996). Teamwork and the need for cooperative learning. *Labor Law Journal, 47,* 564–570.

Milkovich, G. T., & Boudreau, J. W. (1997). *Human resource management.* Chicago: Irwin.

Nahapiet, J., & Ghoshal, S. (1998). Social capital, intellectual capital, and the organizational advantage. *Academy of Management Review, 23,* 242–266.

Peterson's guide to MBA programs 1999: A comprehensive directory of graduate business education at U.S., Canadian, and select international business schools (1998). Princeton, NJ: Peterson's.

Reingold, J. (1998, October 19). Special report: The best B-schools. *BusinessWeek,* 87–92.

Schoonover, S. (1998). *Human resource competencies for the year 2000: The wake-up call.* Alexandria, VA: Society of Human Resource Management.

Stockman, J. E. (1999). Building a quality HR organization at GE. *Human Resource Management, 38,* 143–146.

Strauss, G., & Whitfield, K. (1998). Research methods in industrial relations. In: K. Whitfield & G. Strauss (Eds.), *Researching the World of Work: Strategies and Methods in Studying Industrial Relations,* (pp. 5–30). Ithaca, NY: ILR Press.

Ulrich, D. (1997a). Future directions of human resource management [Special issue]. *Human Resource Management, 36*(1).

Ulrich, D. (1997b). *Human resource champions: The next agenda for adding value and delivering results.* Boston: Harvard Business School Press.

Ulrich, D. (1998). A new mandate for human resources. *Harvard Business Review,* January – February, 124–134.

Ulrich, D., Brockbank, W., Yeung, A. K., & Lake, D. G. (1995). Human resource competencies: An empirical assessment. *Human Resource Management, 34,* 473–495.

Way, P. K. (1996). A survey of curricula of IR/HR master's programs: Common features, new directions. *Labor Law Journal, 47,* 535–539.

Weiss, A. (1997). Slogging toward the millennium. *Training, 34*(4), 51–54.

EXECUTIVE INSIGHTS INTO HR PRACTICES AND EDUCATION

Cristina M. Giannantonio and Amy E. Hurley

ABSTRACT

Over 1,100 Human Resource executives responded to a survey concerning their perceptions of the HR issues their companies are facing; the role of HR in their organization; the skills HR employees should possess; and the substantive HR knowledge that graduates of HR programs should be able to demonstrate. Results suggest the most important issue facing HR executives today is managing change. Executives felt it was extremely important for HR professionals to be able to create a recruitment program in today's labor market. The results of this research provide several implications for the design and the delivery of HR educational programs.

INTRODUCTION

The start of the new millennium provides an opportune time for academics to reflect on the past, present, and future of the field of Human Resource Management. As Human Resource educators, we must assess whether we are meeting the needs of this rapidly changing profession (Dyer, 1999). While there is little doubt that the field of HR has experienced dramatic change during the past several years (Kaufman, 1996), it is less certain which of these changes are the most important to HR practitioners.

Since these changes encompass several dimensions, research is needed which asks HR executives: (1) What are the HR issues of most concern to your organization? (2) What role does the HR department play in your organization? (3) What are the most important skills that HR employees and graduates should possess? (4) What are the most important substantive HR knowledge activities that HR graduate students should be able to perform? The answers to these questions have important implications for both practitioners and educators. Thus, these are the major research questions addressed in this study. The importance of each of these research questions is discussed in the literature review.

LITERATURE REVIEW

The field of Human Resource Management has undergone dramatic changes in the last fifty years (Dyer, 1999; Rothstein, 1999). Among the most important changes are the increasing emphasis on HR as a business partner; a long run strategic perspective; the impact of new technology, and outsourcing (Kaufman, 1996). Two aspects of this change are especially noteworthy. First, HR professionals face an increasingly complex set of issues in the daily practice of their jobs (Kemske, 1998; Sherman, Bohlander & Snell, 1998). Second, the role that HR departments play in organizations has shifted from a purely administrative function to one that includes becoming a strategic partner concerned with adding value to the organization (Kaufman, 1999; Schuler, 1998).

These changes have important implications for educators preparing students to work in the field of HR (Kaufman, 1996). At one level, these changes define the skill sets that HR professionals need to possess if they are to be successful in their chosen field. On another level, these changes have direct implications for the substantive knowledge that graduates of HR programs must master if they are to add value to their HR departments as well as their organizations (Rothstein, 1999). This study examines previous research in four areas of Human Resources practice and education.

HR Issues
A diverse set of HR issues comprises both the internal and the external environments facing HR departments and organizations (Fisher, Schoenfeldt & Shaw, 1999; Sherman, Bohlander & Snell, 1998). The covers of business journals and the headlines of newspapers would suggest that the sheer volume of HR issues confronting managers on a daily basis is overwhelming. HR textbooks written in the late nineties include chapters, topics, and terms that did not exist a decade earlier (Mondy & Noe, 1996).

The first chapter of virtually every HR textbook notes that HR managers must deal with several challenges if their HR departments are to contribute to organizational effectiveness (Sherman, Bohlander & Snell, 1998; Gomez-Mejia, Balkin & Cardy, 1998; Noe, Hollenbeck, Gerhart & Wright, 2000). Among the most commonly cited challenges are rapid change, work force diversity, skill shortages, downsizing, technology, and outsourcing. While these challenges are widely accepted and acknowledged, little research has focused on the most important issues that HR managers believe they confront in the daily practice of their jobs.

A study conducted by Workforce magazine suggested six areas that will be of concern to HR professionals in the first decade of the new century, but did not directly survey HR executives. These areas include workplace flexibility, global business, work and society, workforce development, the definition of jobs, and the strategic role of HR (Kemske, 1998). Schoonover (1998) identified several key challenges facing the HR community. His list includes the development of business partnerships, improved integration across functional, business and global boundaries, accomplishment of business objectives in a challenging operating environment, development of competent HR professionals, and management of on-going, rapidly evolving change.

Although there is agreement that HR managers must deal with numerous issues, little research has focused on the most important issues that HR practitioners face. Research is needed which specifically surveys HR managers about their perceptions regarding which issues are most important. Identifying the most salient issues allows HR educators to address these topics in their classes; offer electives and special topics courses on these subjects; and insures that HR curricula remain current.

HR Roles

Much has been written about the 'new HR manager' and the role that he or she will play in organizations (Dyer, 1999; Kemske, 1998). There is ample evidence that the role of HR departments has changed over the last half of the century (Kaufman, 1996, 1999). The evolution of the IR/HR department's role has included keeping records, advocating employees' rights, insuring legal compliance, facilitating change, and partnering strategically with top management (Kaufman, 1999).

Current perspectives suggest that the HR department is responsible for providing advice and counsel, engaging in service activities, policy formulation and implementation, and employee advocacy (Sherman, Bohlander & Snell, 1998). Schoonover (1998) sees HR professionals fulfilling three roles: HR product and service specialists, HR generalists, and HR strategists. Predictions regarding the future role of HR in organizations suggest that HR professionals will become leaders in affecting organizational performance and will be held accountable for obtaining a competitive advantage through HR (Hunter, 1999; Kempske, 1998).

One way that HR can help organizations obtain a competitive advantage is to offer training programs that are designed to create intellectual capital (Noe, Hollenbeck, Gerhart & Wright, 2000). This type of training is consistent with the idea of creating a learning organization. A learning organization is an organization that is continually expanding its capacity to create its future (Senge, 1990). In his book *The Fifth Discipline,* Senge (1990) suggests that in order for companies to become learning organizations, HR professionals must become coaches and mentors rather than problem solvers. That is, instead of solving the problem for the line manager, the HR professional helps the manager to develop personal skills which will ultimately allow him to solve the problem himself. Senge's ideas suggest yet another role for HR departments to play in their organizations.

Where do HR departments fall along this evolutionary path? Is everyone practicing the 'new HR', or are some departments fulfilling traditional industrial relations/personnel functions in their organizations? These different roles require different skills and substantive knowledge from practitioners. Identifying the roles that HR departments fulfill in organizations, will allow HR educators to assess whether their programs are meeting the substantive needs of the students who work in those departments.

HR Skills
The popular press has long noted the inadequacy of employees' formal training and the skills deficiencies of the American workforce (Rau, 1995). Managers at all levels complain that their recent hires need 'more skills' and could be better prepared for their jobs (Goldberg, 1996). A large body of research has examined HR skills. Kaufman (1996) identified the major changes impacting the field of HR/IR and assessed how these changes influenced the job skills and competencies that companies desire. His research suggests that HR/IR professionals will need management and leadership skills; consulting, advising, and negotiating skills; analytical skills; quality and organizational change skills; computer and information technology skills; and oral and written communication skills.

Hansen and his colleagues (1996) surveyed alumni of the University of Wisconsin's Industrial Relations Research Institute about their perceptions of the skills needed by entry level HR practitioners. After a careful review of the literature, they developed a list of twenty key skills that they believe employers desire in new HR hires. Employers rated each of these skills using a four-point scale. Among the most important skills identified were written communication, active listening, oral communication, decision making, and analytical skills. The study also sought to identify perceived gaps between employers' desires and the training of HR/IR graduate students at one educational institution.

Additional research is needed to assess whether the skills gap experienced by much of corporate America (Rau, 1995), is also occurring within the HR profession. Gathering executives' perceptions of the most important skills for HR professionals and graduates of HR programs is the first step in identifying whether a skills gap exists in HR.

Substantive HR Knowledge
While previous research has examined employer perceptions of the most important skills HR graduates should possess, less research has focused on what it is that graduates of HR programs should know how 'to do' and what types of knowledge they should possess. Hansen and his colleagues (1996) divide knowledge into two categories, substantive and enabling. Substantive knowledge is comprised of 'the subject matter of a field or discipline' while 'enabling knowledge represents the skills individuals possess that allow them to apply their substantive knowledge . . . ' (Hansen, et al., 1996: 524). In HR, an example of substantive knowledge would be write a job description; and an example of enabling knowledge would be analytical skills.

The authors note that "because academic programs focus primarily on subject matter knowledge, students often enter the job market without well developed skills to complement their content knowledge" (Hansen, et al., 1996: 524). In other words they found that HR programs were focusing on substantive knowledge and that students were not obtaining enabling knowledge. Using their terminology, the skills studies described previously have focused on employers' preferences regarding the types of enabling knowledge that HR graduates should possess. Is there a common set of substantive HR knowledge that employers expect new hires to possess? A few studies have assessed the issue of substantive knowledge and they are summarized below.

Way conducted a content analysis of the curricula of IR/HR programs in 1996. He analyzed the curricula of 39 master's programs with specific emphases in either IR or HR. He found that the number of HR programs was increasing while the number of IR programs had decreased. While he found that programs were offering new courses that reflect the changes experienced in the professional environment of IR/HR, such courses were not consistently offered across programs.

Van Eynde and Tucker (1997: 397) asked, "What is a high quality human resource management curriculum from the standpoint of organizations who employ our students?". Using the Delphi technique, twenty-four senior level

HR executives rated the importance of several dozen HR curriculum areas (e.g. compensation, selection, global HRM). The results of their research suggest that HR executives feel that the major topics covered in HR curricula are appropriate. Executives reacted to broad curriculum content areas, not specific substantive HR knowledge activities. No other research was identified which directly assessed HR executives' perspectives on the most important substantive HR knowledge that graduates of HR programs should possess.

Executives' perspectives on substantive HR knowledge could provide a wealth of information to HR program administrators regarding the design of their courses and curricula. HR educators might learn whether some HR functional areas are considered more critical than others and whether graduates should be able to perform more traditional Industrial Relations/Personnel activities or more contemporary Human Resources activities.

This chapter provides evidence of how we will answer these questions by directly surveying HR executives about several aspects of HR practice and education. Executives' insights were gathered regarding the HR issues their companies are facing; the role of HR in their organization; the necessary skills HR employees should possess; and the substantive HR knowledge activities that graduates of HR programs should be able to demonstrate.[1]

METHODS

Survey Design

The purpose of the present study was to directly assess executives' perceptions of several aspects of HR practice and education. A large scale, national study was conducted to address these issues. The survey consisted of five sections: issues, roles, skills, substantive HR knowledge, and background information. To compile the items contained in each section of the survey, a literature search was conducted to identify items used in past research. Recognizing the possible influence of individual, organizational, and industry level factors, three control variables were explored: managerial level, company size, and industry sector (Schneider, 1999).

The first section of the survey asked executives to rate 41 HR issues (e.g. managing change, reverse discrimination, and recruitment) according to how concerned they were with this issue on a scale from 1 to 4, with 1 being 'no concern' and 4 being 'major concern'. The list of issues included items generated from a review of HRM textbooks (Sherman, Bohlander & Snell, 1998; Gomez-Mejia, Balkin & Cardy, 1998; Schuler, 1998; Mondy & Noe, 1996) and research (Wright & Snell, 1991); as well as discussions with local HR executives about the most important issues they face on their jobs. Additional items were identified from the pilot study discussed below.

The second section of the survey included a list of 13 possible roles that HR departments could fulfill in organizations (e.g. internal consultant, strategic partner, and employee advocate). The roles included in this list were gathered from HRM textbooks (Sherman, Bohlander & Snell, 1998; Gomez-Mejia, Balkin & Cardy, 1998; Schuler, 1998) and research (Schoonover, 1998). Respondents were asked to indicate the extent their HR department fulfilled this role in their organization. Each role was rated on a scale of 1 to 4, with 1 being 'not at all' and 4 being 'to a major extent'.

The third section of the survey presented respondents with a list of 28 skills and asked them to rate how important it was for their HR employees to possess each skill. These skills represent traditional labor market skills (e.g. analytical skills, research skills, and communication skills); and are defined as enabling skills by Hansen, et al. (1996). The list of skills in this section included all of the skills used by Hansen, et al. (1996) in their research. Additional skills were included based on a review of the literature and empirical studies (Secretary's Committee on Achieving Necessary Skills, 1994; Kaufman, 1994; Carnevale et al., 1990). In order to replicate Hansen et al.'s (1996) work, respondents rated each skill on a scale of 1 to 4, with 1 being 'not important' and 4 being 'of major importance'. Respondents also were asked to identify the most important skill that graduates of master's level HR programs should possess.

The fourth section of the questionnaire provided respondents with a list of 20 specific HR activities representing substantive HR knowledge and asked them to rate how important it would be for a graduate of a master's level HR program to be able to perform each activity. These examples of substantive knowledge are very specific HR activities; they are not a list of HR courses or curriculum areas. They include items such as calculate absenteeism/turnover rates, conduct a wage survey, and validate a selection instrument. The items were gathered from a review of HRM textbooks (Sherman, Bohlander & Snell, 1998; Gomez-Mejia, Balkin & Cardy, 1998; Schuler, 1998) and previous research (Van Eynde & Tucker, 1997). The scale was identical to the one used for the skills section. In addition, the executives were asked to indicate whether they would be more likely to purchase or outsource each activity, rather than design it in-house.

The last section of the survey asked background information of the respondents. This included questions regarding the respondents' demographics and some information about their employment history with the firm. The respondents also answered questions regarding the companies they worked for such as what industry they operate in and the number of employees.

A pilot study of the survey was conducted on a regional sample of HR executives. Respondents were given the opportunity to list additional items in each section. For example, respondents were presented with a list of HR issues to rate and were provided with space to include other issues they felt were important. The survey was mailed to 48 members of a local Human Resource Executive Forum, comprised of high level HR executives who meet bi-monthly to discuss current issues and trends in the field of HR. Items that were consistently identified by the HR executives were added to the final survey.

Sample

Mailing lists were obtained from the National Society for Human Resource Management (SHRM); a local Executive Human Resource Forum; and the National Human Resource Association. All top and middle level executives in SHRM were surveyed ($N = 7372$). Their names were obtained from the SHRM mailing list. Members of a local Executive Human Resource Forum ($N = 48$) and the National Human Resource Association ($N = 241$) also received surveys. Surveys were mailed to a total of 7,661 HR executives throughout the United States; 1,109 were returned for a response rate of 16.8% (1017 from the SHRM, 16 from the Executive Human Resource Forum, and 76 from the NHRA).

Table 1 shows the available comparisons of respondents to non-respondents for gender, education, company size, and industry. Survey respondents ranged in age from 24 to 79, with a mean age of 45 years. Over 90% of the respondents were white. The average number of years of tenure with their firm was 6.7; and they had an average of 2 years of international work experience. Regarding level, 71% of the respondents were in upper management and 23% were in middle management. Over half of the respondents made between $50,000 to $100,000 in salary; 23% made less than $50,000 and 19% made over $100,000.

A profile of the companies that the respondents worked for revealed that the average number of years their companies had been in business was 46. Over half of them worked at company headquarters, while 20% worked at a single site and 18% were at a branch or a division of a larger company. The average amount of 1997 revenues reported was $540 million.

The respondents were very similar to the non-respondents on most characteristics. Compared with the participants in the study sample, a larger percentage of the non-respondents were female. The respondent sample included slightly more HR executives employed in agriculture, education, and manufacturing than the non-respondents and fewer HR executives employed in government, the medical field and the service industry. The respondents and non-respondents were virtually identical with respect to degrees attained and company size.

Table 1. Comparison of Study Respondents and Non-Respondents

Characteristic	Respondents	Non-Respondents
Gender		
Female	62%	66%
Male	38%	34%
Education		
Bachelor's Degree	44%	46%
Master's Degree	24%	24%
MBA	13%	12%
Other Degrees	19%	18%
Company Size		
<500 Employees	56%	58%
500–999 Employees	16%	15%
>1000 Employees	28%	27%
Industry		
Agriculture/Forestry/Fishing	0.8%	0.6%
Educational/Social Services	5.4%	4.4%
Finance/Insurance/Real Estate	11.7%	11.3%
Transportation/Public Utility	5.1%	5.0%
Construction	1.8%	1.2%
Government	2.6%	3.5%
Medical/Health Services	29.7%	31.5%
Wholesale/Retail	6.1%	6.0%
Services	12.1%	17.4%
Manufacturing	17.1%	14.9%
Other	7.6%	4.2%
N	1109	6552

Analyses

Responses were first analyzed for the entire sample as a whole. The analyses for skills, substantive HR knowledge, roles, and issues included calculating the grand mean and standard deviation of all items in each category of variables. To determine which items executives considered the most and least important, items were delineated into those which were more than 1 standard deviation above the grand mean and those items which were more than 1 standard deviation below the grand mean. To explore the effects of the three control variables (managerial level, company size, and industry sector) the data was split and T-tests were performed. Due to power issues, regression analyses were not performed (Cohen & Cohen, 1983). At the individual level, responses were compared for both upper and middle level HR professionals. At the company level, responses were compared for both small companies (under 500 employees) and large companies (over 500 employees). In addition to identifying the specific industry their firm operated in, respondents indicated if they worked in the service or manufacturing sector.

RESULTS[2]

HR Issues

Respondents were asked to rate 41 different HR issues according to how concerned they were with that issue. Table 2 presents the mean responses for the nine HR issues rated more than one standard deviation above the grand mean and the 10 HR issues rated more than one standard deviation below the grand mean (Mean = 2.46; SD = 0.40). Consistent with predictions from the popular press, rising health care costs and skill shortages also received high ratings of concern. All of the other issues that received high ratings represent the traditional 'outcome' variables that HR departments are held accountable

Table 2. Issues of Concern to HR Executives
1 Standard Deviation Above and Below the Grand Mean
(Mean = 2.46, SD = 0.40)

Issues	Mean Response
1 SD Above Mean	
Managing Change	3.39
Job Satisfaction	3.37
Loyalty & Commitment	3.31
Performance/Productivity	3.30
Skills Shortages	3.16
Rising Healthcare Costs	3.11
Turnover	3.07
Encouraging Innovation	2.98
Strategic HRM	2.96
1 SD Below Mean	
Age Discrimination	2.05
Outsourcing HR Services	2.00
Telecommuting	2.00
Internet Abuse	1.97
Global Competition	1.97
Downsizing	1.94
Elder Care	1.94
Reverse Discrimination	1.79
Immigrant Patterns	1.76
International Assignments	1.46

for in organizations including performance / productivity, job satisfaction, turnover, and loyalty and commitment. Issues which received the lowest ratings of concern include international assignments; immigrant patterns; reverse discrimination; elder care; downsizing; global competition, and Internet abuse.

HR Roles

Respondents were asked to indicate the extent their HR department fulfills each of several roles in their own company. Only one role, implementing HR strategies and programs was rated more than one standard deviation above the grand mean (Mean = 3.36; SD = 0.37). Two items, clerical/processing support and outsourcing HR programs, were rated more than one standard deviation below the grand mean. Other roles receiving high ratings were designing and evaluating HR strategies and programs; monitoring legal compliance; and supporting line management. These results suggest that HR departments are primarily designing, implementing, and evaluating HR programs in their organizations.

HR Skills

Table 3 presents the four skills HR executives felt their HR employees need to possess and which were rated at least one standard deviation above the grand mean and the three skills rated more than one standard deviation below the grand mean (Mean = 3.39; SD = 0.35). As might be expected, the single most important skill executives believe HR employees should possess is people skills. Three out of four of the most important skills reported were communication

Table 3. Skills for HR Professionals and Graduates of HR Programs
1 Standard Deviation Above and Below the Grand Mean
(Mean = 3.39, SD = 0.35)

1 SD Above Mean	1 SD Below Mean	Graduates of HR Programs
People Skills (3.89)	Financial Skills (2.68)	Active Listening
Active Listening (3.88)	Research Skills (2.81)	People Skills
Oral Skills (3.82)	Risk-Taking Skills (2.82)	Leadership Skills
Verbal Skills (3.75)		Customer Service Skills
		Thinking Skills
		Organizational Dynamic Skills
		Decision Making Skills
		Adaptability Skills
		Verbal Skills
		Analytical Skills

skills (e.g. active listening, oral and verbal skills). These findings are consistent with the results of Hansen, et al.'s study (1996).

The five least important skills HR employees should possess are quantitative in nature. They are financial skills, research skills, risk-taking skills, general business skills, and technical skills. Although within one standard deviation of the grand mean, the next lowest rated skills contained process oriented skills including team building, group problem solving, facilitation, and negotiation skills. These results support the stereotype of HR practitioners as 'people persons' uncomfortable with numbers or the hard side of business.

After rating each of the 28 skills, respondents were then asked to indicate the single most important skill that graduates of HR programs should possess. The ten most frequently listed skills are presented in Table 3. Executives wanted HR graduates to possess people skills, active listening skills, and verbal skills.

Substantive HR Knowledge

Respondents were asked to rate twenty substantive HR knowledge activities according to how important it was for HR graduates to be able to perform each activity. Table 4 shows the mean responses for the complete list of substantive HR knowledge activities. The single item rated more than one standard deviation above the grand mean and the four items rated more than 1 standard deviation below the grand mean (Mean = 3.04; SD = 0.42) are also indicated. Executives gave the highest importance rating to create a recruitment program. This may reflect the labor shortage facing organizations for the past several years. Other items receiving high ratings included many of the traditional activities associated with HR practice (e.g. write a job description/job specification; complete a cost/benefit analysis; and conduct training programs).

The lowest rated items were negotiate with unions, validate a selection instrument, conduct a Markov analysis, and implement an assessment center. It is not known whether these activities received low ratings because HR executives do not believe in their importance; do not know how to perform them; find them too expensive to conduct in-house; or believe there are consulting firms which can perform these activities for them.

After rating each of the 20 substantive HR knowledge activities, respondents were then asked to indicate the single most important activity that graduates of HR programs should know how to perform. The most frequently reported activity was write a strategic plan. This may reflect some movement toward the 'new HR' (Dyer, 1999).

Finally, respondents were asked to indicate which of these twenty activities they would be most likely to purchase or outsource. These are indicated in

Table 4. Substantive HR Knowledge
1 Standard Deviation Above and Below the Grand Mean
(Mean = 3.04, SD = 0.42)

Activity	Mean Response
Create a recruitment program [a]	3.49
Write a job description	3.46
Complete a cost/benefit analysis	3.45
Conduct training programs †	3.43
Conduct a wage survey †	3.42
Conduct a job evaluation survey	3.38
Develop a performance appraisal rating instrument	3.34
Insure EEO compliance	3.33
Write a strategic plan	3.25
Design an incentive program	3.22
Conduct a needs analysis	3.22
Conduct a job satisfaction survey †	3.21
Calculate absenteeism/turnover rates	3.06
Develop an HR information system †	3.02
Conduct a utilization analysis	2.99
Engage in HR/succession planning	2.90
Negotiate with unions/handle grievances [b]	2.51
Validate a selection instrument †[b]	2.43
Conduct a Markov analysis [b]	2.33
Implement an assessment center [b]	2.27

† most likely to outsource
[a] rated 1 SD above the grand mean
[b] rated 1 SD below the grand mean

Table 4 and include develop an HR information system; conduct a wage survey; conduct a job satisfaction survey; conduct a training program; and validate a selection instrument.

Control Variables

The effects of three control variables (managerial level, company size, and industry sector) were assessed on executives' ratings of importance for each set of variables. At the individual level, responses were compared for both upper and middle level HR professionals. At the company level, responses were compared for both small companies (under 500 employees) and large companies (over 500 employees). Finally, at the industry level, responses were compared for manufacturing firms and those in the service sector. Given the size of the sample, significant differences are reported at the 0.01 level.

Table 5. T-Tests of Control Variables: Issues of Concern to HR Executives

Issues	Mean	SD	Manufacturing	Service	< 500	> 500	Middle Management	Upper Management
1. Absenteeism	2.62	0.90	2.67	2.60	2.61	2.62	2.61	2.61
2. Affirmative Action	2.24	0.90	2.29	2.22	2.13	2.36	2.36*	2.19*
3. Age Discrimination	2.05	0.81	2.09	2.04	1.92*	2.20*	2.12	2.02
4. Aging of the Workplace	2.24	0.90	2.35*	2.19*	2.10*	2.39*	2.19	2.25
5. Career Plateauing	2.52	0.85	2.50	2.52	2.51	2.52	2.51	2.52
6. Changing Family Patterns	2.41	0.81	2.34	2.43	2.36	2.45	2.27*	2.44*
7. Child Care	2.38	0.83	2.23*	2.42*	2.33	2.42	2.37	2.38
8. Contingent/Temporary Workforce	2.37	0.91	2.45	2.35	2.29*	2.47*	2.30	2.40
9. Downsizing	1.94	0.96	2.09*	1.90*	1.80*	2.11*	1.99	1.91
10. Internet Abuse	1.97	0.78	1.99	1.95	1.91	2.02	1.93	1.97
11. Elder Care	1.94	0.81	1.91	1.93	1.87	2.00	1.86	1.96
12. Employee Privacy	2.16	0.79	2.14	2.17	2.13	2.19	2.18	2.15
13. Equal Employment Opportunity	2.48	0.87	2.40	2.50	2.41	2.56	2.56	2.44
14. Ethics in Business	2.69	0.91	2.58	2.74	2.65	2.74	2.67	2.69
15. Glass Ceiling	2.25	0.87	2.26	2.23	2.13	2.37	2.34	2.20
16. Global Competition	1.97	1.07	2.67*	1.72*	1.79	2.16	1.97	1.93
17. Immigrant Patterns	1.76	0.87	1.98*	1.69*	1.67	1.88	1.78	1.76
18. International Assignments	1.46	0.79	1.80*	1.35*	1.34	1.63	1.46	1.46
19. Job Satisfaction	3.37	0.69	3.23*	3.43*	3.39	3.37	3.37	3.39
20. Loyalty and Commitment	3.31	0.73	3.17*	3.37*	3.32	3.31	3.28	3.33
21. Managing Change	3.39	0.79	3.35	3.41	3.33	3.47	3.30	3.42
22. Career Development Counseling	2.72	0.83	2.69	2.73	2.68	2.75	2.73	2.71
23. Managing Diversity	2.55	0.87	2.45	2.58	2.45	2.66	2.55	2.54
24. Mergers and Acquisitions	2.17	1.11	2.38*	2.12*	1.91	2.51	2.16	2.17
25. More Litigious Workforce	2.82	0.92	2.81	2.83	2.74	2.93	2.72	2.86
26. Motivating Generation X	2.67	0.92	2.57	2.70	2.64	2.70	2.59	2.70
27. Outsourcing Human Resouce Services	2.00	0.86	2.05	1.97	1.89*	2.10*	1.95	1.99

Table 5. (Continued)

Issues	Mean	SD	Manufacturing	Service	<500	>500	Middle Management	Upper Management
28. Performance/Productivity	3.30	0.73	3.34	3.30	3.28	3.34	3.30	3.31
29. Part Time Workers	2.22	0.90	1.97*	2.30*	2.16*	2.30*	2.11	2.26
30. Reverse Discrimination	1.79	0.79	1.78	1.79	1.73	1.84	1.82	1.77
31. Rising Healthcare Costs	3.11	0.85	3.11	3.12	3.17	3.04	3.10	3.12
32. Self Managed Teams	2.20	0.91	2.33*	2.15*	2.16	2.23	2.15	2.21
33. Sexual Harassment	2.75	0.84	2.73	2.75	2.62*	2.89*	2.82	2.71
34. Skill Shortages	3.16	0.84	3.30*	3.12*	3.09*	3.23*	3.10	3.19
35. Encouraging Innovation and Creativity	2.98	0.82	3.01	2.97	2.94	3.02	2.89	3.02
36. Strategic HRM	2.96	0.84	2.90	2.98	2.89*	3.04*	2.87	2.99
37. Substance Abuse	2.30	0.79	2.41*	2.26*	2.24	2.36	2.27	2.31
38. Telecommuting	2.00	0.85	1.93	2.02	1.93*	2.08*	1.96	2.01
39. Turnover	3.07	0.90	2.93*	3.14*	3.09	3.06	3.14	3.05
40. Women in the Workforce	2.23	0.85	2.23	2.23	2.14*	2.34*	2.34	2.20
41. Workplace Violence	2.36	0.84	2.47*	2.32*	2.26*	2.47*	2.30	2.38

* = $p < 0.01$

HR Issues

Table 5 presents the T-test results for level, size, and sector on HR issues. Several interesting differences emerged. It appears that executives in large firms and from manufacturing are concerned about a larger set of HR issues than those in small firms or from the service sector. Executives in the manufacturing sector were more concerned with the aging of the workforce, downsizing, global competition, immigrant patterns, international assignments, mergers and acquisitions, self managed teams, skill shortages, substance abuse, and workplace violence than executives in the service sector. Executives in the service sector were more concerned about traditional HR outcomes such as loyalty and commitment, job satisfaction, and turnover than executives in the manufacturing sector.

Executives from large companies were more concerned with age discrimination, aging of the workforce, contingent/temporary workforce, downsizing, outsourcing HR, part time workers, sexual harassment, skill shortages, strategic HRM, telecommuting, women in the workplace, and workplace violence than executives from small companies. No differences emerged in the other direction. Middle managers were more concerned about affirmative action than upper managers; while upper managers were more concerned about changing family patterns.

HR Roles

The effects of the control variables on HR roles are presented in Table 6. The effect of managerial level was strongest on HR roles. Upper level managers described the HR department as designing, implementing, and evaluating HR strategies and programs, acting as an internal consultant, supporting line management, and being both a member of the executive management team and a strategic partner with top management. Executives from the manufacturing sector reported two roles that HR plays in their companies, that of change agent and outsourcer of HR programs. Executives from small companies reported that their HR departments monitored legal compliance and motivated employees. Executives from large companies reported that their HR department outsourced HR programs.

HR Skills

The effects of the control variables on HR skills are presented in Table 7. Customer service skills are more important to executives in large companies and from the service sector. Executives from small companies gave more importance to organizational skills. No differences emerged between upper and middle level managers.

Table 6. T-Tests of Control Variables: HR Roles

Roles	Mean	SD	Manufacturing	Service	<500	>500	Middle Management	Upper Management
1. Change Agent	3.19	0.85	3.33*	3.17*	3.15	3.27	2.92	3.32
2. Clerical/Processing Support	2.69	0.93	2.69	2.69	2.70	2.68	2.74	2.65
3. Designing HR Strategies and Programs	3.63	0.61	3.61	3.63	3.62	3.65	3.43*	3.72*
4. Employee Advocate	3.52	0.62	3.50	3.53	3.55	3.48	3.47	3.54
5. Evaluating HR Strategies and Programs	3.63	0.61	3.61	3.63	3.61	3.65	3.51*	3.69*
6. Implementing HR Strategies and Programs	3.73	0.51	3.72	3.74	3.73	3.76	3.64*	3.79*
7. Internal Consultant	3.57	0.66	3.54	3.58	3.54	3.61	3.44*	3.64*
8. Member of the Executive Management Team	3.56	0.74	3.63	3.56	3.55	3.60	3.05*	3.77*
9. Monitor Legal Compliance	3.69	0.57	3.68	3.69	3.73*	3.63*	3.63	3.72
10. Motivate Employees	3.09	0.73	3.07	3.10	3.17*	2.99*	3.04	3.12
11. Outsourcing HR Programs	2.26	1.02	2.46*	2.20*	2.14*	2.39*	2.15	2.30
12. Strategic Partner with Top Management	3.54	0.73	3.55	3.54	3.55	3.53	3.15*	3.70*
13. Support Line Management	3.64	0.62	3.68	3.63	3.61	3.67	3.52*	3.69*

* = $p < 0.01$

Table 7. T-Tests of Control Variables: HR Skills

Skills	Mean	SD	Manufacturing	Service	< 500	> 500	Middle Management	Upper Management
1. Active Listening Skills	3.88	0.34	3.84	3.90	3.89	3.88	3.87	3.89
2. Adaptability Skills	3.68	0.50	3.68	3.67	3.66	3.70	3.66	3.68
3. Analytical Skills	3.39	0.58	3.32	3.40	3.39	3.38	3.36	3.40
4. Computer Skills	3.41	0.58	3.39	3.42	3.42	3.41	3.43	3.40
5. Creative Thinking Skills	3.49	0.58	3.47	3.50	3.48	3.51	3.47	3.51
6. Cultural Sensitivity Skills	3.45	0.70	3.42	3.45	3.43	3.46	3.48	3.43
7. Customer Service Skills	3.70	0.54	3.59*	3.74*	3.66*	3.76*	3.69	3.70
8. Decision Making Skills	3.54	0.57	3.55	3.53	3.53	3.56	3.51	3.55
9. Facilitation Skills	3.22	0.72	3.25	3.20	3.20	3.24	3.20	3.23
10. Financial Skills	2.68	0.73	2.70	2.69	2.67	2.71	2.62	2.71
11. General Business Skills	3.07	0.65	3.06	3.07	3.05	3.09	2.98	3.09
12. Group Problem Solving Skills	3.20	0.76	3.24	3.17	3.16	3.24	3.12	3.22
13. Leadership Skills	3.39	0.68	3.41	3.39	3.36	3.44	3.34	3.42
14. Negotiating Skills	3.26	0.80	3.27	3.26	3.22	3.31	3.16	3.30
15. Oral Communication Skills	3.82	0.40	3.81	3.83	3.83	3.82	3.80	3.83
16. Organizational Skills	3.61	0.57	3.55	3.63	3.66*	3.54*	3.59	3.61
17. People Skills	3.89	0.33	3.87	3.90	3.90	3.89	3.87	3.90
18. Planning Skills	3.39	0.63	3.37	3.39	3.41	3.37	3.36	3.40
19. Presentation Skills	3.15	0.72	3.11	3.16	3.13	3.17	3.13	3.16
20. Resourcefulness Skills	3.38	0.67	3.33	3.40	3.41	3.35	3.34	3.40
21. Research Skills	2.81	0.77	2.77	2.81	2.85	2.76	2.80	2.81
22. Risk-taking Skills	2.82	0.80	2.81	2.83	2.79	2.86	2.76	2.85
23. Team Building Skills	3.20	0.76	3.26	3.18	3.17	3.24	3.17	3.23
24. Technical Skills	3.12	0.76	3.11	3.12	3.07	3.17	3.07	3.13
25. Thinking Skills	3.64	0.54	3.67	3.63	3.64	3.64	3.60	3.67
26. Understanding Organizational Dynamic Skills	3.32	0.73	3.30	3.33	3.31	3.33	3.35	3.32
27. Verbal Communication Skills	3.83	0.40	3.79	3.84	3.84	3.81	3.81	3.84
28. Written Communication Skills	3.71	0.50	3.67	3.73	3.74	3.69	3.67	3.72

* = $p < 0.01$

Substantive HR Knowledge

Table 8 presents the results for substantive HR knowledge. Executives from the service sector rated conduct a job satisfaction survey as more important than executives from the manufacturing sector. Engage in HR/succession planning was more important to the manufacturing than the service sector. Upper managers gave more importance to conducting a wage survey than middle managers. Executives from small companies wanted their employees to be able to perform several HR tasks (e.g. develop a performance appraisal instrument, develop an HR information system, and write a job description/specification), since they might not have the resources to outsource these programs. Executives from large companies gave higher ratings to engage in HR/succession planning and negotiate with unions/handle grievances.

Staffing HR Departments

Respondents were asked to indicate what type of degree holders they were most likely to staff professional positions in HR with. In general, there was more preference for individuals with undergraduate degrees than for those possessing graduate degrees. One factor that might explain this finding is the fact that forty four percent of this sample held only an undergraduate degree. Readers should not interpret this finding to mean that graduate degrees are not valued. The role of applicant experience in hiring must also be considered. Examination of the written comments received with the questionnaires revealed that the respondents were interested in hiring employees with undergraduate degrees as long as they had HR experience. Moreover, both manufacturing firms and large firms expressed more interest in staffing the HR department with individuals who possess graduate degrees.

IMPLICATIONS FOR HR PROGRAMS

A frequently cited refrain in both the academic and practitioner literatures is a call for greater collaboration between the world of business and the halls of academia (Miles, 1996). This study attempts to bridge the gap between academics and practitioners by directly surveying HR executives about several aspects of HR practice and education. One of the goals of the study is to provide both Human Resource and Industrial Relations educators with concrete guidelines for improving their curricula. The results of this survey suggest several implications for the design and the delivery of HR educational programs in the next decade.

Table 8. T-Tests of Control Variables: Substantive HR Knowledge

HR Knowledge	Mean	SD	Manufacturing	Service	< 500	> 500	Middle Management	Upper Management
1. Calculate Absenteeism/Turnover Rates	3.06	0.81	2.99	3.08	3.08	3.02	3.06	3.03
2. Complete a Cost/Benefit Analysis	3.45	0.66	3.50	3.44	3.44	3.45	3.39	3.47
3. Conduct a Job Evaluation Study	3.38	0.67	3.38	3.38	3.41	3.33	3.32	3.39
4. Conduct a Job Satisfaction Survey	3.21	0.71	3.11*	3.25*	3.23	3.18	3.18	3.23
5. Conduct a Markov Analysis	2.33	0.84	2.35	2.31	2.32	2.32	2.32	2.31
6. Conduct a Needs Analysis	3.22	0.72	3.25	3.21	3.19	3.26	3.18	3.24
7. Conduct a Utilization Analysis	2.99	0.73	3.02	2.98	2.99	2.98	2.95	3.00
8. Conduct a Wage Survey	3.42	0.70	3.43	3.42	3.46	3.37	3.29*	3.46*
9. Conduct Training Programs	3.43	0.64	3.39	3.44	3.44	3.41	3.39	3.44
10. Create a Recruitment Program	3.49	0.67	3.50	3.50	3.48	3.52	3.45	3.51
11. Design an Incentive Program	3.22	0.72	3.17	3.24	3.23	3.22	3.23	3.23
12. Develop a Performance Appraisal Rating Instrument	3.34	0.73	3.32	3.35	3.43*	3.22*	3.36	3.33
13. Develop an HR Information System	3.02	0.90	2.96	3.04	3.09*	2.92*	2.93	3.04
14. Engage in HR/Succession Planning	2.90	0.84	3.02*	2.86*	2.82*	2.98*	2.85	2.90
15. Implement an Assessment Center	2.27	0.81	2.26	2.27	2.23	2.29	2.21	2.28
16. Insure EEO Compliance	3.33	0.80	3.30	3.35	3.34	3.32	3.33	3.33
17. Negotiate with Unions/Handle Grievances	2.51	1.15	2.61	2.48	2.40*	2.65*	2.46	2.53
18. Validate a Selection Instrument	2.43	0.93	2.44	2.43	2.42	2.43	2.47	2.41
19. Write a Job Description/Specification	3.46	0.69	3.43	3.49	3.54*	3.38*	3.48	3.46
20. Write a Strategic Plan	3.25	0.81	3.25	3.26	3.24	3.27	3.21	3.27

* = $p < 0.01$

Emphasis on HR Issues

The issues that HR executives are most concerned with include virtually all of the traditional outcome variables of HR (e.g. performance/productivity, job satisfaction, turnover, and loyalty and commitment). These issues received higher ratings of concern than did the trendy, topical issues prevalent in the popular press. These findings suggest that HR/IR educators should see that their students are well trained in these traditional measures of a successful employment relationship.

HR/IR educators should show students the links between implementing successful HR programs, and achieving desired HR and organizational outcomes such as performance and satisfaction. It seems unlikely that one required course in Organizational Behavior can provide students with the depth of knowledge necessary to understand such complex human behaviors and reactions. HR programs may want to consider offering courses on managing performance, building commitment, and ensuring job satisfaction. Classes which focus on these types of 'issues', should ensure that HR graduates are able to add value to their organizations.

At the same time, offering special topics courses and current issues in HR classes should insure that HR curricula remain timely and relevant to the business and HR community. For example, the finding that managing change is of great concern to HR practitioners, suggests that HR programs need to teach students how to manage change. This may be accomplished by requiring a class in change; offering it as an elective; or integrating change issues into every course in the HR curriculum.

Emphasis on Skill Development

Employers want their new hires to possess several enabling skills. HR/IR programs must integrate skill development across their curricula and into as many courses as feasible. The importance of communication skills suggests that students need to be given as much practice as possible in developing their writing and presentation skills. Writing requirements such as essay exams and research papers may need to be supplemented with other forms of corporate writing such as proposals, executive summaries, and position papers. Including representatives from the business community in the audience may provide students with valuable feedback on their presentation style during individual and group presentations.

The importance of people skills suggests that students need to be given opportunities to develop processing skills such as managing team projects, motivating group members, and facilitating class discussions. The assignment of group projects is one obvious way of providing students the opportunity to observe group dynamics. The effectiveness of team projects and group exercises may be enhanced if emphasis is placed on debriefing and discussing the process experienced by individual and team members. The careful use of self assessment exercises and self report inventories may allow students to understand their interpersonal and work styles, as well as diagnose their own developmental needs.

The development of quantitative skills presents more of a challenge for HR/IR educators. The results of this study suggest that HR executives do not place great importance on financial, technical, and general business skills. This finding is inconsistent with previous research and predictions regarding the future of the HR field. It seems counterintuitive and heretical to advise HR programs to drop required courses in accounting, finance, statistics, and research methods. We are equally hesitant to suggest that a plethora of 'business-lite' courses be developed for HR graduates (Accounting for HR majors; Finance for HR majors; etc.).

One recommendation is to integrate quantitative skills into specific HR courses. For example, correlation coefficients could be introduced in the Recruitment and Selection class within the context of conducting validity studies and interpreting validity coefficients. Similarly, ratio analysis could be introduced in the Strategic HR class in the context of evaluating firm performance. Students might gain a better understanding of how these quantitative tools can be utilized to help organizations gain a competitive advantage if they learn their applications. Students could be required to develop a portfolio of quantitative applications to bring back to their employers showing how these tools can be utilized to help organizations meet strategic goals and objectives.

Emphasis on the Role of HR in Organizations

Many HR/IR graduate students are full time professionals working in the field of HR. The role that the HR department plays in their current organization is likely to drive their perceptions of what they need to learn in a graduate HR program. HR educators must be sensitive to the differing needs for substantive knowledge and enabling skills that their students will wish to acquire. For example, students working in small companies may be so focused on solving problems on a daily basis that they would be better served by a lecture on how to recruit applicants, than a discussion of HR as a strategic business partner. Program administrators would be well advised to examine whether their HR curricula address the needs of students working in HR departments in different types of organizations.

Executives reported that their HR departments were primarily concerned with designing, implementing, and evaluating HR programs. This suggests that emphasis should be placed on teaching students ways to measure the success of various HR programs. Individual assignments that require students to develop HR programs, should include a component that addresses the evaluation of those programs. Requiring students to design programs within budget constraints, to calculate break even points, and to perform cost/benefit and utility analyses will hold them to the same standards that their colleagues in other functional areas are required to meet.

Emphasis on Substantive HR Knowledge

The body of knowledge comprising the discipline of HR has experienced tremendous growth in the last half century. An entire course could be offered on virtually every chapter in HR textbooks. Executives' ratings of the most important types of substantive HR knowledge included items from every subdiscipline of the field. This suggests that programs which are training their students to be HR generalists will need to offer specialized courses in each of the subfunctions of HR. This does not mean that efforts should not be made to achieve integration across the curricula. It does suggest that students need to be offered experiential learning opportunities within each course so that the emphasis is on being able to demonstrate substantive HR knowledge activities along with developing enabling skills.

The results of this study indicate that graduates of HR programs are expected to know how to do many of the traditional activities associated with the field of HR (e.g. design a recruitment program; write a job description; and conduct a training program). This suggests that HR graduate programs need to teach students how to design, implement, and evaluate HR programs. Graduates will need to demonstrate subject matter expertise in several HR areas to successfully perform in most entry and mid level HR positions. Most graduate programs will need to require that their students complete at least 36 credit hours of course work if they are to adequately cover the material across all subdisciplines of the field.

Finally, HR/IR educators must recognize that the HR issues, roles, skills, and substantive knowledge considered important by HR practitioners will vary depending on students' managerial level, the industry they work in, and the size of their firm. Although HR programs cannot be all things to everyone (Barber, 1999), acknowledgement of these types of control variables should be integrated into HR courses and curricula.

Future Research

The start of the new millennium provides an opportune time to reflect on whether HR educators are meeting the needs of this rapidly changing profession. If we are to have a clear picture of what HR curricula should include to prepare our students for HR in this millennium, academics must continue to work collaboratively with HR practitioners to gain their insights into the field of HR. Surveys such as the present study are one way of bridging the gap between HR practitioners and HR educators.

Future research could extend the present study by examining the perspectives of organizational groups such as managers in other functional areas; employees at several levels in the organization; and members of the senior executive team. Insights regarding their perceptions of the role of HR in organizations, the issues facing their company, and the substantive knowledge and required skills HR employees should possess are important. Their insights would provide a more complete picture of how HR is perceived by people outside the field, and allow HR practitioners to better serve diverse constituency groups inside the organization.

One of the contributions of this study was the ability to examine differences in the sample according to company size, managerial level, and industry sector. Future research should continue to explore the role of control variables such as individual difference variables among HR executives, company level variables, regional and geographic differences, and more specific industry differences. Research of this nature will insure that HR programs continue to prepare students to work in one of the most challenging, dynamic, and exciting fields of business.

NOTES

1. It should be noted that since HR and IR graduate programs often largely differ in name only, for purposes of exposition we will refer to them both as HR throughout the chapter.
2. The correlation matrices for issues, roles, skills, substantive HR knowledge, and control variables are available from the authors.

ACKNOWLEDGMENTS

This study was supported by the Executive Human Resource Forum of Orange County, California. The authors would like to thank Dr Tom Buckles for his assistance with the initial questionnaire.

REFERENCES

Barber, A. E. (1999). Implications for the Design of Human Resource Management – Education, Training, and Certification. *Human Resource Management, 38*, 177–182.

Carnevale, A., Gainer, L .J., & Meltzer, A. S. (1990). *Workplace Basics: The Essential Skills Employers Want.* San Francisco: Jossey-Bass.

Cohen, J., & Cohen, P. (1983). *Applied Multiple Regression/Correlation Analysis for the Behavioral Sciences*, 2nd Edition. Hillside, NJ: Erlbaum Associates, Publishers.

Dyer, Jr., W. G. (1999). Training Human Resource Champions for the Twenty-First Century. *Human Resource Management, 38,* 119–124.

Fisher C. D., Schoenfeldt, L.F., & Shaw, J. B. (1999). *Human Resource Management* 4th Edition. Boston: Houghton Mifflin Company.

Goldberg, M. A. (1996). The Case Against 'Practicality' and 'Relevance' as Gauges of Business Schools. *Journal of Management Inquiry, 5,* 336–349.

Gomez-Mejia, L. R., Balkin, D. B., & Cardy, R. L. (1998). *Managing Human Resources* 2nd Edition. Upper Saddle River, NJ: Prentice Hall.

Hansen, W. L., Berkely, R., Kaplan, D., Yu, Q. S., Craig, C., Fitzpatrick, J., Seiler, M., Denby, D., Gheis, P., Ruelle, D., & Voss, L. (1996). Needed Skills for Human Resource Professionals: A pilot study. *Labor Law Journal, 47,* 524–534.

Hunter, R. H. (1999). The 'New HR' and the New HR Consultant: Developing Human Resource Consultants at Andersen Consulting. *Human Resource Management, 38,* 147–154.

Kaufman, B. (1999). Evolution and Current Status of University HR Programs. *Human Resource Management, 38,* 103–110.

Kaufman, B. (1994). What Companies are Looking for in Graduates of University HR Programs. *Labor Law Journal, 44,* 503–510.

Kaufman, B. (1996). Transformation of the Corporate HR/IR Function: Implications for University Programs. *Labor Law Journal, 47,* 540–548.

Kemske, F. (1998). HR 2008 A Forecast Based on Our Exclusive Study. *Workforce, 77,* 46–60.

Kraut, A. I., & Korman, A. K. (1999). *Evolving Practices in Human Resource Management.* San Francisco, CA: Jossey-Bass.

Miles, R. E. (1996). Some Further (and Future) Thoughts on Practicality and Relevance. *Journal of Management Inquiry, 5,* 352–354.

Mondy, R. W., & Noe, R. M. (1996). *Human Resource Management* (6th ed.). Upper Saddle River, NJ: Prentice Hall, Inc.

Noe, R. A., Hollenbeck, J. R., Gerhart, B., & Wright, P. W. (2000). *Human Resource Management: Gaining a Competitive Advantage* 3rd Edition. Boston: Irwin McGraw-Hill.

Rau, J. (1995). A Business School Seeks Customer Opinions. *HR Focus, 72,* 8–11.

Rothstein, H. R. (1999). Recruitment and Selection: Benchmarking at the Millennium. In: A. I. Kraut & A. K. Korman (Eds.), *Evolving Practices in Human Resource Management* (pp. 170–182). San Francisco, CA: Jossey-Bass.

Schneider, B. (1999). Is the Sky Really Falling? A View of the Future. In: A. I. Kraut & A. K. Korman (Eds.), *Evolving Practices in Human Resource Management.* (pp. 328–357). San Francisco, CA: Jossey-Bass.

Schoonover, S. (1998). *Human Resource Competencies for the Year 2000: The Wake Up Call.* Alexandria, VA: Society for Human Resource Management.

Schuler, R. S. (1998). *Managing Human Resources* 6th Edition. Cincinnati, OH: South-Western.

Senge, P. M. (1990). *The Fifth Discipline: The Art and Practice of the Learning Organization.* New York: Doubleday.

Sherman, A., Bohlander, G., & Snell, S. (1998). *Managing Human Resources* 11th Edition. Cincinnati, OH: South-Western.

U.S. Department of Labor, Secretary's Commission on Achieving Necessary Skills (SCANS), 1994. *What Work Requires of Schools: A SCANS Report for America 2000.* Washington, D.C.

Van Eynde, D., & Tucker, S. (1997). A Quality Human Resource Curriculum: Recommendations From Leading Senior HR Executives. *Human Resource Management, 36,* 397–408.

Way, P. (1996). A Survey of Curricula of IR/HR Master's Programs: Common Features, New Directions. *Labor Law Journal, 47,* 535–539.

Wright, P. M., & Snell, S. A. (1991). Toward an Integrated View of Strategic Human Resource Management. *Human Resource Management Review, 1,* 203–225.

DEVELOPING NEW PROFICIENCIES FOR HUMAN RESOURCE AND INDUSTRIAL RELATIONS PROFESSIONALS[1]

W. Lee Hansen

I. INTRODUCTION

Recent changes in the roles of human resource and industrial relations (HR/IR) professionals place new demands on them if they are to operate successfully in a shifting business environment. These demands are reflected in what are often described as the 'core competencies' or the 'knowledge, skills, and abilities' required of human resource professionals. Whatever term is used, these requirements go well beyond what traditionally has been regarded as essential for HR/IR practitioners. How to change the culture of the field and in turn nurture these competencies has received much discussion.

Much less attention has been given to preparing new HR/IR job entrants so that they can operate not only as traditional HR/IR professionals but also later as key business partners in their organizations. Particularly for those educated and trained in professional, masters degree programs, these programs must be changed to help prepare HR/IR students to meet the evolving demands of the workplace. The challenge to academic programs is determining how to adapt their instruction to this new environment. Concentrating on traditional content knowledge will no longer suffice. Greater emphasis must be given to cultivating a broad set of skills to complement the standard array of knowledge taught in regular courses. In short, HR/IR graduates must show that they can do more than simply pass courses and complete formal program requirements.

The most appropriate way of achieving this goal is to focus on developing in students what are described here as 'proficiencies'. Proficiencies reflect the capacity of new graduates to combine their content knowledge and acquired skills in creative ways that add value to their new employers. Put another way, we can think of content knowledge and acquired skills as inputs to a production process whose output is proficiencies. Proficiencies differ from both core competencies and knowledge-skill-ability requirements by emphasizing the developmental aspects of the education-training process for HR/IR students; they also provide a benchmark against which to evaluate both new graduates and the programs from which they graduate.[2]

Before proceeding, the HR/IR linkage needs elaboration. Industrial relations is a broad social science field that focuses on all aspects of the employment relationship; its history is rooted in the analysis of labor problems and the role played by unions and government in the amelioration of these problems. With the waning of union strength in recent decades and the growing need for human resource experts, masters degree-granting industrial relations programs have become more like human resource programs in business schools. Increasingly, these programs are renaming themselves to reflect this shift in emphasis. Meanwhile, what used to be called personnel management in business schools has been broadened and recast as human resources or human resource management. Though, the two fields of industrial relations and personnel management are converging, important differences remain in terms of the training provided.[3]

Four questions are posed here. First, what proficiencies need to be developed for HR/IR practitioners? Second, what priority should be given to developing these proficiencies? Third, to what extent do HR/IR academic programs develop the knowledge and skills needed by graduates to demonstrate these proficiencies? Fourth, how can HR/IR programs change to enhance the knowledge and skill development that leads to these proficiencies? The first question is answered through a review and analysis of recent human resource literature. The second is answered using a quality function deployment process to assess the leveraging power of different skills and content knowledge on proficiencies. The third and fourth questions are answered largely through a content analysis of the literature, plus a detailed knowledge, complemented by survey results, of the University of Wisconsin-Madison's masters degree program in industrial relations, offered by its Industrial Relations Research Institute (IRRI). Particular attention is given to that part of the program pursued by students interested in human resources; hence, the references throughout the chapter to HR/IR.

II. LITERATURE RECAP

Beginning in the middle 1980s, studies by human resource and industrial relations managers and scholars began highlighting the rapid transformation of many American companies and discussing the implications of this transformation for human resource management (e.g. Kochan, Katz & McKersie 1986; Dyer, 1988; Schuler, 1991; Legge, 1995; Ulrich, 1997). The dynamic new environment they describe stems from significant changes in external and internal forces affecting the nation's business enterprises. Global competition, rapid technological advances, shortages of highly skilled employees, growing diversity in the work force, customer demands for quality, increased employee demands, and heightened expectations among the general population top the list of challenges companies faced (Carnevale 1991). American business organizations began responding, with shifts in corporate vision, strategic planning, and responsiveness to customers. The implications of these changes are captured in several recent studies, most notably, those by Kaufman (1994, 1996), Connolly and Mastranunzio (1994), and the Conference Board (1994a, 1994b, 1994c, 1995a, 1995b). These studies not only delineate the changing dimensions of the human resource field, but they also outline new roles and responsibilities expected of human resource professionals. They go on to specify the capabilities organizations need to meet these new challenges and outline the core competencies required of human resource professionals (Schoonover, 1997; Ulrich, 1998).

Business leaders see new roles and responsibilities emerging for human resource managers (Conference Board, 1995b). Most important, human resource managers must play a more central by understanding the business direction of their companies, including what products and services it produces, who are its typical customers, and how it is positioned competitively in the market place. Moreover, they must help bring about this transformation by adding significant value to the business through facilitating change with the help of well planned strategies and processes. They also need to deliver functional expertise for traditional human resource activities, whether the functions are performed internally or contracted out. Last, human resource professionals must continue to serve as employee advocates, looking out for the people-related processes needed to gain the high commitment and performance that leads to business success.

In the past, human resource managers were often seen as playing a largely administrative role in their organizations, occupying staff positions that dealt with traditional functions, including hiring, training, salary, benefits, and the like. Because many did not fully understand business fundamentals, human resource practitioners and their various functions were never perceived as being 'critical' to the overall success of the organization. Continued adherence to this traditional role has led to what the Conference Board (1995b) recently described as a "crisis of confidence and credibility" for human resource professionals as the world of business undergoes dramatic changes.[4]

In the new competitive environment, human resource professionals must be equipped to deal with a much wider range of people-related business issues. While continuing the bread and butter work of human resources, meeting this challenge requires rethinking their responsibilities and holding them accountable for developing the essential competencies required to carry out those responsibilities. Indeed, business leaders argue that academic HR/IR programs should focus on developing new capabilities to overcome these deficiencies. Among the capabilities most frequently noted are consulting, organizational development, business/financial analysis, process improvement, and global awareness. Others include team building, consulting-advising, and leadership styles that emphasize facilitation and coaching. In addition, business savvy and knowledge, change management, and global perspective are also viewed as competencies expected of human resource professionals.

The fact that the business community is redefining the role of HR/IR professionals and the core competencies, or the knowledge, skill, and ability they must bring to their jobs, does not mean that academic programs should be overhauled explicitly to meet these demands.[5] On the other hand, at least some faculty believe that academic HR/IR programs do not provide their graduates with the right amounts and mixture of knowledge, skills, and abilities needed for them to fulfill their new roles (e.g., Kaufman, 1994, 1996; Grossman, 1998; Way, 1996; Way, 1999; Johnson & King, 1999). Thus, it is crucial for academia to look closely at changes in the HR/IR function, contrast them with how students are being educated and trained in current HR/IR programs, and then decide what if any response is appropriate.[6]

III. IDENTIFYING PROFICIENCIES

What proficiencies are expected, if not required, of HR/IR professionals in the new economy of the 21st Century? This project's central challenge is finding a way of translating the changing role of HR/IR professionals, reflected in what are often called the core competencies or knowledge-skill-ability requirements, into a meaningful set of proficiencies that can give focus to HR/IR programs. The term used here, 'proficiencies', describes people's capacity to combine their content knowledge and acquired skills so they can fully meet the requirements of their jobs. Since this study focuses on new graduates of HR/IR programs, proficiencies reflect the capability of students to combine their subject matter learning with an array of skills, and thereby demonstrate that they can apply what they know and can do the full range of practical activities they are expected to perform on the job.

Meeting this challenge began with an exhaustive search of the literature to define and identify the proficiencies. This process focused on identifying what HR/IR practitioners do in their jobs, drawing on studies discussed above as well as related literature on business education (e.g., Porter & McKibbin, 1988). Participants in this process were forced to identify the essence of what practitioners do and what knowledge and skills contribute to their performance (Hansen et al., 1999a).[7]

Four broad categories of proficiencies emerged: HR/IR Proficiencies, Business Proficiencies, Leadership Proficiencies, and Learning Proficiencies. The first, *HR/IR Proficiencies,* represents the traditional knowledge and skills required by people working in this particular field of employment. The next two proficiencies capture the broader role HR/IR professionals are being called upon to play within their organizations. One is *Business Proficiencies* which reflects the new role of HR/IR professionals in helping create profitable enterprises that serve their customers effectively. The other is *Leadership Proficiencies* which reflect the new role of HR/IR professionals not as staff people but as part of the core decision-making groups leading these enterprises. The fourth, which we label *Learning Proficiencies,* is quite different. It reflects the demands of a new knowledge-based economy where success lies in creating and sustaining learning organizations whose members bring the best newly discovered knowledge to their work and are able to continue learning over their professional careers. These proficiencies run the gamut, from the most general Learning Proficiencies to the most specific HR/IR Proficiencies, with Business Proficiencies and Leadership Proficiencies standing in the middle.

After these broad proficiencies were identified, they had to be elaborated in what can be viewed as sub-proficiencies. To the extent students can demonstrate all of these sub-proficiencies, they can be assumed to demonstrate the broad proficiency. At the same time, these sub-proficiencies provide guidance in curriculum development. Without the right mix of content knowledge and skills, students will experience difficulty demonstrating these proficiencies. In addition, students must gain experience in demonstrating these sub-proficiencies.

No explicit attention is given to how the need for these proficiencies changes over the life cycle careers of practitioners. It is clear that program graduates must be prepared to operate effectively not only in entry-level jobs but later as managers and still later as leaders. Though considerable uncertainty exists about what their future jobs will be and when they will occupy them, students must be prepared to look beyond their entry-level positions. For this reason, the proficiencies are designed to reflect their career rather than their immediate entry-level needs. It should also be noted that the sub-proficiencies are limited to four (five in the case of Learning Proficiencies), to keep the presentation manageable.

A. Elaboration of HR/IR Proficiency

The bread and butter of HR/IR practitioners is knowing the nuts and bolts of their field. Key components include traditional personnel management, union-management relationships, workings of the labor markets, plus the impact of government regulation, and more recently, diversity in the work force. All of these topics receive strong emphasis in the IRRI's program's human resource track.

Definition
Possesses a broad, in-depth knowledge and understanding of all aspects of the HR/IR function in an organization.

(1) Facilitates and Maintains Employment Relationship. Handles organization's traditional personnel functions. Knows how to attract and retain employees. Recognizes how changes in the labor market affect the organization's employees.
(2) Manages Diverse Workforce. Is aware of the role that the economic and social environments have on developing human resource policies. Knows how these policies, once formulated, are implemented within the organization.
(3) Handles Organization's Labor Relations and Employment Agreements. Understands the evolution, current state, and future of employee-management relations in the United States, including a union and non-union perspective.
(4) Maintains Compliance with Government Regulations/Guidelines. Knows and understands labor and employment law principles developed by the courts governing employer-employee relations in the work place and how to interpret them.

B. Elaboration of Business Proficiency

The need for a deeper knowledge of business by HR/IR practitioners is readily apparent from the literature reviewed above. Because the IRRI program is interdisciplinary with a strong social science orientation, it does not emphasize the standard foundation business courses (finance, accounting, management, marketing, etc.) that are required of Master's degree students who specialize in

Management and Human Resources in the School of Business. Although HR/IR students now take more business courses than previously, they still need a more systematic knowledge of business and the broader business environment.

Definition
Understands the business and acts as a value-adding partner by aligning HR/IR activities with the business needs in a bottom-line orientation of increasing profits and containing costs.

(1) Designs HR/IR Strategy to Meet Current Business Needs. Designs HR/IR projects to achieve goals in the current year. Revises/designs new HR programs (e.g., a recent purchase of a new product line requires revision of some current HR programs/policies).
(2) Designs HR/IR Strategy to Meet Future Strategic Business Goals. Designs HR/IR Project to meet strategic business goals associated with acquisition of new business unit. Analyzes current HR programs/policies to update them with the goal of providing the company with a competitive advantage in the future.
(3) Analyzes Economic Impact of HR/IR Programs. Conducts cost-benefit analysis of new HR programs/policies/contracts to determine whether they should be implemented.
(4) Participates on Cross-Functional Teams. Performs on cross-functional business teams that address business issues (e.g., development of the business unit's strategic plan).

C. Elaboration of Leadership Proficiency

A knowledge of leadership and management is essential to the success of today's HR/IR practitioners. Courses in leadership are relatively new in academe though management courses have been taught for many years. Several reports of the Conference Board indicate that many leading organizations are demanding that HR/IR professionals lead change within the organization to enhance quality and performance. In addition, Kaufman (1996) reports that leadership is a competency that companies are looking for in HR/IR graduates in order to fulfill their future roles as top HR/IR professionals. The particular leadership proficiencies described here come from several sources (Carnevale, Gainer & Miltzer, 1990; Critten, 1993; and Legge, 1995).

Definition
Leads, influences, and inspires others to align the organization toward realizing its vision.

(1) Facilitates Effective Working Relationships with Internal and External Customers. Influences and inspires others toward organization's vision. Plans, allocates, and evaluates work carried out by teams and individuals that motivates others.
(2) Empowers Individual/Team Development to Enhance Organizational Performance. Facilitates others/teams. Creates, maintains, and enhances effective working relations through perceptive facilitation processes and conflict resolution.
(3) Pursues Organizational Vision and Continuous Learning. Empowers others. Develops teams and individuals to enhance performance in carrying out duties aimed at obtaining company vision.
(4) Acts as Change Agent. Initiates and implements change or improvement in services, products and/or systems.

D. Elaboration of Learning Proficiency

The inclusion of Learning Proficiencies reflects several recent developments, among them a growing emphasis on knowledge work (Drucker, 1992; Garvin, 1993), creating learning organizations (Senge, 1990), and the more-central role of HR/IR practitioners in their organizations (Conference Board, 1995b). The specific Learning Proficiencies come from earlier work that proposed five learning proficiencies in the context of educating undergraduate economics majors (Hansen, 1986). These learning proficiencies take on added significance because they happen to be so similar to those emerging from a more recent study on improving knowledge work processes in industry (Davenport, Jarvenpas & Beers 1996).[8]

Definition
Locates and uses new and existing knowledge, creates new knowledge, and fosters a spirit of curiosity and inquiry.

(1) Accesses Existing Knowledge. Displays good library and electronic search skills, and wide acquaintanceship with information sources
(2) Displays Command of Knowledge. Evidences wide ranging reading and networking to build personal knowledge base that will be of use to organization
(3) Assembles and Packages Knowledge. Demonstrates good thinking, writing, and organizing skills that enable individual to produce in timely fashion well-organized and effectively composed presentations
(4) Applies Existing Knowledge. Sees how to bring knowledge to bear on new issues and problems

(5) Creates New Knowledge. Recognizes the constant need to develop new knowledge, and knows how to do this effectively.

IV. HOW KNOWLEDGE AND SKILL CONTRIBUTE TO PROFICIENCIES

What kinds of knowledge and skills contribute to the capacity of students and of graduates to demonstrate these proficiencies? The answer to this question comes from two sources. One is an earlier study (Hansen, Berkely, Kaplan, Yu, Craig, Fitzpatrick, Seiler, Derby, Gheis, Ruelle & Voss 1996, henceforth referred to as Hansen et al., 1996). It identified through a content analysis of the syllabi from courses taken by students specializing in human resources what kinds of knowledge and skills were taught in the Wisconsin program. The published study focused on the 20 identified skills. In broadening that study to examine the link between proficiencies and both the knowledge and skills on which those proficiencies rest (Hansen et al., 1999a), the list of skills remained essentially unchanged; however, the number of knowledge categories grew from 15 to 20.[9] The list of knowledge and skill categories used here appears in Table 1.

Table 1. Skills and Knowledge Needed by Human Resources/Industrial Relations (HR/IR) Professionals

Knowledge	Skills
Accounting	Active Listening
Benefits	Adaptability
Budgeting	Analytical
Compensation	Computer
Employee Analysis	Creativity
Equal Employment Law	Decision Making
Finance	Facilitation
Job Analysis	Group Problem Solving
Labor Markets	Initiative
Labor Law	Leadership
Management	Negotiation
Marketing	Oral Communication
Negotiation/Mediation	Organiz. Dynamics
Organizational Behavior	Planning/Organization
Production Processes	Research
Public Policy	Resourcefulness
Recruitment	Risk Taking
Staffing/Evaluation	Sensitivity to Diversity
Quality Improvement	Team Building
Training	Written Communication

Exactly how important is each of these knowledge and skills categories in contributing to each proficiency? In particular, how can we identify the leveraging effect on proficiencies of instruction that gives greater emphasis to the various knowledge and skill categories? This question is answered with the help of a modified quality function deployment process widely used in quality improvement efforts in the private sector. It starts with matrix listing the proficiencies in the rows and the individual knowledge and skill categories in the columns. The process of completing the matrix calls for those doing the rating, the authors of the 1999 study, to indicate the importance of each knowledge and skill category in contributing to the development of each sub-proficiency and ultimately to each broad proficiency.[10] The results indicate where additional emphasis on knowledge and skills can have the greatest effect on proficiencies and, hence, indicates the priorities for changing the program's emphasis.

To bring out the leveraging effect on proficiencies, a 9–3–1–0 scale is used to rate the importance (9 = very strong, 3 = moderately strong, 1 = weak, and 0 = no relationship) of each knowledge and skill category to each sub-proficiency. This scale gives greater weight to extreme values and thus helps pinpoint those factors that provide maximum leverage in producing change. It is worth noting that this scale is widely used in the quality improvement literature (Imai, 1986; King, 1989); it has recently been used by the author to analyze how to improve access and persistence in higher education (Stampen & Hansen, 1999).

To illustrate this rating process, consider the four sub-proficiencies that contribute to the broad HR/IR Proficiency in Table 2 which is a part of the more detailed Proficiencies Knowledge Priority Matrix. For the first of the four sub-proficiencies, Facilitates Employment Relationship, (ignoring the first column and reading across the row) 11 of the 20 types of knowledge categories display Priority Values of 9. This means that all of them have very strong effects on this proficiency. No category has a Priority Value of 0, and only three have a rating of 1. By contrast, for the fourth sub-proficiency, Maintains Regulatory Compliance, only seven types of knowledge gain ratings of 9; once again, there are no zero ratings and only 3 ratings of 1.

The entries in the first column reflect what are called Proficiency Weights. They indicate the relative importance of each of the four sub-proficiencies in contributing to overall HR/IR Proficiency.[11] These Proficiency Weights are used to aggregate the specific Priority Values for the four proficiencies in rows 1–4. The result, the aggregated Priority Values for the HR/IR Proficiency, is shown in the fifth row. These aggregated Priority Values are then ranked from highest to lowest to yield the Priority Rankings which indicate the relative effect on the broad HR/IR proficiency of giving greater emphasis to each knowledge category.

Table 2. Proficiencies Knowledge–Skill Matrix: Knowledge Priority Rankings

Proficiencies HR/IR PROFICIENCIES	Proficiency Weights	Accounting	Benefits	Budgeting	Compensations	Employee Analysis	Equal Employ Law	Finance	Job Analysis	Labor Markets	Labor Law	Management	Marketing	Negotiation/Mediation	Organizational Behavior	Production Processes	Public Policy	Recruitment	Staff/Evaluation	Quality Improvement	Training
Facilitates Empl. Relationship	3	3	1	9	1	9	9	3	9	9	9	9	1	3	3	9	3	9	9	3	9
Manages Diverse Workforce	3	3	1	9	1	9	9	3	9	3	9	9	1	1	3	9	3	9	9	9	9
Handles Coll. Bargaining	3	3	9	9	9	9	9	3	9	3	9	9	1	9	9	9	9	1	3	3	1
Maintains Regulatory Compl.	2	3	3	9	3	3	9	3	3	1	9	9	1	1	3	9	9	9	3	3	3
PRIORITY VALUES		33	39	99	39	87	99	33	87	47	99	99	11	41	48	99	63	75	69	51	60
PRIORITY RANKINGS		11	10	1	10	2	1	11	2	8	1	1	12	9	7	1	5	3	4	6	4

Priority Values are the Proficiency Weights times the importance ratings for each Knowledge category, summed for each broad proficiency and for all proficiencies. Subtotals for the Learning Proficiencies are normalized to equal the other subtotals.
Source: Knowledge–Skill Matrixes from Hansen et al. (1999a).

Table 3. Broad Proficiencies Knowledge–Skill Matrix: Summary: Knowledge Priority Rankings

Proficiencies	Accounting	Benefits	Budgeting	Compensations	Employee Analysis	Equal Employ Law	Finance	Job Analysis	Labor Markets	Labor Law	Management	Marketing	Negotiation/Mediation	Organizational Behavior	Production Processes	Public Policy	Recruitment	Staff/Evaluation	Quality Improvement	Training
HR/IR PROFICIENCIES																				
Priority Values	33	39	99	39	87	99	33	87	47	99	99	11	41	48	99	63	75	69	51	60
Priority Rankings	11	10	1	10	2	1	11	2	8	1	1	12	9	7	1	5	3	4	6	4
BUSINESS PROFICIENCIES																				
Priority Values	90	12	90	18	72	23	90	72	44	16	90	30	11	72	90	17	38	30	24	28
Priority Rankings	1	11	1	8	2	7	1	2	3	10	1	5	12	2	1	9	4	5	6	4
LEADERSHIP PROFICIENCIES																				
Priority Values	12	11	12	12	81	17	33	81	23	23	99	12	69	81	33	11	27	81	51	81
Priority Rankings	9	10	9	9	2	8	5	-2	7	7	1	9	3	2	5	10	6	2	4	2
LEARNING PROFICIENCIES																				
Priority Values	12	12	12	12	17	22	12	17	26	22	12	12	22	25	12	22	12	12	26	17
Priority Rankings	5	5	5	5	4	3	5	4	1	2	5	5	3	2	5	3	5	5	1	4
ALL PROFICIENCIES																				
Priority Values	147	74	213	81	257	161	168	257	140	160	300	65	143	226	234	119	152	182	152	186
Priority Rankings	11	16	5	15	2	9	8	2	13	10	1	17	12	4	3	14	10	7	10	6

Priority Values are the Proficiency Weights times the importance ratings for each Knowledge category, summed for each broad proficiency and for all proficiencies. Subtotals for the Learning Proficiencies are normalized to equal the other subtotals.

Source: Knowledge–Skill Matrixes from Hansen et al. (1999a).

Table 4. Broad Proficiencies Knowledge–Skill Priority Matrix: Summary: Skill Priority Rankings

Proficiencies	Active Listening Skills	Adaptability	Analytical Skills	Computer Skills	Creativity	Decision Making Skills	Facilitation Skills	Group Problem Solving Skills	Initiative	Leadership Skills	Negotiation Skills	Oral Communication Skills	Organizational Dynamics	Planning/Organization Skills	Research Skills	Resourcefulness	Risk Taking	Sensitivity to Diversity	Team Building Skills	Written Communication Skills
HR/IR PROFICIENCIES																				
Priority Values	81	51	81	21	29	99	47	51	99	41	51	81	69	69	31	51	41	81	47	63
Priority Rankings	2	5	2	10	10	1	6	5	1	8	5	2	3	3	9	5	8	2	6	4
BUSINESS PROFICIENCIES																				
Priority Values	42	33	90	48	42	72	54	33	90	54	27	72	78	60	44	42	30	27	27	60
Priority Rankings	8	9	1	6	8	3	5	9	1	5	11	3	2	4	7	8	10	11	11	4
LEADERSHIP PROFICIENCIES																				
Priority Values	69	69	99	11	69	99	99	69	99	99	69	99	51	81	11	33	41	99	63	63
Priority Rankings	3	3	1	7	3	1	1	3	1	1	3	1	5	2	11	6	5	1	4	4
LEARNING PROFICIENCIES																				
Priority Values	40	40	86	27	63	40	29	30	86	40	8	86	25	63	63	75	25	11	14	75
Priority Rankings	5	5	1	8	3	5	6	6	1	5	12	1	9	3	3	2	9	11	6	2
ALL PROFICIENCIES																				
Priority Values	232	193	356	107	203	310	229	183	374	234	155	338	223	273	149	207	137	218	151	261
Priority Rankings	8	14	2	20	12	4	9	15	1	7	16	3	10	5	18	13	19	11	17	6

Priority Values are the Proficiency Weights times the rating of importance for each Skill category, summed over each broad proficiency and over all proficiencies. Subtotals for the Learning Proficiencies are normalized to equal the other subtotals.

Source: : Knowledge–Skill Matrixes from Hansen et al. (1999a).

A sharper picture of the relationship between knowledge and skill categories and the proficiencies emerges when this process is repeated for each of the broad proficiencies. The aggregated Priority Values and the resulting Priority Rankings are shown in Table 3. Comparable results for skills are shown in Table 4.

What do we conclude from this exercise? Consider first the traditional HR/IR Proficiencies shown in the top panels of these two figures. Overall, the most highly ranked knowledge categories (Table 3) include: Budgeting, Equal Employment Law, Labor Law, Management, and Production Processes which are all tied for 1st place in the Priority Rankings based on their Priority Values of 99. By contrast, Accounting with a Priority Value of 33 is tied for 11th place and Finance with a Priority Value of 11 is 12th in the Priority Rankings. The most highly ranked skill categories (Table 4) include: Decision Making Skills, and Initiative (tied for 1st place), and Active Listening Skills, Analytical Skills, Oral Communication Skills, and Sensitivity to Diversity (all tied for 2nd place). By contrast, Computer skills and Creativity are tied for 10th place.

Readers can observe for themselves how the Priority Values and Priority Rankings differ among the broad proficiencies. The similarities and differences in the knowledge and skills needed for each of the broad sets of proficiencies are apparent from examining the overall Priority Values and Priority Rankings in the bottom section of each panel in Tables 3 and 4. Six types of knowledge, namely, Employee Analysis, Job Analysis, Management, Production of Services, Staff/Evaluation, and Training, rank among the top five in each of the four broad proficiency groups. When averaged over all proficiency groups, the top five knowledge categories are in order of importance, Management, Employee Analysis, Job Analysis, Production, and Organizational Behavior, followed by Training. In a sense, these can be viewed as representing the field's core knowledge.

With respect to skills, six of them – Analytical, Decision Making, Initiative, Oral Communication, Planning/Organization, and Written Communication – are ranked among the top five skills in each broad proficiency group. When averaged over all proficiency groups, the top five skill categories are, in order of importance, Initiative, Analytical, Oral Communication, Decision Making, and Planning/Organization, followed by Written Communication. These can be taken to represent the field's core skills.

To sum up, the Priority Rankings pinpoint the leveraging effects on proficiencies of giving greater emphasis to knowledge and skills. This leveraging effect emerges because of the heavier weight given to the knowledge and skills that are expected to have a greater effect on proficiency development.

V. PROGRAM EMPHASIS ON KNOWLEDGE AND SKILLS

HR/IR student perceptions about what knowledge the program should emphasize can be compared with student perceptions about how much that knowledge is emphasized in the program, obtained from surveying IRRI students focusing on human resources, based on both published and unpublished data (Hansen et al., 1996). Such comparisons assume that HR/IR students are reasonably well informed about what recruiters look for in job applicants, even though at least some student respondents were still in the middle of their two-year program.

Responding students identify extensive gaps between the knowledge they believe the program should provide and what they believe it does provide (Table 5). The largest gaps are in knowledge of Training, Quality Improvement, Job Analysis, Recruitment, and Compensation. The smallest gaps are in Labor Law and Negotiation/Mediation. Interestingly, students report more than adequate

Table 5. Gaps between Labor Market Entry Knowledge and Knowledge Emphasized in Program

Knowledge	Market Entry Knowledge Needs, as Seen by Students (1)	Knowledge Emphasized in Program as Seen by Students (2)	Gap between Col. (2)–(1) (3)
Benefits	3.1	2.1	1.0
Compensation	3.2	2.1	1.1
Equal Employment Law	3.2	2.2	1.0
Empirical Analysis	2.6	2.9	-0.3
Job Analysis	2.8	1.6	1.2
Labor Markets	2.3	2.7	-0.4
Labor Law	3.1	2.7	0.3
Negotiation/Mediation	2.8	2.4	0.4
Organizational Behavior	2.9	2.1	0.8
Public Policy	2.7	2.1	0.6
Recruitment	3.0	1.8	1.2
Staffing/Evaluation	3.0	2.1	0.9
Quality Development	2.8	1.5	1.3
Training	3.1	1.6	1.5

Needed and Actual Program Skills Emphasis levels in columns 1 and 2 are averages of Strongly Emphasized = 4; Emphasized = 3; Somewhat Emphasized = 2; and Not Emphasized = 1. At the time these data were gathered, the importance of the additional knowledge categories established in the Hansen et al. 1999a study were not yet known.
Source: Unpublished data from Hansen et al. (1996).

emphasis on Empirical Analysis (interpreted as research) and Labor Markets, as indicated by the negative gaps.

Information is also available on skill gaps, as viewed by both students and by HR/IR professionals who were graduates of the Wisconsin program over the previous half-dozen years. Students were questioned about skills in the same way as they were asked about knowledge. In addition, HR/IR professionals were asked about the skills expected of new graduates hired for entry level jobs. The largest gaps based on data for students, shown in Table 6, column 3, are for Facilitation, Organizational Dynamics, Oral Communication, and Leadership, followed by Computer, Decision-making, and Team Building. The smallest gap is for Analytical, while the gap for Research is negative, indicating that students believe it is given excessive emphasis.

If, however, HR/IR professionals are viewed as better judges of what skills are needed by new entrants, on average the gaps between what the labor market requires and what students believe the program emphasizes remain about the same but the mix differs somewhat, shown in column 5 (column 4 minus column 2). The largest gaps are for Active Listening, Oral Communication, Decision Making, Facilitation, Computer, Organizational Dynamics, and Risk Taking. Analytical displays the smallest gap. Once again, the gap for Research is negative, with students responding to the heavy emphasis it receives in the program.

What commonalities exist among these different sets of skill gaps? Five of the top-ranked skills – Facilitation, Oral Communication, Organizational Dynamics, Decision-making, and Computer – are common to both gap measures. There is also agreement about the smallest gap (Analytical) and the negative gap (Research). Thus, whether the rankings are done by students or HR/IR professionals, the pattern of skill gaps that emerges is surprisingly consistent. This finding suggests that student perceptions of the skills needed in the labor market are in close touch with labor market realities, thereby lending some credence to the accuracy of the proficiencies analysis in Part III above. This finding also suggests that the Priority Values and Rankings for skills, determined on the basis of extensive input from advanced IRRI students have some validity, and by extension, so also do the Priority Values and Rankings for knowledge.

What is the likelihood that high priority values, indicating the leveraging effect on proficiency development, are consistent with the gaps between what knowledge and skills are needed and what the program provides? If there were a strong association, programmatic efforts to enhance the knowledge and skill categories could be expected to narrow these gaps. On the other hand, a weak association suggests that increased student knowledge and skills would produce relatively small reductions in the gaps. And, if the gaps were large, the likelihood of enhancing HR/IR proficiencies would be slim. In fact, the relationships appear

Table 6. Gaps between Needed Labor Market Entry Skills, and Skills Emphasized in Program

Skills	Needed Labor Market Entry Skills as Seen by Students	Skills Emphasized in Program as Seen by Students	Gap between Needed and Emphasized Skills as Seen by Students Col. (1)–(2)	Needed Labor Market Entry Skills as Seen by HR/IR Profs.	Gap between Needed Skills as Seen by HR/IR Profs and Emphasized Skills as Seen by Students Col. (4)–(2)
	(1)	(2)	(3)	(4)	(5)
Active Listening	3.1	2.0	1.1	3.6	1.6
Adaptability	3.1	2.1	1.0	3.3	1.2
Analytical	3.2	3.0	0.2	3.4	0.4
Computer	3.2	2.0	1.2	3.3	1.3
Creativity	2.8	1.7	1.1	2.8	1.1
Decision Making	3.2	2.0	1.2	3.4	1.4
Facilitation	3.0	1.5	1.5	2.9	1.4
Group Problem Solving	3.4	2.6	0.8	3.1	0.5
Leadership	3.0	1.7	1.3	2.9	1.2
Negotiation	2.7	1.9	0.8	2.7	0.8
Oral Communication	3.5	2.1	1.4	3.6	1.5
Organizational Dynamics	3.2	1.7	1.5	3.0	1.3
Planning/Organization	3.1	2.3	0.8	3.3	1.0
Presentation	3.3	2.2	1.1	3.3	1.1
Research	2.8	3.3	–0.5	2.6	–0.7
Resourcefulness	2.8	2.1	0.7	3.2	1.1
Risk Taking	2.4	1.4	1.0	2.7	1.3
Sensitivity to Diversity	3.2	2.1	1.1	3.3	1.2
Team Building	3.2	2.0	1.2	3.0	1.0
Written Communication	3.5	2.8	0.7	4.0	1.2

Needed Entry Skill levels are averages of Very Skilled = 4; Skilled = 3; Somewhat Skilled = 2; and Not Skilled = 1. Needed and Actual Program Skills Emphasis levels are averages of Strongly Emphasized = 4; Emphasized = 3; Somewhat Emphasized = 2; Not Emphasized = 1.
Source: Hansen et al., 1996.

to be weak, suggesting that no simple rule is available to use in prioritizing efforts to enhance knowledge and skill development.

A comparison of the values and gaps indicates that developing the proficiencies of entry-level HR/IR practitioners requires a complex array of knowledge and skills, that some types of knowledge and skills have greater leverage than others on the development of proficiencies, and that, most important, skill and knowledge gaps are independent of priority values. What does remain clear is that a considerable number of knowledge and skills are not sufficiently emphasized in the Wisconsin program.

VI. WHAT DO COURSES CONTRIBUTE?

Based on the foregoing analysis, how much do the Wisconsin program's courses contribute to building the knowledge and skills that lead to HR/IR proficiencies? With unpublished data available from the earlier study (Hansen et al., 1996), this question can be answered in several ways.

The most obvious approach is to examine the gap between the knowledge that courses in five broad program areas emphasize and what knowledge students believe they need. The gaps for IR Core (IR Theory and two courses in IR Methods), Labor Markets/Employment Policy, Unions/Collective Bargaining, and Comparative/International are all small. Most students express strong interest in knowing more about Current Trends/Issues in HR/IR, but this is neither a program area nor a course. Two gaps stand out. Students specializing in human resources would like to get more out of their human resource courses. They also believe their IR Methods courses are overemphasized.

Whether and how the IRRI program should respond to these results is an open question. Creating a course emphasizing Current Trends/Issues is difficult; encouraging faculty to infuse more current developments in their regular courses would probably be more effective. In any case, students should be encouraged to take more responsibility for acquiring such knowledge on their own through reading current periodicals and journals. Whether the two-semester sequence in IR Methods should be reduced in duration is a perennial question among faculty. They believe, however, that any reduction in this requirement would seriously impair the ability of HR/IR practitioners to keep abreast of new research and developments in the field. But, as shown below, this course is also important for student skill development.

The extent to which existing instruction meets student needs for knowledge is illuminated by survey evidence compiled by a major employer of Wisconsin's HR/IR graduates (Goodson, 1994).[12] Employees who graduated from the Wisconsin program were asked to indicate how well they thought their courses prepared them for their current jobs which, at that time, they had occupied for an average of three years. The results are available by program area as well as by individual course. By program area, the most favorable rankings go to Labor Market/Employment Policy, followed by HR Management, IR Core, Unions/Collective Bargaining, with Comparative/International bringing up the

Table 7. Average and Range of Skill Rankings For IR Core and HR Courses, and for Two Highest Ranked Courses

Skills	IR Core Courses Average (1)	IR Core Courses Range (2)	HR Courses Average (3)	HR Courses Range (4)	Employment and Training Course Average (5)	IR Methods II Course Average (6)
Active Listening	2.8	2.7–2.9	2.6	1.3–4.0	3.4	2.9
Adaptability	2.4	2.3–3.2	2.2	1.7–2.7	3.2	2.4
Analytical	3.4	2.8–4.0	2.6	1.7–3.7	3.2	4.0
Computer	1.9	1.0–2.9	1.7	1.0–4.0	1.2	2.9
Creativity	1.8	1.8–2.9	2.5	2.0–3.0	2.9	2.0
Decision Making	2.4	2.0–2.9	2.4	1.3–3.5	2.6	2.9
Facilitation	1.9	1.7–2.7	2.1	1.0–3.5	2.7	2.3
Group Problem Solving	2.5	1.7–3.4	2.2	1.0–3.5	3.4	3.3
Leadership	1.8	1.3–2.4	1.8	1.0–2.5	2.4	2.3
Negotiation	1.8	1.5–2.3	1.6	1.0–2.5	2.0	2.3
Oral Communication	3.0	3.0–3.7	2.7	1.0–4.0	3.7	3.3
Organizational Dynamics	2.0	1.3–2.1	1.9	1.0–3.0	3.1	3.3
Planning/Organization	2.6	2.2–3.3	3.1	2.3–3.7	3.2	3.6
Presentation	2.2	1.3–3.6	2.3	1.0–3.7	2.4	3.7
Research	2.8	1.8–3.7	2.9	2.0–4.0	2.6	2.3
Resourcefulness	2.2	2.2–2.6	2.4	1.3–4.0	2.3	1.9
Risk Taking	1.8	1.7–2.3	1.8	1.0–2.5	2.1	1.1
Sensitivity to Diversity	1.6	1.1–2.1	2.1	1.0–2.5	2.3	3.0
Team Building	2.2	1.7–3.0	1.9	1.0–2.5	2.1	1.3
Written Communication	3.1	2.6–3.6	3.3	2.5–4.0	3.3	3.6

Based on same 4–3–2–1 scale used in prior tables.
Source: Based on student responses in Employment and Training Course. Spring 1996.

rear. The most favorable responses for individual courses, based on 8 of the 18 courses that were rated by at least three of the 11 respondents, go to Employment and Training Programs, Equal Employment Policy and Practice, Labor Relations Law, Tutorial, Personnel Staffing, Organizational Behavior, Employee Benefits Management, and HR Management.

The final piece of evidence comes from previously unpublished responses of IRRI students who collaborated on the Hansen et al (1996) paper.[13] At the semesterís end, students were asked to rate the emphasis given in their IR Core courses (IR Theory and the two IR Methods courses) and their HR courses on each of the 20 skill categories. The average ratings of 2.4, based on the same 4–3–2–1 scale (see Table 2 Notes), were identical for IR Core and HR courses. Of the 11 courses for which data are available, four rated 2.7 and above, five rated from 2.3–2.6, three rated from 1.9–2.2, and one rated below 1.9 (Table 7).

More pertinent is the extent to which IR Core and HR courses emphasize specific skills, as indicated by the average ratings and range of ratings for courses in each group. The IR Core courses proved to be strongest in promoting Analytical, Written Communication, Oral Communication, Active Listening, and Research skills, with average ratings of 2.8 and above. The potential impact of these courses on skills is considerably greater, with nine of the 20 skills having upper range of ratings of 3.0 or above.

The rankings for HR courses proved to be more uniform, with only two of them, Written Communication and Planning/Organization, receiving ratings of 3.0 or above. HR courses with the lowest ratings are similar to the IR Core list, the only notable exception being the stronger rating given to creativity by those taking HR courses. Still, the potential of these courses is substantial, as shown by the upper end-of-range ratings for individual courses; for all but four skills the upper end-of-range ratings are 3.0 or above.

Two courses deserve separate treatment because of their strong impact on skill development, notably Employment and Training and IR Methods II. Employment and Training rated high in developing these skills: TQM Processes (though not included in the list, several respondents noted this topic), Oral Communication, Active Listening, Group Problem Solving, Written Communication, Adaptability, Analytical, Presentation, and Planning/ Organization – all rated 3.0 or above in their effect. At the same time, Computer, Negotiation, Sensitivity to Diversity, Organizational Dynamics, and Risk Taking all rated below 2.4; the explanation is that these skills were not emphasized. The ratings for IR Methods II are also high, exceeding 3.0 for the following skills: Analytical, Research, Presentation, Written Communication, Group Problem Solving, Oral Communication, Planning/Organization, and Team Building. Of course, both courses had small enrollments and were taught by instructors dedicated to skill development.

VII. CONCLUSIONS AND IMPLICATIONS

This analysis is predicated on the assumption that HR/IR students need to acquire a set of knowledge and skill-based proficiencies if they are to perform effectively in their future jobs and over their careers. The central question is how to narrow the gap between what the changing labor market for HR/IR practitioners demands and the proficiencies brought to the labor market by newly graduated HR/IR masters degree holders. The analysis concentrates on identifying the range of proficiencies required of HR/IR practitioners, determining what kinds of knowledge and skills are required to build these proficiencies, and trying to quantify the relative importance of the knowledge and skill categories in enhancing each proficiency. The study suggests but does not take the next step, which is to assess what particular types of instruction and learning opportunities can make the greatest contribution to developing the skills and knowledge required to demonstrate the essential proficiencies. The larger purpose, then, has been to establish the linkages among proficiencies and the skills and knowledge that contribute to building these proficiencies.

What remains unclear is how best to enhance these proficiencies through changes in academic programs and thus lay the basis for acquiring through job experience and further training the proficiencies demanded of HR/IR professionals in a changing economic world.[14] Several positions can be taken. One, leave matters as they are; let academic programs do what they have always done by focusing on teaching content knowledge, even if this requires employers and their employees to remedy whatever knowledge and skill deficiencies may exist. Two, adapt academic program requirements and instructional pedagogies to foster development of proficiencies. Three, find better ways for academic programs and employers (and indeed, employees) to work together, sharing in the continuing development of HR/IR professionals.

This study elaborates a rationale for the second position. It does so by analyzing how academic programs can think more productively about what they might do to enhance the knowledge and skill development of their students, using proficiencies as both a guide for that process and to assess the progress of students in developing these proficiencies. The analysis demonstrates that certain categories of knowledge do not receive sufficient emphasis. It reveals even more dramatically that skill development receives relatively little emphasis. In short, substantial gaps exist between what employers seek to find, and what students believe they should be getting from these programs, if they are to be adequately prepared for ever more challenging employment opportunities (Johnson & King, 1999; Way, 1996; Way, 1999).

Several steps need to be taken. One is to examine the impact of HR/IR programs on the development of knowledge and skills. Such a study would inquire how proficiencies and the knowledge and skills needed to demonstrate them are promoted through both instruction-centered and program-associated learning opportunities. The options include: (1) curriculum with its traditional focus on courses and requirements, (2) instructional-learning strategies employed in these courses,[15] and (3) extracurricular learning opportunities. With about two dozen courses, perhaps a half-dozen instructional-learning strategies used in existing courses, plus numerous extracurricular learning opportunities, trying to determine how each affects knowledge and skill development is a daunting task.

Second, methods must be developed to assess the ability of students to demonstrate proficiencies because traditional examinations cannot do that effectively.

This is a difficult challenge because the complex demonstrations required call for qualitative assessments that are demanding and for faculty time consuming. However, the rapidly growing literature on assessment approaches points to what can be done. Finally, academic programs must find some way to discuss how they can best move away from the current course- and requirement-centered approach toward a proficiencies-based model of learning. Only then can the linkages between academic programs and labor market demands be strengthened.

NOTES

1. This chapter draws in part on a longer, more detailed paper (Hansen, Mehlek, Murphy & True 1999a, hereafter referred to as Hansen et al., 1999a). The author is indebted to the editors of this volume, Bruce Kaufman and David Lewin, for their penetrating criticisms of several earlier drafts and their constructive suggestions.

2. The concept of proficiencies was developed by Hansen (1986) for the economics major. Its development was influenced in part by the author's exposure at the University of Maastricht to problem-based learning which was being instituted in the mid-1980s (Boud, 1985 and Boud & Feletti, 1992). Application of the proficiencies concept has been advanced by Hansen (1991), Wyrick (1994), Salemi and Siegfried (1999). For a description of the economics major, see Siegfried, Hansen, Bartlett, Kelley, McCloskey and Tietenberg (1991).

3. The fact that many people in the human resource field are graduates of MBA programs is acknowledged but is not discussed in this work; for a description of the MBA program approach, see Lewin (1997).

4. One referee points out that while the human resource function may be changing in large firms, the work of most human resource personnel continues to be much like it was in the past.

5. Space limitations prevent more detailed discussion of this issue.

6. For more on knowledge and learning in the professions, see Eraut (1994) and Schon (1987).

7. These proficiencies were developed with the help of student collaborators as part of a graduate course project; for details, see Hansen et al. (1999a). However, time did not permit elaborating how on these proficiencies might be assessed at the time students complete their academic programs.

8. The importance of continuous learning is described more fully by Argysis (1991), Davis and Botkin (1994), and Senge (1990).

9. The process for identifying these categories of knowledge and skills is described in Hansen et al. (1996), with some subsequent modifications in Hansen et al. (1999a). Thus, the latter study adds the following knowledge categories: Finance, Accounting, Budgeting, Management, Production Processes, and Marketing. In retrospect, these additions are not too surprising, representing as they do the core business foundation courses required in most MBA programs, including that at Wisconsin. IRRI students are not required to take any of these courses though a few undoubtedly take one or more of them. Only one item was added to the skill categories, something called Initiative, which may be more akin to a personal attribute than a skill. One skill category was deleted,

namely, Presentation, on that grounds that it was covered by Oral Communication. In retrospect, this latter skill should have been retained to emphasize the greater attention it requires in the instruction-learning process.

10. To sharpen the results, the entries shown in lines 1–4 of Table 2 reflect a consensus ranking arrived at by the authors rather than an average of their individual rankings.

11. Proficiency Priority Weights reflect the possibility that some proficiencies are more important than others. To allow for this possibility, weights of 3–2–1, with a 3 representing the most important, are assigned to the specific proficiencies within each broad proficiency. Because the list of proficiencies has already been screened for importance, the weights do not differ by much.

12. Goodson, then at IBM, surveyed 12 IRRI graduates then employed at IBM, receiving responses from 11 of the 12 graduates.

13. A brief comment on the author's Employment and Training course which enrolled 11 students and is traditionally taught in seminar fashion and always conducted on two parallel tracks, the first devoted to expanding students' content knowledge and second devoted to an individual or team research project. On this occasion I formulated a set of group projects that involved everyone in the class, with the idea of promoting the Learning Proficiencies. At the same time, I was groping toward the development of broader set of HR/IR proficiencies. Thus, in responding to this end of the semester questionnaire, the students displayed heightened awareness about what courses were doing for skill development. Interesting, the highest ranking went to a 'skill' not included on the list, Quality Improvement, which provided a framework for the course.

14. While the focus is on Wisconsinís IRRI program, much of what is said applies to similar programs elsewhere.

15. These strategies, detailed by Angelo and Cross (1993), Barnett (1993), Becker and Watts (1999), Christensen, Garvin, and Sweet (1991), Hansen (1999b), Ramsden (1992), Walstad and Saunders (1998), open possibilities for not only developing a wider array of skills (wider than does the traditional lecture approach) but also reinforcing content knowledge.

REFERENCES

Angelo, T. A., & Cross, P. K. (1993). *Classroom assessment techniques: A handbook for college teachers.* San Francisco: Jossey-Bass.

Argyris, C. (1991). Teaching smart people how to learn. *Harvard Business Review, 69,* 3, 99.

Barnett, R. (1992). *Improving higher education: Total quality care.* London: Open University Press.

Becker, W. E., & Watts, M. (Eds.) (1999). *Teaching undergraduate economics: Alternative to chalk and talk.* Boston, MA: Kluwer Academic Publishers.

Boud, D. (1985). *Problem-based learning in education for the professions.* Sydney: Higher Education Research and Development Society of Australia.

Boud, D., & Feletti, G. (Eds.) (1992). *The challenge of problem based learning.* London: Kogan Page.

Carnevale, A. P. (1991). *America and the new economy.* San Francisco, CA: Jossey-Bass.

Carnevale, A. P., Gainer, L. J., & Meltzer, A. S. (1990). *Workplace basics: The essential skills employers want.* San Francisco, CA: Jossey-Bass.

Christensen, C. R., Garvin, D. A., & Sweet, A. (Eds.) (1992). *Education for judgment: The artistry of discussion leadership.* Cambridge, MA: Harvard Business School Press.

Conference Board (1994a). *The changing global role of the human resource function: A research report.* Report Number 1062–94-RR. New York: Conference Board.
Conference Board (1994b). *Closing the human performance gap: A research report.* Report Number 1065–94-RR. New York: Conference Board.
Conference Board (1994c). M*aximizing performance through human resources: A conference report.* Report Number 1069–94-CH. New York: Conference Board.
Conference Board (1995a). *Rewriting the rules of human resources: A conference report.* Report Number 1108–95-CH. New York: Conference Board.
Conference Board (1995b). *Rethinking human resources: A research report.* Report Number 1124–95-RR. New York: Conference Board.
Connolly, T. R., & Mastranunzio, J. P. (1996). *Global challenges require new HR capabilities.* Armonk, NY: IBM Corporation.
Critten, P. (1993). *Investing in people: Toward corporate capability.* Oxford: Butterworth-Heineman.
Davenport, T. H., Jarvenpaa, S. L., & Beers. M. C. (1996). Improving knowledge work processes. *Sloan Management Review, 37*(4), 53.
Davis, S., & Botkin, J. (1994). The coming of knowledge-based business. *Harvard Business Review, 72*(5), 165.
Drucker, P. F. (1993). *Post-capitalist society.* New York: Harper.
Dyer, L. (Ed.) (1988). *Human resource management: Evolving roles and responsibilities.* Washington, DC: Bureau of National Affairs.
Eraut, M. (1994). *Developing professional knowledge and competence.* London: The Falmer Press.
Goodson, M. Letter to P. Voos, IRRI Director, January 20, 1994, and attachment '1993 Wisconsin IR Survey'.
Grossman, R. J. (1998). An interview with E. J. Lawler. *HRMagazine*, July, 94.
Garvin, D. A. (1993). Building a learning organization. *Harvard Business Review, 71*(4), 78.
Hansen, W. L. (1986). What knowledge is most worth knowing for economics majors? *American Economic Review, 76*(2), 149.
Hansen, W. L. (1991). The education and training of economics doctorates: Major findings of the executive secretary of the American Economic Association's commission on graduate education in economics. *Journal of Economic Literature, 29*(3), 1054.
Hansen, W. L., Berkley, R. A., Kaplan, D. M., Yu, Q., Craig, C. J., Fitzpatrick, J. A., Seiler, M. R., Derby, D. R., Gheis, P., Ruelle, D. J., & Voss, L. A. (1996). *Needed skills for human resource professionals: A pilot study.* Proceedings of 1996 Spring Meeting (pp. 524–534). Madison, WI: Industrial Relations Research Association.
Hansen, W. L., Mehlek, N., Murphy, M., & True, D. (1999a). Adapting a quality function deployment model to optimize professional education in human resources/industrial relations. In: J. Hommes, P. K. Keizer, M. Pettigrew, & J. Troy (Eds.), *Educational Innovation in Economics and Business IV: Learning in a Changing Environment.* (pp. 191–227). Boston: MA: Kluwer Academic Publishers.
Hansen, W. L. (1999b). Integrating the practice of writing into economics instruction. In: W. Becker, & M. Watts, (Eds.), *Teaching Economics to Undergraduates: Alternatives to Chalk and Talk.* London: Elgar.
Imai, M. (1986). *Kaizen: The key to Japan's competitive success.* New York: McGraw Hill.
Johnson, C. D., & King, J. (1999). *Are we properly training future HR/IR practitioners? A review of the curricula.* Presented at Second Innovative Conference on Teaching in Human Resources and Industrial Relations. Atlanta, GA. June.

Kaufman, B. E. (1994). *What companies are looking for in graduates of university HR programs.* Proceedings of 1994 Spring Meeting (pp. 503–510). Madison, WI: Industrial Relations Research Association.

Kaufman, B. E. (1996). *Transformations of the corporate HR/IR function: Implications for university programs.* Proceedings of 1996 Spring Meeting (pp. 540–548). Madison, WI: Industrial Relations Research Association.

King, B. (1989). *Better designs in half the time: Implementing QFD quality function deployment in America.* (3rd ed.). Meuthen, MA: GOAL/QPC.

Kochan, T. A., Katz, H.C., & McKersie, R. B. (1986). *The transformation of American industrial relations.* New York: Basic Books.

Legge, K. (1995). *Human resource management: Rhetorics and realities.* London: Macmillan Press.

Lewin, D. (1997). *Different approaches to teaching human resource management (HRM)/industrial relations (IR) in MBA Programs.* Presented at 49th Annual Meeting of the Industrial Relations Research Association, New Orleans, LA.

Porter, L. W., & McKibbin, L. E. (1988). *Management education and development: Drift or thrust into the 21st century.* New York: McGraw-Hill.

Ramsden, P. (1992). *Learning to teach in higher education.* London: Routledge.

Salemi, M. K., & Siegfried, J. J. (1999). The State of Economic Education. *American Economic Review, 89*(2), 355.

Schoonover, S. C. (1997) New HR Skills Needed for a New Work Environment. *Employment Relations Today, 24* August, 21.

Schon, D. A. (1987). *Educating the reflective practitioner: Toward a new design for teaching and learning in the professions.* New York: Basic Books.

Schuler, R. S. (1991). *Managing HR in the information age.* Washington, DC: Bureau of National Affairs.

Senge, P. M. (1990). *The fifth discipline: The art and practice of the learning organization.* New York: Doubleday.

Siegfried, J. J., Hansen, W. L., Bartlett, R. L., Kelley, A. C., McCloskey, D. N., & Tietenberg, T.H. (1991). The economics major in American higher education. *Journal of Economic Education, 22*(3), 197.

Stampen, J. O., & Hansen, W. L. (1999). Improving higher education access and persistence: New directions from a 'systems' approach. *Educational Evaluation and Policy Analysis, 21*(4), 417–426.

Ulrich (1997). *Human resource champions: The next agenda for adding value and delivering results.* Boston: Harvard Business School Press.

Ulrich (1998). A new mandate for human resources. *Harvard Business Review,* 124.

Walstad. W. B., & Saunders, P. (1998). *Teaching undergraduate economics: A handbook for instructors.* New York: Irwin McGraw-Hill.

Way, P. K. (1996). *A survey of curricula of IR/HR master's programs: Common features, new direction.* Proceedings of 1996 Spring Meeting (pp. 535–539). Madison, WI: Industrial Relations Research Association.

Way, P. K. (1999). *What HR/IR knowledge, competencies and business awareness students need and what IR/HR master's degree program offer.* Presented at Second Innovative Conference on Teaching in Human Resources and Industrial Relations. Atlanta, GA. June.

Wyrick, T. L. (1994). *The economist's handbook: A research and writing guide.* St. Paul, MN: West Publishing Co.